Gender Inequality and Welf ⌐ ⅲ Europe

Gender Inequality and Welfare States in Europe

Mary Daly

Department of Social Policy and Intervention, University of Oxford, UK

Edward Elgar
PUBLISHING

Cheltenham, UK • Northampton, MA, USA

Published by
Edward Elgar Publishing Limited
The Lypiatts
15 Lansdown Road
Cheltenham
Glos GL50 2JA
UK

Edward Elgar Publishing, Inc.
William Pratt House
9 Dewey Court
Northampton
Massachusetts 01060
USA

Paperback edition 2020

A catalogue record for this book
is available from the British Library

Library of Congress Control Number: 2019952420

This book is available electronically in the **Elgar**online
Social and Political Science subject collection
DOI 10.4337/9781788111263

ISBN 978 1 78811 125 6 (cased)
ISBN 978 1 78811 126 3 (eBook)
ISBN 978 1 80037 383 9 (paperback)

Typeset by Servis Filmsetting Ltd, Stockport, Cheshire

Contents

Figures and tables

FIGURE

TABLES

Introduction

This book assesses the relationship between gender and social policy, for the purpose of both taking stock and sketching out a future research agenda. Having the benefit of decades of scholarship and policy enables us to take the long view in surveying developments over time. As well as an examination of the main theorizations, a series of empirical analyses are undertaken to identify key developments and reflect upon what we know about women's and men's situations in regard to social policy and what remains unknown. The gap that the book seeks to fill is a lack of convincing assessments of both progress already made and the significance of a range of social policy approaches in this context.

Looking back some 40 or so years, much has changed from when, first, women-oriented and, then, gender scholarship started to take hold in the analysis of social policy. In the mid 1980s, for example, the average proportion of women in the labour market in the European Union (EU) was 45 per cent; in 2017 it was 66.4 per cent (European Commission, 2019). One of the lowest ever gender gaps in employment in the EU was recorded in 2017, an 11.5 percentage point difference between women (66.4) and men (77.9). A higher female presence in parliamentary representation across Europe and beyond represents a similar story. And yet, the scale of contemporary gender gaps and inequalities in living situations and access to resources is striking. For example, in the EU women expend five times more of their time than men in caring and household duties; 40 per cent of women live in a single-person household compared with 19 per cent of men; the pay gap between women and men has hovered for years at between 15 and 20 per cent; the average gender pensions gap is of the order of 38 per cent (European Commission, 2017a, p. 16). On a global basis, the United Nations (UN) estimated that in 2015 women earned 24 per cent less than men on average and performed two and a half times more unpaid care and domestic work (UNRISD, 2016). If we start to pick away at these statistics, we will find many differences, with mothers generally earning less than non-mothers and women of ethnic minority background even more poorly placed still (LSE Commission on Gender, Inequality and Power, 2015). While acknowledging that such differences and inequalities play out differently for different subgroups, gender inequalities combine

1

to systematically undermine women's chances of economic independence, making them far more likely than men to fall into poverty and to be low or secondary earners throughout their lives.

However, there has been action to counter gender inequality. The 50 years have been busy (although admittedly not all of them), playing host to different types of policy response – even pioneering an approach in gender mainstreaming. The three decades from the 1970s to the start of the new millennium saw much policy reform in the EU. With gender strongly present in these years, the period oversaw an assault on direct and indirect discrimination against women in regard to access to employment and some welfare benefits as well as measures to improve working conditions and address the intersection of family and work lives. Gender inequality came to be a 'problem' known to and recognized by policy makers. However, since then – and especially for at least the last decade or so – gender inequality has been a fading star in social policy reform in Europe. The former thrust towards equalizing entitlements to welfare benefits and opportunities for women as individuals has come to a halt and there is growing (re)centring of familial situation for the purposes of benefit and service design and access. This, the subject of so much feminist critique as prolonging women's dependency, suggests strong continuities with the (deeper) past.

In Europe, the great recession which started in 2008 was generally taken as an opportunity to deepen neoliberal impulses in social policy. What this spells, inter alia, is a policy reform portfolio that seeks to cut back and reduce the scope of welfare state services and benefits, remove or downgrade rights-based conceptions of social policy and shepherd the core service institutions (income support, health, education) in the direction of market principles and away from a public bureaucratic ethos (Yeatman, 2018, p. 21). The impact has been deep, in fact far deeper than many realize. The LSE Commission on Gender, Inequality and Power (2015), among other contributions, pinpoints women as being disproportionately affected by a crisis which it sees as also normalizing austerity policies. The EU Gender Equality Index – which measures six dimensions of inequality – recorded only marginal progress between 2005 and 2012 (European Institute for Gender Equality, 2017a). With an overall score of 52.9 out of 100 in 2012, one interpretation is that the EU remained in 2012 only halfway towards equality, having experienced a meagre rise of 1.6 percentage points in the index since 2005. This has since improved, but not hugely. The most resilient gender gaps are in the distribution of unpaid work and domestic activities and men's over-representation in all areas of decision-making, despite marked increases in women's representation in the political sphere. Moreover, any changes in gender equality have gone hand-in-hand with soaring socio-economic inequality in most parts of the world (Watkins, 2018, p. 7). These are global trends, leading to strong commonalities among world regions (although the scale of the gaps and the presence and impact of supportive architecture vary hugely and should not be under-estimated) (UNRISD, 2016; Nieuwenhuis et al., 2018).

We are making our way out of the recession now and the changes effected are becoming visible, at home and abroad. It is generally agreed that social policy played a key role in the European states, in either exacerbating or ameliorating the impact of the crisis (depending on the countries in focus) (Ólafsson et al., 2019). It is also clear that burdens and disadvantages were not equally shared. As well as robust gender effects, a social class gradient saw to it that across countries it was the three lowest income deciles that suffered the greatest setback in income (with Iceland as a notable progressive exception in this respect) (Ólafsson et al., 2019). When we probe for the living situations of those most affected, we find among them the unemployed, the low paid, immigrants and lone-parent families or those of two parents with more than one child. It has also taken longer for these sectors to recover from the impact. Indeed, full recovery may be impossible for some (Cavaghan and Dwyer, 2018). Beyond doubt is that the globalized neoliberal paradigm that has been predominant for some decades continues to hold sway (Ólafsson et al., 2019). That said, there is no one generally accepted roadmap for the future. Social investment policies have been inserted or sit alongside austerity approaches, for example, and this has seen selective and particular social investment accompany disinvestment. The contemporary consensus appears to agree on stronger policies for labour activation and human capital development, especially for the youngest cohort through childcare and early education, and disinvestment in income maintenance more broadly (Morel et al., 2012). However, there are trends that might up-end this settlement. The growth of right-wing politics across the EU is one such trend and Brexit is another. It is not easy to decipher the specific social policy project inherent in either. What they appear to share in common is a favouring of conservative gender and nationalist values. Hence, we might expect such politics to call forth a social policy in the image of the traditional, male-fronted family with migrants conceived in terms of 'undeserving other' (Erel, 2018). And in regard to Brexit in the UK, it has been pointed out that gender issues, while among the most significant in terms of likely impact, are downgraded if not silenced in the debates and politics (Guerrina and Masselot, 2018; Women's Budget Group et al., 2018).

It is interesting to observe in this context how some policy-related agency, and in particular that of the EU, some international organizations and some national governments, is turning to women, tapping the 'empowering' and freeing up of women's economic engagement and female initiative as a way forward as male incomes and economic growth both stall. This kind of emphasis is to be found in the EU's turn to social investment policies for example, which foreground the promotion of labour market participation (especially for women) and human capital development as the appropriate role for social policy (Morel et al., 2012). Such policies have purchase for both women and men, emphasizing labour market engagement and policy environments that are supportive of family life by enabling a better balance between work and family (Jenson, 2009). A modernized family model is called for especially in a world where the main purpose of the welfare state is seen to be as an investor in human capital. Only a limited understanding of social and economic life as gendered underlies this perspective (Saraceno, 2015; Jenson, 2018).

The need to take stock also arises from the existence of research from which to learn. On the back of some 30–40 years of researching gender-equality developments, we are in a position to interrogate the range of perspectives that have prevailed as well as identify the impact and shortcomings of particular intellectual and policy approaches. There have also been some developments that were not fully anticipated. The great recession, for example, which, as well as authoring a substantial change in social policy and reducing standards of living for most Europeans, has occasioned structural change in the economy affecting, for example, employment levels and demand for skills, and potentially lengthening young people's dependence (Eurofound, 2015). Nor did we expect that social policy would go inside the family in the way that it has and seek to influence the practice and texture of family life to quite a fine degree (especially through parenting-related measures which will be detailed in Chapter 7). Another unexpected occurrence was the undermining of what is in many respects a feminist ideal – the Swedish welfare state model. Among the changes made there are greater privatization of social services, extensive reforms effecting greater diversity in both service and provider, and changes in the scale of state provision on the grounds that people prefer choice and are prepared to assume greater responsibility for themselves and their families (Burström, 2015). The Swedish commitment to social equality – including gender equality – and universal rights has weakened. This has delivered a blow to envisioning a different gender order although it might, viewed in a different light, prove to be a fillip to scholarship, moving us beyond a rather one-dimensional idealization of the Swedish model for its institutionalized model of gender equality (Gornick and Meyers, 2009; Martinsson et al., 2016).

One of the questions that especially arises is what happened from the 1990s on to break a momentum that appeared progressive. In this regard it helps particularly to take developments in feminism into account for it has played a large role in the fields of interest in this book, both as scholarship and political/policy engagement. Feminism has been and is present today but the kinds of gender politics that prevail now are noticeably particular, especially in the liberal countries of the UK and US (among others).[1] Observing the self-identification as feminists of high-profile businesswomen like Cheryl Sandberg of Facebook and Anne-Marie Slaughter, analysts speak of a 'neoliberal feminism' (Fraser, 2009, 2013; McRobbie, 2013; Rottenberg, 2014, 2018). What is being referred to here is the rehabilitation – and transformation – of feminism as 'a broad constellation of socio-political interest converging around the category of woman' (McRobbie, 2013, p. 120). This feminism is hallmarked by an individualist orientation, a belief in formal equality, a valorization of self-responsibility and self-realization, and a downgrading of the significance of material conditions as defining features of life situation. Maternity is a central consideration, with women urged not to turn away from maternity but to postpone or manage it in such a way that it can be the subject of a chosen personal engagement and 'balanced' with other achievements (Rottenberg, 2018). Good timing and planning for positive affect and material success is essential. Policy has little place in this landscape and when considered it is mainly corporate policy that is addressed.

The '#MeToo' movement, the international campaign raising awareness around sexual assault and harassment, is also significant, spearheaded as a Facebook campaign by high-profile women largely from the world of entertainment (although its roots are earlier and less celebrity oriented). Its modus operandi has been to shame male public figures accused of sexually inappropriate behaviour, while at the same time giving women a voice and creating empathy for them. The #MeToo movement does call for collective action and has feminist underpinnings in that the underlying problem is seen to be male power and a societal tolerance of – if not support for – a form of masculinity characterized by aggressive and sexualized male behaviour. To the extent that it targets change, it is change in the law's approach to male violence against women that appeals, including reform of the procedures for reporting incidences of violence and harassment, and the ways such reports are received and handled by the authorities. Since it is still new, it is difficult to predict how it will develop and whether it will evolve to become a broad-based social movement oriented to societal transformation and a shift in power structures from a gender perspective.

---

[1] However, see Watkins (2018) for an account of very different feminist approaches in Europe and North America, as well as some Asian countries. Fraser et al. (2018) also covers this theme, among others.

At present, it has many 'silences', especially in regard to the experiences of minority women (Tambe, 2018). We have to keep open, therefore, the question of whether and how these developments map onto feminist critiques of the dominant political order and liberalism's promotion of a form of gender equality and economic model that both tolerates and deepens exclusions and inequalities.

THE BOOK'S APPROACH

Situated within the fields of social policy and gender studies, the book uses the latest evidence to reveal the reality of core aspects of women's and men's everyday lives and enquire into how social policy is implicated. The quotidian focus comes out of a long tradition of feminist social policy research on the reality of people's situation and the conditions under which women especially live their lives (as will be outlined in Chapter 1). In key ways, it pinpoints social location, a concept and approach prioritized especially in identity and intersectional studies. 'Quotidian' here does not spell an exclusive focus on the micro; rather, it seeks to reveal how people's lives are lived out in the shadow of policy. The core orientations can be appreciated from the kinds of research questions that guide the book: How do women's and men's living situations compare and what role does social policy play in affecting these and shaping gender patterns? What are the different ways of addressing gender inequality in social policy and with what results? How is the intersection of gender with other inequalities managed, reproduced or changed by social policy? And what are the constituent elements of a research agenda for the future that identifies the most pertinent theoretical frameworks and asks the most penetrating research questions going forward? Where these questions are to be answered through empirical data, the analysis mainly concentrates on empirical data from 2005 on. However, these are data points and do not define the book as a whole, which, throughout, aims for a historically informed discussion.

The approach taken to answering these questions and developing a research agenda has a number of hallmark features. First, I am convinced that a comprehensive investigation of the relationship between social policy and gender should examine not only the content or make-up of social policies and their associated outcomes but also the ways these are studied and understood (the 'knowledge' about them). Hence, the underlying epistemology encapsulates both theoretical and empirical developments. This and the task of constructing a future research agenda are also informed by an interdisciplinary approach. As well as gender and social policy studies, knowledge and insights from sociology and political science are central. These are disciplines convinced that the transformations (or not) in women's and men's lives matter.

A further notable feature is the book's international and comparative scope. An active search for variation leads the way, rooted in a conviction that only when we comprehend versions or forms of a phenomenon in varied contexts can we truly understand it. Broad-based comparison is the main method used, with the usual health warning that, while this enables us to overview developments in a systematic manner, it tends to under-appreciate relevant phenomena as features of particular settings. The book is especially oriented to developments and experiences in the EU. The EU is taken not as a unit of convenience but because it has a strong history as an anti-gender inequality, supranational project. It also offers us the convenience of engaging with a large chunk of the existing scholarship, especially that which seeks to categorize and compare countries in terms of historically embedded policy models. This literature has organized itself comparatively around the existence of systematic social policy variation in European countries, differentiating between the Nordic countries, the Continental European countries, the liberal countries (especially UK and Ireland) and the Mediterranean nations (Esping-Andersen, 1990; Ferrera, 1996). My core interest is in identifying systematic patterns and pathways within and across countries and not regimes per se. There are two methodological points to note about the EU focus. First, with 28 member countries it implies a 'zoom-out' lens rather than a 'zoom-in' perspective.[2] The empirical analyses, therefore, will concentrate on the broader EU picture. A second point to note about the EU focus is that it steers us generally in the direction of the high-income/developed welfare state nations and hence the rich capitalist democracies of the global North. Of course, not all of the member states are wealthy but they are all part of a political and economic bloc that, in a world context, constitutes an area of very high income and political and economic weight, and they all have a history of the welfare state (although again there are significant variations in the nature and depth of the welfare state in particular national settings).

---

2   At the time of writing the UK is in the process of exiting the EU, which will leave 27 member states. It might be helpful to note at this stage – given the significance of the EU for gender equality policy – that the Union expanded in waves. To the original six member states the so-called BENELUX countries (Belgium, France, Germany, Italy, Luxembourg, the Netherlands), Denmark, Ireland and the UK joined in 1972. Greece joined in 1981 and was followed by Spain and Portugal in 1986 and Austria, Finland and Sweden in 1995. These are often known as the EU-15. All further expansions were to the south and the east. Ten countries joined in 2004: Cyprus, the Czech Republic, Estonia, Hungary, Latvia, Lithuania, Malta, Poland, Slovakia and Slovenia. Bulgaria and Romania joined in 2007 and Croatia was the last to join in 2013.

While the book does not systematically examine wider processes beyond this region, it is sensitive throughout to wider global developments and accepts as a first principle the impossibility of separating developments in one part of the world from everywhere else. But every focused project has to set boundaries, even if recognizing that these are porous.

KEY CONCEPTS

Some words are in order at this stage about the key concepts, and in particular the meanings of 'gender', 'gender inequality' and 'social policy' as they are used throughout the book.

Gender has now become one of those taken for granted words in both academic scholarship and public discourse. Harewood (2014), in a review of over 160 articles published in sociology journals between 2006 and 2010, found that gender is rarely defined explicitly and that the terms 'sex', 'female' and 'male' are used frequently – and often unreflexively – in work that is gender focused. She coined the term 'gender reduction' to describe a particular feature of the way the term 'gender' is used to limit and simplify complex issues. This suggests the need to be explicit about the particular gender approach being adopted.

Gender is an ambiguous concept, although it is now widely understood to refer to a socially constructed rather than a biological category (Milkman and Townsley, 1994). It is a strongly relational term, conceiving of women and men in comparison to each other and as engaged in complex relations at different levels (Scott, 1986). Apart from the relationality aspect, one of the key elements of gender as a lens for analysis is that it signposts particular domains of life. Bradley (2013, p. 16) guides us here: "gender refers to the varied and complex arrangements between men and women, encompassing the organization of reproduction, the sexual divisions of labour and cultural definition of femininity and masculinity". Connell and Pearse (2015, p. 11) are equally clear about focus when they claim gender as "the structure of social relations that centres on the reproductive arena, and the set of processes that bring reproductive distinctions between bodies into social processes". Both Scott (1986) and Ferree (2010) remind us – more generally – that gender is a relationship of power connected to and realized through institutional and normative processes.

Informed by the above but drawing explicitly from Joan Acker's work (e.g. 1992), gender is conceived of here to refer to constituent elements of social relations and social structures which are based on and lead to differences and inequalities between women and men as individuals and social categories, and is a primary signifier of power in regard to access to resources and status. What about gender in social policy analysis? Taking such a lens, Shaver (2018, p. 2) defines gender as "the basis of complex, social inequalities, taking the forms of both material inequalities of income, assets and social status and social inequalities reflecting unequally valued social identities". We can connect the welfare state in this view to a system of social distribution. The study of gender connects us especially – but not exclusively – with work that is 'feminist' in orientation. Orloff (1996, p. 52) defines her feminist approach to analysing the welfare state as taking "gender relations into account as both causes and effects of various social, political, economic and cultural processes and institutions" that produce ". . . gender differentiation, gender inequalities and gender hierarchy in a given society".

The term 'feminist' is used in this book to apply to work which has as a germinal interest the unequal positioning of women vis-à-vis men and the processes, relationships and structures that constitute this. Feminism's spring-loading of a critical approach especially appeals. It spells, among other things, a privileging of the experiences of women and a commitment to using 'voice' to convey and enable agency (as set out by Gottfried, 1996). Ackerly and True (2013, p. 136) point out that for feminist research a commitment to a process and set of research ethic(s) is more important than following a lock-step set of rules. They regard a critical feminist methodology as hallmarked by the following commitments (inter alia): attentiveness to unequal relations of power; attentiveness to relationships; attentiveness to boundaries of inclusion–exclusion and forms of marginalization; and situating the researcher in the research process. Not all of these are relevant to the current endeavour but they do seem like worthwhile principles by which to be guided.

Gender scholarship over the last few decades has been hallmarked by engagement with intersectionality as a promising and challenging development. This perspective eschews single axis analyses of the dynamics of difference and sameness, and views gender as intersecting with other inequalities and subject to multiple causality (Cho et al., 2013). It challenges our usual habits of argument by positing overlaps and conflicting dynamics among race, gender, class, sexuality, nation and other inequalities (Lykke, 2011). To the extent that intersectionality has been applied in social policy analysis, it has mainly been utilized to recognize women's multi-positionality and/or explore the situation of subgroups of women. However, these are just some of the possible applications (Choo and Ferree, 2010; Cho et al., 2013) as will be discussed further in Chapter 2. For now suffice to say that intersectionality is taken forward in a number of ways in this book. First, an attempt will always be made to go beyond universal categories and identify how the 'categories' of women and men are permeated by other differences and divisions. This means that we view women and men not as singular monoliths but as differentially placed regarding social class and also ethnic background, age/generation and other relevant markers of intersectional location and political and structural inequalities. Second, the book is intersectional by virtue of its approach to policy – seeing it as a set of cross-cutting policy (life) domains rather than a series of separate policy spheres. This has the added advantage of pointing us in the direction of the general architecture of the social policy system and away from particular programmes (singular programme specificity being a strong characteristic of gender and other scholarship in the last decades). Thirdly, the empirical chapters – especially 3, 4 and 5 – are organized around cross-cutting resources of income, work and time.

The foregoing may well prompt a question in the reader's mind about men and where they fit into the book's canvas. Of course, men have always had a central (if unacknowledged) place in welfare and other scholarship, because it was their typical life experiences that formed the basis for much of the analysis. A gender approach creates an opening to analyse the situation of men more explicitly because it means that they are no longer the 'silent counterfactuals'. However, that opening has not been widely taken up, and certainly not in comparison to the women-oriented scholarship. It is in their role as workers that men most appear on the pages of the gender and welfare state scholarship but there is work also engaging with domestic violence and young men's vulnerability. There is also some discussion of social policy's engagement with masculinities and men as actors with gendered subjectivities in the broader sociological literature (well outlined and considered by Ferree, 2010 and Hearn et al., 2018). But in social policy research that guides this book, the main engagement has been with men's status and agency as fathers and as members of families (in terms, for example, of their participation in the family/household division of (caring) labour and their role as breadwinners) (Hobson, 2002; Hearn, 2010). It has taken a long time for a scholarship on men to build up (perhaps because this required recognition that, while structures might favour and reproduce male privilege, the experience and agency of individual men was taken for granted and was ultimately not as powerful as that of women in revealing hidden structures).

Gender inequality is a second leading concept. It too requires some clarification at the outset. I am primarily interested in it as a 'problem' or goal-set for policy. And, as befits a social policy discussion, my focus is on material inequality rather than status in the sense of essential difference/recognition. Although academic and policy debates have operated with different versions of equality, one robust differentiation is that between equality of access and equality of outcome. The former, access, view of inequality centres upon the starting conditions and in particular the absence of legal and institutional barriers to entry or participation, whereas equality of outcome refers to the distribution of economic and other resources and benefits and therefore is focused on tangible results (Rees, 1998). 'Equality of opportunity', embracing the capacity and resources to participate, falls somewhere between the two. One could argue at length about the appropriate conceptualizations of equality – and the relative success of EU and other types of equality policy – but I treat it here as a multi-layered concept which means that, inter alia, equality of access becomes an essential first step towards a higher-order equality. Htun and Weldon (2018, pp. 6–7) offer a good definition: "We understand gender equality as an ideal condition or social reality that gives groups constituted by gender institutions similar opportunities to participate in politics, the economy, and social activities; that values their roles and status and enables them to flourish; in which no gender group suffers from advantage or discrimination; and in which all are considered free and autonomous beings with dignity and rights". One of the key analytic questions that the book addresses is what outcomes were targeted by policy in regard to gender inequality and whether these have changed.

Social policy is the book's third anchoring focus. As used, it refers to publicly organized and funded benefits and services to achieve goals around public welfare and social protection (recognizing that these are contested terms) and interventions in the distribution of income, earning and opportunities, and resources over the life course in market-based societies. The focus on social policy directs us to the material elements of gender inequality – such as income and employment – but these are not treated independently of relational elements. In terms of the usual social policy fields, income-support measures, employment policy, family policy and social services feature prominently since these are the most relevant domains of social policy for the present purpose. I do not draw a rigid boundary around these, however, and include also other service areas and policies which affect social and economic organization and gender relations more generally (directly or indirectly). These include taxation, social care policy and also, on occasion, early education policy. As mentioned, policies are treated as intersecting – hence I do not interrogate them individually but combine them for how they contribute to setting up the environment and resource sets within which women and men conduct and manage their lives as individuals and members of collective units. The one exception made is for (gender) equality policy (which receives a chapter of its own – Chapter 6). This is because gender inequality was specifically problematized in its own right by the EU and so merits scrutiny and critical assessment as a case study of the achievements and limits of targeted policy.

The concepts of 'social policy' and 'welfare state' are used interchangeably, in recognition of the systematic elements and relationships involved, and to foreground the state (or the public authorities) as a key political actor.

BOOK STRUCTURE

Excluding this introduction, the book consists of eight chapters, divided into three main sections. The first reviews existing literature; the second undertakes empirical analysis of developments relating to access to income, employment and resources; and the third part undertakes a review of policy. This vision provides the book's organizing structure – the set of chapters identifying what is happening empirically is bookended by two other sections, and two short intermezzo passages connect the different parts of the book. The purpose of the latter is to provide connecting threads, especially in terms of making clear the lines of investigation and framework of analysis followed.

The structure is as follows:

1. Women, gender and social policy in early work
2. Contemporary approaches to gender and social policy: bringing scholarship up to date
3. Income, wealth and poverty
4. Access to employment
5. Inequalities of time use and life satisfaction
6. The EU, equality and social policy
7. Gender and social policy more broadly
8. Scoping a future research agenda

To offer a more detailed outline, the first two chapters are scene-setting, engaging in an intellectual history of the key concepts and approaches on the basis of the substantial 'archive' that has been built up over a remarkably short period. The first chapter sets out the early evolution and the extant theoretical approaches and main concepts while the second tracks the themes, theories and questions that have dominated since the 1990s. To some extent the date point at which to break the chapters is arbitrary, although there was a significant change of direction from the 1990s. Together, these two chapters mine the existing literature for insights, frameworks and policy approaches. We are fortunate here in that, while the currency of gender inequality in popular discourse and as a motivator of policy reform has varied over time, no one could deny the influence of gender as a 'social problem' for academic work. Even more, social policy is one of the domains where gender made an early and relatively strong impact on scholarship (as we shall see in Chapter 1). As well as calling for historical sensibility, this means that a body of work exists which can be drawn upon to illustrate how the welfare state was gendered historically and, going forward, interrogate the reforms undertaken to see if they addressed the intricate ways in which gender differences and inequalities have taken shape.

These two chapters also function to identify emerging insights over time which serves as a bridge between the first part of the book and the analysis undertaken in the second part (with key insights highlighted explicitly in the form of a short intermezzo that sets out the theoretical/empirical framework). These three empirical chapters examine access to particular resources, outlining in turn access to income, employment and time. What they seek to do, in essence, is to identify the prevailing female/male comparison in access to different types of resources in the broader context of living patterns and existing institutional arrangements. Each makes an attempt to link the patterns found to broader questions relating to inequality and change. Chapter 3 considers women's access to income and relative financial well-being. It examines in turn comparative financial equality, wealth and the gender distribution of poverty. It then goes on to explore how access to welfare state-related benefits is associated with gender inequalities, paying particular attention to old-age pensions and gender gaps therein. Chapter 4 scrutinizes women's access to employment. In focus here is the patterning of gender and other axes of inequality in regard to engagement with the labour market. As well as absolute employment levels, the chapter also looks at part-time work and pay-related and other inequalities. In the second part, Chapter 4 considers the factors that contribute to inequalities, interrogating the latest evidence to explain inequalities in women's labour market engagement and relative pay. The third empirical chapter – Chapter 5 – looks at time as a resource and how this is associated with the arrangement of family/home life and satisfaction therewith. The chapter considers in turn work–family forms and arrangements, and how these are changing, the volume and distribution of paid and unpaid work, changes in time use, life satisfaction and the role of attitudes, culture and other factors in explaining developments and persisting inequalities.

The final section of the book turns to policy review. The three chapters comprising this part scrutinize some of the main relevant policy developments and draw conclusions about where we might go from here, especially in terms of a research agenda. It is preceded by another short intermezzo section that sets out the rationale for what is considered.

Chapter 6 looks at gender equality in policy, focused on the EU approach. What this chapter seeks to reveal is the policy approach that has been taken to gender inequality and how this has changed, or not, over time. As mentioned, the EU is the focus because it has a long history of problematizing gender inequality and has sought to develop a policy portfolio around gender inequality, and in more recent times other inequalities. Chapter 7 aims to enquire into gender-related social policy reform more generally, and so defines relevance beyond policy with gender equality in its nomenclature or discrimination in its targeting. The first part of the chapter discusses two important policy frames or rubrics: work–life balance and social investment. Subsequent chapter sections analyse the policy reforms that have sprung from these and other dominant considerations, considering in turn measures investing in parenting, childcare and care for older people. This is followed by a concluding chapter which sets out an over-arching research agenda, drawing together conclusions about what is clear but also remains unknown from the domains considered in the preceding chapters. The chapter especially sets out some 'knotty issues' that scholarship (and policy in practice) has to deal with.

I should note that I am forced to exclude important areas – such as violence and health and reproductive rights.[3] This is regrettable, given that these are fields of experience and policy that profoundly shape women's lives and well-being.[4] Justification for their exclusion includes constraints imposed by word limits but, especially, the book's core focus on social policy. This, as mentioned, is taken to refer especially to income, employment and family life in a perspective that is most sensitive to material resources and organization, and policy's role in regard to people's status, access to resources and opportunities and redistribution. I am also forced to exclude women's representation (and therefore matters of political representation and associated contestation and causality). The detailed consideration necessary is not possible in the context of space limitations. But to some extent also, it is not essential to the book's purpose, which is to examine both the nature and consequences of policies rather than explain them as the outcome of political engagement. That said, not only am I mindful of the signature importance of politics, I take forward insights from that body of work implicitly if not explicitly – they are inherent in my complex conception of the state, for example, in the book's understanding

---

[3] See the study by Htun and Weldon (2018) which looks at the factors affecting the institutionalization of a range of women's rights relating to violence against women, family and employment law, reproductive rights, and parenting-related leave and childcare.

[4] See the LSE Commission on Gender, Inequality and Power (2015) for a very good discussion of gender-based violence and gender in the media and culture and communications.

of the political interests associated with gender, the awareness that all social policy is in key ways a product of political engagement and political interest, and that the issues of gender, women's and men's paid and unpaid work and family are fundamentally associated with the distribution of power and authority.

1. Women, gender and social policy in early work

This chapter overviews the early work on gender and social policy, looking especially at how thinking and research unfolded over time. It starts back in the late 1960s and proceeds to around the 1990s.

One could summarize endeavour in the field by viewing it in terms of two main orientations: first, the women-oriented work and, second, scholarship adopting a gender perspective. The former sought to unearth the relationship between women and social policy as it was embedded in the system of public support (including welfare benefits and services). It proceeded on the basis of themes such as women's situation vis-à-vis income and other resources and the role played by social policy in this; the specificity and uniqueness of women's experience of claiming benefits and services; systemic positioning of particular subgroups of women, especially those with home responsibilities; and the consequences in terms of living situation, personal prospects and inter-personal relationships of being dependent on the state. While still often focusing on women, the gender work was oriented more to questions around how social policy contributes to creating and perpetuating gender differences and inequalities with particular reference to unequal resources and opportunities. This led to an analysis of social policy as both promoting and potentially undoing gender-based power relations, especially through its effect on access to material resources and a range of other forms of support. It is important not to set up a strong divide between the scholarship on women and that on gender, though, for they are each products of their time to some extent, and reflect emerging insights and changing analytic and theoretical preferences over time. In addition, for long periods both sets of work have proceeded side by side, feeding into each other in key ways. As these are still vibrant fields of enquiry, I tend to use the present tense when discussing them.

Somewhat more controversially perhaps, I use the generic label 'feminist' for both sets of endeavour. This is for two reasons, both reflecting my view of the field. First, I see common cause or shared intent connecting both types of work and, second, I observe a rather swift evolution towards a feminist – primarily power based – understanding which showcases the gender system as a system of stratification and segregation. That said, we should be mindful of the distinction between feminist work that adopted an 'explicitly feminist orientation' – in the sense of purposefully aiming to uncover and address women's relative powerlessness, oppression and disadvantage vis-à-vis men – and that which could be described as 'feminist-oriented' – in the sense of viewing differences between women and men as non-accidental and consequential and not necessarily an expression or result of power and hence requiring political and structural transformation. Such differences persist and are to be found in scholarship today as well.

We should note that the literature considered is grounded in social policy in the developed countries, especially Western Europe, America and the Antipodes (Razavi and Staab, 2018). It is important to bear in mind, therefore, that the perspectives and theories considered generally omitted the situation and experience of other world regions and were in key respects focused on the bounded nation state as the unit of analysis. In fact, a lot of the work was country specific; most of the early feminist critique emanated from the UK, the US and some of the Nordic countries, for example. Not only did the literature and research considered in this chapter mainly originate from these parts of the world but it was the so-called liberal welfare systems (the UK and the US especially, but also Australia and to a lesser extent Canada, Ireland and New Zealand) which provided the substance of analysis. This does not make the literature theoretically flawed but it does render it theoretically specific. This is true for other reasons as well, especially in light of the critique that emerged over time pointing out that it was the lives of white women that were in focus (Glenn, 2002) and that the story of the US welfare state in particular cannot be told without centrally integrating race into the picture (Mink, 1990; Quadagno, 1994).

A working research question for the chapter reads as follows: What was problematized when women and gender were the focus of early critical social policy thinking? The chapter is divided into two main parts. Following a brief overview, the first section sets out the main lines of research and investigation and the second looks at the sets of explanations offered, considering a range of feminist perspectives.

1.1 ORIGINATING CONCERNS AND ORIENTATIONS

There were a number of spurs to enquiry in the early years. In particular, poor outcomes for women in a range of areas, such as poverty and low personal income, financial dependence and lack of employment participation and other opportunities, directed the spotlight at the extent and details of social policy provision. Feminist scholars realized early on that they should not only highlight the impact of the design and operation of social policy but dissect assumptions, patterns of thought and modes of analysis. This extended the 'critical gaze' to dominant philosophies, concepts, methodologies and frameworks in academic work as much as the norms and assumptions in policy itself. In some key respects, this approach prefigured mainstream scholars' somewhat later adoption of 'ideas' as signature influences on welfare state (re)design and reform (in approaches that attribute a driving force to the promotion of or adherence to particular ideas, ideologies and world views) (e.g. Blyth, 1997; Campbell, 2002; Béland and Cox, 2011).

Thinking in this way laid bare that the use of gender-neutral concepts, in both extant scholarship and policy, was a form of dressing that concealed the categories of analysis as themselves gendered and sex selective. This meant that part of the critical analyst's task was to 'denaturalize' key concepts like 'family', 'old age', 'childhood', and even 'woman and man' (Rose, 1981, p. 496). But more than this: there was, along with a male bias, an absence of women from much of the work. There are two points of note here. The first is that the aspects or areas of social policy that are studied matter. Social insurance – the foundation for much of the classic social policy research – is a benefit for workers, conceived as replacing and sometimes supporting the male (breadwinner) wage and hence excluded women in large numbers until it was reformed from the 1970s on. The 'bias' was built in from the beginning in the institutional focus of research but it took a long time for this to be noticed.[1]

The second is that the underlying assumptions, ideas and framings of analytic and policy approaches are as worthy of study as the outcomes – for they form what Pascall has called the 'underlay' (Pascall, 1986, p. 197).[2] To find them one has to dig deep and also think intersectionally, as they often hide in other categories.

Many taken-for-granted conventions in research played a role. One is the practice of compartmentalization or 'siloing'. The sidelining of the study of the family and 'private life' from more 'public' and research-friendly spheres – such as employment or retirement – was especially consequential. Some suggest that it made for a schism between male and female subjects (Pascall, 1986). A statist bias in the prevailing mode of social policy analyses may be another factor complicit in sidelining gender (Sainsbury,

---

[1]   I am grateful to Sheila Shaver for this point.
[2]   Gender scholarship has taken up the notion of frames quite assiduously – see Bacchi (1999).

1996). The relative invisibility of women and gender was exacerbated by a lack of reflection on or acknowledgment of the male orientation or bias. A further – perhaps the most – fundamental critique of social policy (and the way it was studied) was that it telescoped its analysis of power on socio-economic factors and class relations. Of concern here was a failure to appreciate how social and other policies engaged in the distribution of power between women and men and played a role in women's relative powerlessness vis-à-vis men and societal institutions. As it emerged in the 1970s, aspects of the feminist critique dovetailed with an emerging critique of British social policy as 'apolitical', given its dominant interest in the modalities of policy and their effectiveness in solving problems, especially from an administrative (efficiency) perspective (Williams, 1989).[3]

Lack of gender analysis and the virtual exclusion of women's situation had profound consequences. It meant, first, that many of social policy's most important influences and outcomes were not being fully investigated and, second, that some policies and organizing principles of the system of welfare had yet to be studied (Gordon, 1990). Consider, for example, two possibilities: first that welfare state policies and programmes are directed differentially at women and men and, second, that the underpinning logic of women-oriented programmes is different to that in programmes focused on supporting men and typically male risks. In such instances, the 'norm' (derived as it was from the study of male-oriented programmes such as social insurance and other employment-oriented benefits) would actually not be representative of the system as a whole (Gordon, 1990). Missed also would be the possibility that social policy discriminates against women and is active in reinforcing women's subordination, in the family, economy and society for example. Were this to be the case – and we now know it to be true so we can move out of a subjunctive mode of expression – the entire structure of relations involved in state welfare needs to be reconsidered. While all of this might seem self-evident nowadays, the situation was completely different in the 1970s. Writing in 1983, Gillian Pascall (1983, p. 94) identified the analytic task as to find ways of demonstrating the centrality of the welfare state's concern with male/female relations as well as identifying how the structures of dominant trends of thought were conducive to excluding this possibility from view.

There were three main points of entry for gender appraisal, all inflected one way or another by an awareness of relative power and resource inequalities.

---

[3] This was a dominant analytic tradition of British social policy historically – see Donnison and Chapman (1965), Rose (1981), Lee and Raban (1988) and Chapter 1 in Williams (1989). For a feminist critique, see Pascall (1986) and Williams (1989).

1.1.1   Revealing Women's Experiences

One strand of work examined women's experiences of welfare. Much of this focused on the micro level, starting from the reality of women's lives and experiences and chronicling how the programmes (and via this the state itself) treated women and helped to construct their work as paid or unpaid. The idea of women's relationship to the welfare state was born; if not (yet) connecting the personal to the institutional then at least revealing how people approached the state for support and the reality of what being a client of the state meant, especially if one were a woman (Shaver, 1990). In later literature, this would be depicted as uncovering women's situated agency. This work started to look at how different groups of women – especially those without a man to support them – accessed assistance through the public system, the conditions attaching to the support given and the consequences flowing from it. Problematizing 'welfare' and underlining the considerable effort involved in attaining it, studies indicated that women had at least two relationships to the welfare state: as worker and as client. In the former regard, it is striking how much the European welfare states were built on women's labour in social, educational and health services, and how female-dominated many of these sectors were (and still are). We may associate this with the Scandinavian countries – and we would be correct – but it is a feature of the welfare state in Europe more broadly. For example, the workforce of the National Health Service (NHS), the single largest employer in Britain, was 77 per cent female in 2014.[4] Most of the feminist appraisal, though, focused on women's relationship to the welfare state as client, in a literature that was generally highly critical, even if some were at pains to point out that the welfare state bestowed real gains on women, especially if viewed historically, and was actually welcomed by some women activists (Hernes, 1987; Blackburn, 1995).

This work highlighted the coalface of accessing public benefits and services, conceiving the process of claiming as an act of agency, whether on the part of the 'claimant' or the bureaucrat charged with delivery, or both. Welfare was uncovered as local and particular by studying everyday practices and adopting a critical approach to decoding institutional practice and language as well as attitudes and behaviour. This work was in some ways a reflection of a feminist epistemological commitment to giving 'voice', focused on the experience of the everyday, the doing of welfare (within and outwith a family setting), the receiving of public support, in order to reveal the experiences, agency and personhood of those who are

---

[4]   See infographic at http://www.nhsemployers.org/case-studies-and-resources/2014/03/ women-in-the-nhs-infographic.

relatively powerless in the system. It had resonance with the idea of gender as process and performance – in West and Zimmerman's (1987) terms: 'doing gender', wherein welfare could be seen to constitute people as 'male' or 'female' and, in the process, force them to perform appropriately.[5]

Revealed in large print were the many details of what it was like to approach the public authorities requesting help – something previously considered relatively mundane, uninteresting and self-evident. As Mary McIntosh (1981, p. 32) described it, "the queues and the forms, the deference, the anger, the degradation, the sense of invisibility and the loss of autonomy". Laid bare too was the frequently humiliating nature of means tests and other assessments of 'deservingness'. This was a more widespread experience for women because they were more likely than men to be claiming social assistance or benefits that were discretionary and not available as a right. Here moral probity rivalled financial need as the basis for judging people and their claims and this occasioned not just affirmation and sanction but a form of close surveillance of people's lives. This, too, may have reached women in greater numbers than men given that they were more often approaching the public authorities in precarious or potentially 'norm-breaking' situations, like unmarried or extra-marital child bearing/rearing (although one should not underestimate the extent to which the treatment of men or women in situations of unemployment was also coloured by the perception of people in this state as morally dubious). It is for this kind of reason that the differentiation between rights-based and non-rights-based provisions was to assume such a pivotal role in feminist research and political engagement.

Women's contribution as producers of welfare was one of the new insights here. The family as a location of welfare-related work and industry was another important contribution (Hartmann, 1979), especially as regards the economic character and function of housework (Oakley, 1974a, 1974b). As Hilary Rose (1981, p. 497) explains: despite huge public welfare budgets "most of welfare/personal production and reproduction still takes place within the home". Conceiving of reproductive work as care came later; in the earlier studies it was women's contribution in the family as a unit of welfare production that was highlighted.

---

[5]   As well as highlighting agency, this kind of work reveals the fluidity and complexity of sex and gender categories (Bradley, 2013, p. 22). According to Risman and Davis (2013, p. 741) the 'doing gender' framework has become perhaps the most common perspective in contemporary sociological research in the US.

1.1.2   Probing Underpinning Values and Assumptions

A further focus of attention was the philosophical foundations of social policy. The assumptions underlying social policy have always seemed to be more important as an analytic lens in feminist work as compared with more mainstream scholarship where they tended to be taken for granted. Why the feminist interest? One of the founding feminist scholars, Elizabeth Wilson, explains: "the Welfare State is not just a set of services, it is also a set of ideas about society, about the family, and – not least important – about women" (Wilson, 1977, p. 9). Such ideas serve a powerful legitimizing function. But there is another reason also – once you know the assumptions you are better placed to discern two component features. The first is the underpinning social architecture (especially if that is hidden or unstated). The second is the underlying power relations, especially what we might call 'power with a small p': that is, social relations not conventionally thought of as political but where power is lodged in taken-for-granted assumptions and practices and assumes forms that may not necessarily involve force or threat (Glenn, 2016, p. 115).

The evidence, once unearthed, showed that assumptions about inherent differences between women and men and their respective and appropriate roles were widespread in social policy and that on the basis of this the system of which it was a part set up a clear division of identity and labour (and hence power) that was sex- or gender-based (Shaver, 1990). Pascall (1986, p. 198) summarizes some such key assumptions of social policies in the 1970s UK: "... (1) that women are available to do housework and care for children and elderly relatives, without pay; (2) that couples consist of one full-time worker (usually a male breadwinner) and one 'housewife' whose work outside the home is insignificant, being merely for 'pin-money'; and (3) that women can look to men for financial support".

Policy's modus operandi was to represent certain practices and arrangements as normal. The patriarchal family, for example, was part of the natural order of society according to the prevailing social policy of the time (Wilson, 1977). Ideologies around the female role and contribution, and by implication the appropriate role of men as husbands and fathers, were germinal. While social policy held a strong normative position on the family, it was reluctant to look inside, preferring to keep the focus on an aggregated (rather than disaggregated) collective unit. Motherhood dominated the female register in that maternalism made (common) sense as a way of supporting women. The earliest women-specific benefits therefore were maternity-related benefits. Protecting women and recognizing their contribution as mothers was also a focus of some early mobilizations of women (Koven and Michel, 1993; Orloff, 1996). Along with maternalism, welfare states historically also subsidized marriage (Shaver and Bradshaw, 1993; Scheiwe, 1994; Montanari, 2000). This was an early example of an approach informed by insersectionality whereby marriage and motherhood intersected as ideals and policy categories. Of the possible arrangements, marriage within a nuclear family context was the preferred arrangement in most countries. And, of course, marriage was a heterosexual institution. Montanari's (2000) analysis of policy developments cross-nationally between the 1930s and the 1990s shows how the architecture of family benefits and services was accompanied by a parallel architecture supporting the married family arrangement and that such subsidies existed in practically every high-income country for much of the twentieth century. What she is referring to here are taxation-related arrangements, such as tax splitting between members of couples, tax allowances and tax credits. To the extent that welfare states supported marriage, what they were in effect doing was reinforcing marriage as the institution through which women should be compensated for their unpaid care; to the extent that they paid benefits directly to women they were bypassing marriage (Scheiwe, 1994).

And yet it was recognized that the welfare state also provided many services that were essential to women's well-being and, indeed, was a major source of employment for women. On this account, the relationship between women and the welfare state was a complex one. On the one hand, welfare states provided women with material and social improvements, needed services and in some cases employment. On the other hand, however, the form of provision and gender-based differences in generosity of social policy circumscribed women's lives and gave them a secondary status to men (Pascall, 1986; Williams, 1993). Rose (1986, p. 82) summarizes well – the system turns on the enforced dependency of women and yet at the same time provides the preconditions (through support and so forth) through which women increasingly challenge both its form and content. For some, this meant that the welfare state's relationship to women was contradictory (as drawn out in Elizabeth Wilson's 1977 work and also by Land, 1978, 1980; Pascall, 1983; and Siim, 1987). These kinds of contradictions – while perhaps today more explicitly targeted through new policy rubrics such as 'work–life balance' – have not gone away.

1.1.3 Analysing Benefit Organizational Structure and Access

A third seam of feminist work turned the spotlight on the structure of social policy and especially the organization of the benefit system itself (in some ways encompassing and bringing to fruition the insights of the first two seams). With the goal of pinpointing the specific structural mechanisms, in focus here were the design and operation of social programmes.

Looked at over time, this was arguably the largest body of feminist work in social policy – there were numerous investigations of the fine detail of provision, focused on individual countries but also – over time – more comparative work (as we shall see also in Chapter 2). Seemingly small details – the fine print of entitlement – were shown to matter for the way the system 'positioned' women and their circumstances. There were two main strands of work here that take us further into the organizational detail of programmes and social policy itself: one was on the 'risks' or contingencies which women typically face or encounter and how the social policy system treated these; the second studied the unit of entitlement for eligibility purposes and the related conditions attaching to benefits and services. It was around these – especially the latter – that the momentum for social policy reform cohered in subsequent years (see Chapter 6).

A foundational aspect of the structure and positioning associated with the welfare state is how social risks are defined and covered. Social insurance is after all a system of risk protection through collectivization. This is significant from a gender perspective because, while they share some risks in common, women and men also experience different risks of loss or insufficiency of income and resources. Historically for men (and still today), their income level and security are mainly endangered by interruption or loss of earned income, through illness, accident, unemployment and old age for example. These are (the) classic male risks to which the welfare system was developed to respond, with class-based politics playing a key role as sectors of the working population exposed to market risks sought protection (Baldwin, 1990; Van Kersbergen and Vis, 2014). While women are also vulnerable to such risks, they are subject to them to a lesser degree than men and are also prone to a set of risks that are but indirectly related to such market-induced uncertainties. Unique income risks for women are defined by the female biological constitution (birth-giving), the social construction of marriage/partnership as an institution of female support and of caregiving (mothering especially) as primarily a woman's role. Women, therefore, experience a number of additional risks:

- loss of a male income (through widowhood, divorce and separation);
- loss of own income through pregnancy and child-rearing;
- loss of own income through the need to care for others (either adults and/or children).[6]

---

[6]   Another risk event for women, married and cohabiting women especially, is if men fail to share their usually larger income with their partners and children. However, this has never been taken up as a major risk by most welfare states.

Notice the focus on 'own' income here – it underlines a concern with independent access to income for women.

European and other welfare systems have always been very particular about which risks they collectivize, through social insurance especially. Of what we might call 'classically women's risks', only pregnancy and widowhood ever achieved the status of a social insurance risk. Divorce and separation have not been specifically provided for as risks in their own right through the welfare state (although there is provision in some systems for the state to provide 'income maintenance' to women should the father(s) of their child(ren) fail to do so). Loss of income through the need or obligation to provide care – a situation widely the case for mothers and other female family members – has tended to be recognized and legitimated more as a weak claim (that is, through social assistance rather than under the rights-based and usually more generous social insurance – although in the last decades Austria, Germany and some Asian countries have instituted long-term care social insurance). Such structural differentiations led some scholars to claim that social insurance was male and social assistance female, and also to talk of a two-channel welfare system (Nelson, 1990).

The second structural element examined in the search for the gender basis of the welfare state was the unit of entitlement and other programmatic rules governing the social support system. As with the assumptions underlying policy, this was seen to be a vital link in the chain of understanding how the welfare state affected women's status and participation in public life as well as the material living conditions of women vis-à-vis men.

As regards the unit of entitlement,[7] social entitlements are usually thought of as individual-based – the individual earns them usually through making paid contributions into the designated funds. Hence, they are rights accrued and claimed by individuals. Across and within national settings, the basis of entitlement varies widely, however, and individual rights constitute only one basis of entitlement. There were two gender particularities of note. In social insurance where benefits are typically organized on an individual, life course basis, many women entered the system of coverage by virtue of their relationship to a man or through some recognition of their entitlement through their home duties (as in pension credits for example). Hence, they constituted a different 'class of beneficiaries' and only women who could approximate the male norm of uninterrupted working life claimed on a full individual, like-for-like basis. A second gender imprinting was inscribed

---

[7]   In relation to the British welfare state, Roll (1991, p. 22) conceptualizes this interface in terms of the 'benefit family' and problematizes the claiming process in the following four-fold way: who is entitled to make the claim; who is taken into account by the various rules of entitlement; who is the payment intended to cover; who is entitled to receive the payment.

in the use of the male head of household as the conduit of benefits for the household in the case of means-tested benefits. This, coupled with the fact that women were not employed in anything like similar proportions as men, copper-fastened a secondary or subsidiary role for women. Feminist policy analysis identified numerous conventions (institutional practices) in the system leading to such an eventuality. Some such examples include the cohabitation rule (which was applied to unmarried couples and vetoed the paying of a benefit to a woman if she were co-resident with a man); in the UK and Ireland the so-called 'married woman's option' (whereby women could voluntarily opt out of paying for (and thereby receiving) a social insurance benefit (such as an old-age pension) in their own right), electing instead to be treated as the 'dependant' of their husbands.[8] Furthermore, welfare benefits indirectly (and in some cases directly through rules about other income for example) shaped the labour market role and choices of the female partner, either by specifying the permissible degree and form of economic activity or by making it a rational decision for only one partner to be employed. Many rules continue to exist today and, although they may be different in nature, they have the similar effect of circumscribing choice and patterning behaviour for those subject to them (see Millar and Bennett, 2017, for analysis of UK reforms).

The use of family status for the purposes of the benefit system and assumptions about women's capacity and dependency have the potential to be positive and negative for women. When family status is a criterion for paying benefits to women – maternity benefits, survivor benefits, children's allowances, some payments for caring – it helps overall to reduce male/ female differences in income level and can enable some financial independence for women (Daly, 2000). Widows are the most universal classic case (but note the rather obvious point that these benefits can be claimed only when the husband/partner has died). Other women – such as lone mothers – were rarely provided with benefits in their own right, usually having to make recourse to a general claim to social assistance. In sum, while these benefits do help individual women, their distinct character and typically lower than average generosity put a brake on the extent to which family status-based benefits erode gender inequalities. The other side of the family status criterion is when it was used as a justification to pay higher benefits to those with family obligations. In this guise it often acted, indirectly, to increase male incomes and hence gender inequalities (men being more likely to claim for adult 'dependants' than women). So there are two countervailing forces pulling against each other.

---

[8]   The option was phased out in the UK in 1978.

Overall, the strong message from feminist appraisal was that gender was a major organizing principle of the welfare (state) system.

1.2 EXPLAINING PRACTICES AND RELATIONSHIPS

While it might appear from the foregoing that research activity was mainly focused at the empirical and experiential level, in fact the field was from the start strongly theoretical. Offering a theoretically-informed critique of the gender divisions in social policy was a founding aim. Feminist work on the welfare state, in the first decade or so anyway, was closely connected to the re-emergence of the women's movement in the 1960s, which Watkins (2018, p. 50) eloquently characterizes as "a starburst of original thinking". Bennett describes some of the context for the UK in the 1970s (1983, p. 194): many active feminists were also members of Left groups and wanted to bring a feminist perspective to bear on discussions about the state's economic and ideological functions as well as its relationship with capitalist production and reproduction. Analysis therefore also served the purpose of identifying effective points of intervention for political mobilization.

Feminism is therefore an important place to look for theoretical work on gender and the welfare state. The feminist critique drew from and enlarged a range of theoretical perspectives and so there is no single feminist social policy approach (Pascall, 1986). Williams, writing in 1989, reveals the diversity and richness. She considers six approaches in her review: libertarian feminism, liberal feminism, welfare feminism, radical feminism, socialist feminism and black feminism.[9] The prominence of each of these strands in social policy varies – the bulk of the work was actually by social-ist feminists, with significant contributions by liberal and radical feminists also. These are the main fields I will review here. Throughout though, we need to be mindful of Williams's point that there were other perspectives apart from these and in particular that a significant critique was developed by black and Third World feminists.

The criteria used by Williams (1989, p. 42) to interrogate the femi-nist positions are helpful for critical thinking. These criteria are: the significance they attribute to women's biology in their explanations; whether they emphasize the public sphere of work and politics or the private sphere of home and caring, or both; and the degree of focus on the generality of women's oppression or the differentiated needs and

---

[9] See Ferguson (2017) for a more up-to-date engagement with feminist ideologies and Rottenberg (2014, 2018) for a review of contemporary liberal feminism and its critiques.

experiences of particular groups of women. Williams also examined whether the approaches are individualist, materialist or idealist.

Liberal feminism's axis of explanation centres on sex discrimination as an underlying cause of gender inequalities within and outwith the welfare state. The lack of recognition and rights for women as mothers and tolerance of sexual violence and repression are core sites of theory building. The state is taken to be more or less neutral and it is assumed that welfare institutions can be reformed from within (O'Connor, 1996, p. 4). If discrimination is the primary medium through which inequalities are perpetuated, then it follows that a reform programme to address discrimination (especially legislation and other measures to counter prejudice and stereotyping) is the way forward. Power is regarded positively ('power to') and women can and should aspire to the power and opportunities that men possess (Kantola and Lombardo, 2017a, p. 52). In regard to the conditions of motherhood, the demands of what Williams (1989, pp. 49–52) labels 'welfare feminists' – such as Eleanor Rathbone in the UK – were primarily concerned with women's welfare within the home and family. Liberal feminism works with a conception of women and men as equal but different – hence motherhood should be deserving of rights and protection from the state. Of course, this means the continued separation of public from private and the privileging of the public remaining relatively unchallenged. There is a strong rights foundation to the liberal feminist approach, the ultimate goal of which – when applied to the welfare state historically – was equal rights for women to work and benefits, and supportive services to enable that to happen. Actions in the public sphere therefore are prioritized over those in the private sphere which is not generally highlighted as a location of reform (Williams, 1989, p. 46). An understanding of gender as a structural feature of the economy and society is not foregrounded in this perspective and this has been a cause for critique. On this account, liberal feminism can be criticized for underestimating the structural forces limiting women's equality and underemphasizing the need to attend also to women's role and work within the private sphere. Furthermore, women and men are seen to form coherent, unified and binary categories. In sum, what a critical approach to liberal feminism teaches us is that, while measures to address discrimination are necessary, the full cause of gender inequality will never be found solely within the benefit or welfare state system itself or its discriminatory orientation to women.

Radical feminists proposed a theory of gender inequality as resulting from the sexual division of labour that is reproduced through patriarchy in reproductive relations, the family and sexuality (Bradley, 2013, p. 44). They led the call for the abolition of the nuclear family (e.g. Firestone, 1970). Patriarchy was a key concept/theorization here (in the work of Millett,

1970, especially; see also Walby, 1990). In their welfare state-focused analyses, radical feminists turned the spotlight on the role of welfare systems in maintaining the sexual division of labour and how this benefits men (public patriarchy). The sexual division of labour was seen to have a strong material character (in the sense of the division of labour and responsibility and the opportunities seen to be appropriately open to each sex) but also a symbolic expression. Male power – in the form of the patriarchal system – is the root causal factor of inequalities in this view and the welfare state is one institutionalization of that power system. In a system bent towards men, social policies exert control over women and play a key part in keeping the accepted sexual and reproductive order as it is (through mechanisms such as those we have seen in earlier parts of the chapter). That order, and the legitimacy of the state, is not challenged by moves towards rights for mothers or anti-discrimination (Williams, 1989, p. 48). In fact, women are oppressed as a group. Different writers within this approach stress different aspects of the patriarchal system, but men's effective control over women's sexuality and reproductive capacity and the prevalence and functional purpose of sexual violence (especially in the domestic setting) are usually somewhere close to the centre. This strand of feminism championed and pioneered new models of service provision to address especially (but not exclusively) social and health problems experienced by women. They have been leaders in advocating for alternative health services and abortion clinics for example. Overall, though, women and men are inherently oppositional categories in this perspective (Ferree, 2015, p. 7).

Of all three, it was perhaps for the socialist feminists that the welfare state as a system of social policy was of most theoretical interest. This is the strand of feminist work that is most prominent among the early theorists of the gender dimension of the welfare state and social policy (although liberal feminism is also very strong and has had major influence on social policy discourse and reform in the US – see Orloff, 2009). Socialist feminists – drawing from Marxism and a critique of other types of feminism – emphasized the significance of material factors, attributing the capitalist economic system a pivotal role. However, the conventional Marxist perspective is critiqued for its economistic concern with the reproduction of labour rather than, for example, what one might crudely call 'the production of people' (Hartmann, 1979; Barrett, 1980; Pascall, 1986). The core claim centres around the complicity of the welfare state in articulating productive activity with reproduction through a set of material and ideological divisions that are in core respects based on sex and gender. Socialist feminists conferred a broad meaning and high theoretical purpose on social reproduction. It covers "... not only the process of bearing children, but also the physical, emotional, ideological and material processes involved in caring for and sustaining others – not just children" (Williams, 1989, p. 42). Women's economic dependency was both a central assumption and functional pre-requisite of the welfare state. Any boundaries between paid and unpaid work were artificial. A key mechanism through which the system operates is the promotion of the nuclear, male breadwinner household or family form by the welfare state (McIntosh, 1978; Land, 1980). Here the family wage was pivotal, providing both the financial conditions and the ideological justification (Land, 1980; Gordon, 1990). This brings feminists in conflict with the labour movement for the family wage was one of their demands (Sapiro, 1986). This analysis not only connected organized social policy to reproducing the fundamental conditions of capitalism but it also suggested that Marxist analysis placed the concerns of class over gender (Hartmann, 1979).

A key question pursued by socialist feminists was who benefits from women's unpaid reproductive work and caring labour? In reply, they spotlighted the privileging of capitalism and men through particular state forms and conventions. They saw women as being exploited and oppressed as a class (e.g. Beechey, 1982). The interweaving of the state, family and economy was an important theoretical insight that predated Esping-Andersen's (1990) work on welfare regimes (e.g. Showstack Sassoon, 1987), and was in any case developed much more profoundly in feminist conceptions. According to Williams (1989, p. 64), there are two core theoretical positions that most socialist feminist accounts have in common and try to integrate: a recognition of the existence of institutionalized power relationships between women and men and their significance in reproducing gender inequality; and a recognition that capitalism gives rise to different experiences of oppression by women located differently. Hence, while levelling criticism against conventional Marxism for ignoring women and gender, socialist feminists were conscious of the differences among women as well as those between women and men. In some respects, this perspective prefigured the growth of intersectionality since it countenances class and gender as being reproduced within the same system. However, it devoted relatively little attention to care as we understand it today. This was interesting mainly because it was a form of labour – the idea of it as a type of human interconnection was not really part of socialist feminist thinking.

1.3 CONCLUSION

All told, focusing on women and gender added a new set of complexities to the study of social policy. It peeled away the layers and started to investigate theoretically and empirically elements that had previously been either hidden or taken for granted (such as the process of accessing and claiming benefits and assumptions and norms underpinning the system of public support). Not only was the welfare state brought to life as a presence and actor affecting the everyday lives and choices of women and men, but a focused and layered understanding was offered of how it actually functioned. And in its operation gender was revealed to be a fundamental organizing principle. Social policy's assumptions, rules and procedures were shown to encode norms and practices directing women and men towards different paths (sometimes through directly controlling behaviour and sometimes through more indirect means) and constraining women's independence and participation in public life. It is impossible to overestimate the significance of the detailed conditions, conventions and local functioning of social policy in early feminist appraisal. They were freighted with meaning and significance. In the process of revealing these, this work has raised for debate the ideologies embodied in welfare and put on the table for our consideration the ways in which social policy operated to a sex- and gender-differentiated understanding of entitlement and citizenship. These are themes that will recur throughout this book.

In peeling away the layers, a number of mechanisms were theorized as crucial. One of these was the (constructed) divide between public and private that social policies helped to erect and maintain. Of course, this is not static and shifts over time (as we shall see in later chapters) but the mechanisms whereby some matters are considered 'public' – and therefore worthy of social concern and perhaps even public support – while others are constructed as 'private' – in the sense of being beyond or outside public purview and governance – are enduring features of welfare systems. Second, theorizing the family and its role in social and economic organization was considered a vital exercise. In this regard, feminist work showed how – for social policy purposes – women and even men are situated centrally in a family setting – they are family actors. Study after study showed the welfare state's role in drawing the borderline between itself, society and family and its significance in 'managing' and 'policing' this and other boundaries. Of crucial import here was the family's (and women's) role as a site and conduit of unpaid labour. Social reproduction was a core line of theorizing to explain why women (and men) were positioned as they were by welfare state, economy and society. Taken together, the work showed the merits of shifting the ground from the analysis of production to that of production and reproduction. Despite significant reform, the inherent tensions and contradictions continue.

It is important to add that the foregoing analysis does not tell the story of women everywhere, and indeed of all women. The US is a good case to point out that its welfare state cannot be understood in the absence of an analysis that considers racial issues centrally. This prism reveals how racial divisions and concerns in the US meant that citizenship never developed as a social political paradigm, unlike in Europe where the development of the welfare state system turned on distributional politics, especially those associated with class and gender within relatively homogeneous and united populaces. In the US, says Mink (1990, p. 99), social politics took shape within a paradigm drawn by diversity and democracy whereas in Europe it was the relations between capitalism and democracy that shaped them. Given this, it is important to bear in mind that the category of 'dependant' and the gender division of labour do not accurately describe the lives of women in some racial minorities, who were much more likely to be self-supporting, to be engaged in paid domestic work, to live without male support and to be in relationships of subservience to other women. Race has generally been ignored or underplayed in the social policy scholarship (Williams, 1989).

Before concluding this chapter, it is interesting to note how some of the originating insights and approaches of the early gender work have made a broader impact. Take the interest in examining the assumptions underpinning social policy. The early interest shown in this by the gender-focused social policy analysis is now also to be seen in more general analysis of social and public policies especially in the growing body of work focusing on ideas in explaining the reform of the welfare state (e.g. Béland, 2005; Béland and Cox, 2011). Feminist influence is also to be seen in a related development – the growth of the framing approach as a mode of analysing policy change, drawing especially from Carol Bacchi's (2009) work and that of Lombardo et al. (2009). Highlighting discourse, the hallmark of this approach is to identify and critique the construction of the 'problem' by policy, to treat this as political and assign policy analysis the task of revealing not just what is being problematized but what is left unproblematized in the 'problem representation', and the consequences that are likely to follow from such a representation of the 'problem'. Finally, one can see elements of the feminist focus on risks in the new social risks literature (e.g. Taylor-Gooby, 2004; Bonoli, 2005). While it sees risks as shaped by life courses and tends not to problematize gender inequalities, its fundamental insights draw from a recognition of the specificities of the female life course and differences in this regard between women and men.

As will be obvious, this chapter has spoken in general if not universal terms. There has been little consideration of cross-national variations or the situation of subgroups of women or men. In some respects, this reflects the literature considered and its orientation towards grand theorizing and making universal claims around sex and gender. There is no doubt that it was theorizing from both a narrow base and a unified conception of woman. But the enduring power and application of many of the ideas – and the longevity of concepts like choice and social reproduction – makes this a non-fatal critique. However, the downplaying if not exclusion of some groups and associated political interests – particularly along ethnic and racial lines – is important to note. The generalist focus is overtaken in the next chapter which covers a period in which scholarship became much more attuned to variation and difference. A key set of questions that we now turn to centres upon what has happened in the intervening period and whether the developments depicted in this chapter are now history.

2. Contemporary approaches to gender and social policy: bringing scholarship up to date

This chapter takes up the story of how the study and conceptualization of the relationship between gender and the welfare state proceeded from the 1990s. It will show the picture to be one of both continuing interest in some of the older issues as well as significant new trends and conceptual orientations.

In broad strokes, I read feminist work from the 1990s on social policy and the welfare state as marked by two characteristics. First, it was middle range theoretically, working with what Joan Scott (1986, p. 1055) has termed "usable theoretical formulations" rather than broad-ranging theories. Prominent among such formulations were gender-based typologies, processes of familialization/defamilialization, and care (understood in terms of both giving and receiving it). Second, it favoured structural analyses (over, say, more discursive or constructivist approaches) – continuing the study of the linkages between social policy as part of the organization of a range of social, economic and political institutions, and agency and circumstances in real life. This is reflected in a shift from social policy to the concept of the welfare state which became more prominent in feminist work from the 1990s on. An outgrowth of this was a more systemic focus on state patterning and a larger picture view of both power relations and the ways that these were embedded in political constellations and more global systems of relationships. The investigation of policies as an expression of deeper interest group politics and ideologies was one line of analysis; another was the enduring impact of welfare's organizational or institutional patterns (even after reform). A key strand of feminist work sought to continue to broaden the focus beyond relations of production, and situate reproductive relations in the political economy approach (Orloff, 1993). Another hallmark of feminist scholarship from the 1990s was the strong comparative focus. This led to a body of work identifying and explaining cross-national variations in welfare state policies. This too was focused mainly on the high-income countries.[1] Here, feminist work dovetailed with the very influential typologizing literature (e.g.

Esping-Andersen, 1990), which, through comparisons of variation, helped internationalize the study of social policy and associated models of political economy (although it also tended to reconfirm the nation state as the appropriate unit of analysis). The classic European welfare state models that emerged from this work were the social democratic (to be found mainly in the Nordic countries of Denmark, Finland, Norway and Sweden), Continental European (characteristic of the systems prevailing in Austria, Belgium, France, Germany, Luxembourg and Italy) and the liberal model to be found in Ireland and the UK. Others have added a set of Mediterranean countries (Ferrera, 1996). And of course there are the Central Eastern European and Baltic countries which have been less integrated into the welfare state regime literature but are also characterized by sui generis policy models (Pascall and Lewis, 2004; Javornik, 2014). In gender hands, a large body of comparatively-informed research has been built up over nearly three decades which analyses and critiques variations in social policy and welfare state politics from a woman's and/or gender perspective. This sits alongside – rather than necessarily being integrated into – the conventional welfare state analysis which understands political economy mainly from a social class perspective.

This chapter concentrates on further conceptual developments from the 1990s. To signpost what lies ahead, I review what I see as four main lines of analysis: elaborations of the underlying system; conceptions of processes and end states; the emergence and growth of the concept of care; the growing interest in gender as one of a number of intersecting inequalities.

2.1 SYSTEM-ORIENTED WORK

We saw in the last chapter that one of the key insights of early scholarship was that welfare programmes not only kept women subordinate but did so in a way that supported a whole social system in which such subordination was consequential (Gordon, 1990, p. 183). Three causal linkages in the relationship between the welfare state and unequal gendered outcomes were highlighted: the family wage system which resourced men as heads (patriarchs) of families; a gendered division of paid and unpaid labour; and a division between public and private relations and spheres. These themes were taken forward in later work also but to a differential degree and also sometimes through different lenses.

As mentioned, comparison and a systemic focus was a hallmark of

---

[1] For early reviews, see O'Connor (1996) and Orloff (1996). By 'high-income' here I mainly mean the countries of Europe as well as Australia, Canada, New Zealand and the US.

feminist work from the 1990s. Comparing systems had three main forms of appeal: the capacity to take forward the long-standing feminist interest in the organizational features of social policy; the possibility of embedding these in the wider political economy of varying welfare states; and the chance to connect the organizational features of the state system to other 'systems' (e.g. those of family, market and nation). In the process, the feminist approach to the welfare state has come to be marked by a perspective which focuses not only on the complexity and reality (particularly from a woman's perspective) of social policy in national settings but also – and especially – using and problematizing variation within and across welfare states as a lever to improve understanding. This, it seems to me, has seen a greater influence of political science frameworks and thinking in feminist work as compared with the past. At the risk of over-simplifying a complex field, in addition to the existing focus on a comparison of programme rules and philosophies, a second stream endeavoured to counter or complement mainstream work by producing typologies founded on gender-centred criteria. Both streams of work have been generally faithful to earlier concerns and an interest in the identification of underlying models is common to both. We consider each briefly in turn.

2.1.1   Institutions, Ideologies and Rights

The work of Diane Sainsbury is exemplary here. In a series of papers and books produced in the early- to mid-1990s, she undertook gender-based comparisons across a number of countries of the conditions attaching to pensions, unemployment, sickness and public assistance benefits to see how women and men were placed as beneficiaries in different welfare systems. She was especially interested in whether social rights were individualized or more family based. Among the factors scrutinized to reveal this were the bases of entitlement, benefit levels, conditions of entitlement, coverage of eligible population, and so forth (see also Gornick et al., 1997; Daly, 2000). This strand of work also sought to bring conceptual order to the broader approaches and underpinning logics governing the treatment of different groups of women (and men) in social security and tax provisions. Among the logics or mechanisms identified by Sainsbury and others (present in countries to differential degrees) were the subsidization of marriage as against parenthood (Scheiwe, 1994), different models of motherhood (employed as against home based for example) (Leira, 1992; Koven and Michel, 1993) and the mechanics of states' support for a wifely and/or motherly role for women (Shaver and Bradshaw, 1993).

Moving one step back – or up – there was also a continued interest in linking ideology to organizational form, with an elaboration of the family

Table 2.1   Capturing variation in the gender dimension of social policies

Dimension	Male breadwinner model	Individual model
Familial ideology	Privileging of marriage strict division of labour husband = earner wife = carer	No preferred family form shared roles father = earner/carer mother = earner/carer
Taxation	Joint taxation deduction for 'dependants'	Separate taxation equal tax relief
Employment and wage policies	Priority to men	Aimed at both sexes
Sphere of care	Primarily private	Strong state involvement
Caring work	Unpaid	Paid component

Source: Adapted from Sainsbury (1996, p. 42, Table 2.1).

wage system in terms of the male breadwinner model especially prominent. Indicators became more systematized and sophisticated. Comparing countries suggested that, while at first glance they appeared to differ hugely, in actual fact they were characterized by similar features but to a differential degree. Hence, Sainsbury (1996) showed through the aforementioned comparison that one could conceptualize the relevant set of welfare arrangements in the Netherlands, Sweden, the UK and the US as lying along a continuum which is bounded at one end by a male breadwinner/ housewife model and at the other by a model with an individual focus. As can be seen from Table 2.1, the indicators she uses relate to the underlying ideology in regard to family, the appropriate divisions of labour between the sexes and views on the appropriate location of care (in terms of both responsibility and work) between the public and private spheres. It can be seen to be more than a one-dimensional framework in that she considers a range of policy spheres and also looks at the policy arrangements that flow from particular ideological orientations.

Some of the deeper roots, especially the political foundations, were theorized through the concept of citizenship. Bringing in both the state and the political community, work here was especially concerned with the degree to which women had access to social rights, the conditions attaching to such rights and the extent to which citizenship arrangements promote or hinder women's autonomy and economic independence, especially those with caring responsibilities. The resultant work drew attention to citizenship as a (gender) differentiated concept and set of institutions and practices (Pateman, 1988; Fraser, 1989; Lister, 1990, 1997a, 1997b; Leira,

1992; O'Connor, 1992; Orloff, 1993; Fraser and Gordon, 1994). Fraser and Gordon (1992) and also Lister (1997b) explored the differentiation between civil and social citizenship. The former establishes the rights deemed necessary for individual freedom (such as rights to property and personal liberty and the right to justice) whereas social citizenship embodies the rights to public support we have been talking about to date in this chapter and the last. Again feminist work showed that these two institutions were shot through with gender-related and other differentiations. The work of Pateman (1988), for example, showed that social rights historically attached to those who are 'independent'.[2] Looking at the US historically, Fraser and Gordon (1994) researched the long-range career of 'dependency' in welfare ideology and practice, revealing the convention of opposing 'dependence' to an idealized 'independence' and a lack of problematization of the state of 'dependence' as well as the situation of those (especially women and people of colour) seen to be 'dependent'. One important legacy of the prominence of citizenship in feminist thinking is the use of law to craft a programme and project of change. This will figure prominently in Chapter 6, when we look at how claims for equality in social policy were framed, especially in the context of gender discrimination (Brocas, 1988; Meulders-Klein and Eekelaar, 1988; Sohrab, 1996).

2.1.2 Types and Regimes

The second focus of comparative work has been on typologizing, engaging with the idea that social policy comes in types and that – taking account of a range of different factors – these might be conceptualized as regimes or systems. This work was fuelled by the typologizing turn in conventional welfare state studies from the late 1980s. Part of the originating desire was to add a gender-focused approach to the comparative field, given that Gøsta Esping-Andersen's widely influential 1990 book – *The Three Worlds of Welfare Capitalism* – was largely based on men's relationship to the welfare state (without any real acknowledgment of that specificity). Everyone knew the workers were men, and that men were genderless. The closest Esping-Andersen came to gender was family, suggesting that different types of policy regime co-exist with different roles for the family. Yet his work gave no more than a taste of such inter-relations because neither the family nor household was integrated systematically into his analysis

---

[2] Three elements of classical independence on which citizenship was founded were: the capacity to bear arms, the capacity to own property and the capacity for self-government (Pateman, 1988, p. 238). See also Skocpol (1995).

of welfare state variations, or at least not to the same degree as his other concepts of decommodification and stratification (Daly, 2000).

The most noted gender typology is that offered by Jane Lewis (1992) and Lewis and Ostner (1991). This was defined in terms of the degree of adherence to the male breadwinner model, the classic version of which valorized heterosexual marriage and a preferred division of labour between husband and wife whereby he was employed and responsible for securing the family income (hence the reference to 'breadwinner') and she was a full-time carer in the home (Sainsbury, 1994, 1996, used similar categories of analysis). Lewis based her models on many of the elements of welfare systems described in the last chapter and in earlier paragraphs above – like the entitlement units for benefits and services, the conditions attaching, the extent of support for married fathers and what kind of role was endorsed for women. Lewis's great accomplishment was to treat the breadwinner as a series of models rather than a single entity. On her account, three variants of gender regime exist: those with strong, moderate and weak male breadwinner models. Britain and Ireland are categorized as strong male breadwinner countries, because they tended to draw a firm dividing line between public and private responsibility and to treat married women as dependent wives for the purposes of social entitlements. France is categorized as a moderate male breadwinner state because women there gained entitlements as both citizen mothers and citizen workers. Female labour market participation was encouraged but, at the same time, the policy framework was strongly supportive of families. Motherhood is treated as a social function rather than a private matter by family-centred, pronatalist-inspired social policies. Post-1970 Sweden and Denmark constituted the third variant in the typology, described as 'weak male breadwinner states'. Social democratic governments in these countries and elsewhere in the Nordic region took conscious steps to make the 'two breadwinner family' the norm, transforming the basis of women's social entitlements and the conditions of their lives so that they could be workers and mothers.

This work has been very influential, providing a foothold and focus for subsequent scholarship to develop along several lines. In actual fact, the inter-relations between the state, the market and the family proved a magnet for researchers and subsequent years saw work on intergenerational regimes (Saraceno and Keck, 2010), care regimes (Bettio and Plantenga, 2004) and family policy regimes (Leitner, 2003; Keck and Saraceno, 2013) (to name just some). A second contribution was to use the typologies – actually underpinning models – to identify trends and pinpoint emerging policy trajectories as the old breadwinner model started to be reformed. From this work the notion of the 'adult worker model' was born. Jane Lewis contributed centrally to this also, naming it in the first instance and identifying a number of empirical features of the associated social policy template, while underlining that it was a policy ideal rather than a reality (Lewis, 2001). Distilling this down, it would appear that for Lewis there are three main indicators of a move to an adult worker model (developed especially through analysis of the UK and broader EU social policy context over the course of the 1990s). Of significance, first, is the impulse to encourage employment on the part of both parents – a widespread development in Europe (and a central goal at EU level) as European welfare states confront problems with their labour markets. A second relevant direction of policy highlighted by Lewis was some 'defamilialization' of care, whereby states seem more willing to either offer or subsidize relevant services, also often for the purpose of freeing women up for labour market participation. A third associated trend which to Lewis signalled a move to an adult worker model is reform in the direction of individualization for the purpose of entitlement to social security benefits. There was a flood of such reforms in the EU in the 1980s and 1990s and when this is put together with a general move to tighten the relationship between labour market participation and eligibility for benefits and services it weakened the privileging of family-related status, especially marital status. We should note that many of these changes have not in the intervening period progressed on the rapid course they seemed to be on in the 1980s and 1990s. Other attempts at classifying underlying models include those of Crompton (1999) and Daly (2011). Notably, this work did not engage in producing typologies based on race or ethnic origin or, indeed, other axes of inequality.

The general consensus in the field on the basis of the gender-oriented typologizing is that the countries of the EU cohere into five main groupings in terms of their family/gender model: the Nordic countries, the Continental European countries, the Mediterranean nations, the liberal countries of UK and Ireland, and the Central Eastern European states (with some question over whether the Baltic states form a stand-alone grouping – Kováts, 2017) (Bettio and Plantenga, 2004; Saraceno and Keck, 2010). They differ in the commitment to gender equality – with the Nordic countries most committed to gender egalitarianism. European countries differ also in their vision of gender equality. The Nordic countries (especially Sweden) and also the Central Eastern European and Baltic countries tend to follow a gender sameness understanding of equality. In many of the other countries, equality – to the extent that it is a priority – is understood more in terms of differences between women and men or a mix of sameness and difference. Family considerations, not least the understanding of the mother's role and appropriate child-rearing practices, play a major role. Family is prominent especially in the Continental European and also the

Mediterranean countries and this makes for more gender traditionalism in these countries. In the UK and Ireland, under-development of the services aspect of the state, rather than necessarily gender traditionalism, sees a mixed approach to gender equality. While not engaging in a typologizing analysis as such, I will return to the matter of country groupings through-out Chapters 3, 4 and 5 when we look at the empirical variations in the interconnections between women's and men's individual lives and welfare state organization and patterning.

2.2   CONCEPTUALIZING PROCESSES AND ENDPOINTS

A lot of thought has been devoted to conceptualizing the processes and outcomes generated by the welfare state. This has been considered from both a woman's perspective and a more gendered perspective. For women at the micro or individual level, original formulations thematized especially their degree of independence, autonomy and self-reliance. O'Connor (1992) spoke of personal autonomy or insulation from dependence; Hobson (1990) viewed the end points in terms of exit (from a bad marriage or unsatisfactory relationship for instance); Orloff (1993) thought in terms of the capacity to form and maintain an autonomous household which was in turn interpreted as freedom from compulsion to enter into potentially oppressive relationships (to be able to survive and support their children without having to marry to gain access to a breadwinner's income). More recent work on processes and outcomes deepens the recourse to freedom by thinking in terms of the capabilities approach developed originally by Amartya Sen and Martha Nussbaum (e.g. Lewis and Giullari, 2005; Hobson, 2014). Rather than generosity and inclusiveness as valued in their own right, this shifts the focus to more general conditions and quality of life and the extent to which state policies (inter alia) allow or enable people the means and capabilities (e.g. resources and opportunities) that can be converted to realize their preferred outcomes (functionings) (Sen, 1985; Nussbaum, 2000; Robeyns, 2003; Kurowska, 2018). As Ciccia and Sainsbury (2018, p. 101) point out, this approach recognizes the existence of both diversity in preferences and inequality of conditions among women (which they say gives it affinity with an intersectional approach).

Freedom from what? Family loomed large here. One of the foremost conceptual tools was the familialization/defamilialization continuum. This, too, was primarily developed as a comparative tool. The concept derives from feminist work (Lister, 1994; McLaughlin and Glendinning, 1994), although it is now used in comparative welfare state studies more broadly (e.g. Esping-Andersen, 2009). It is in some ways a development of Jane Lewis's ideas on the male breadwinner model (in its focus on the degree and nature of gender difference and inequality). But it is also – and perhaps more directly – traceable to critique of Esping-Andersen's (1990) concept of decommodification and its relative neglect of women's situation. Women's dependence on the family is almost a mirror image of men's dependence on the market. Hence, Esping-Andersen's use of decommodification captures only a part of the significance of the welfare state and is potentially illogical if applied to women. McLaughlin and Glendinning (1994) developed defamilialization to pick up on this, conceptualizing it to refer to the terms and conditions under which "people engage in families and the extent to which they can uphold an acceptable standard of living independently of (patriarchal) 'family' participation" (p. 65).

More recent comparative work has developed the familialization/ defamilialization continuum in two registers: at an individual and institutional level. Both are measured by the degree to which policies redistribute the responsibility for and practice of care-related tasks and associated dependencies away from the family – for example, the extent to which the state substitutes for the family as a service provider, 'socializes' or subsidizes family-related tasks or functions, and treats family members as individuals (in terms of rights, status, obligations and sources of support) and potential earners (Leitner, 2003). Its core reference is to responsibility for and execution of care but Saraceno (2011) uses it also to refer to which family members are legally obliged to offer intergenerational financial support (which used to be quite widespread in Europe in the past). Investigated and developed especially by Leitner (2003) and Leitner et al. (2008), it has a proven proficiency in aggregating and synthesizing the composition and aims of different social programmes and considering outcomes for women and men. So Leitner (2003), for example, distinguished between four directions or end points of social policy regarding the family: defamilializing, implicitly familialistic, explicitly familialistic and optionally familialistic. One of the insights of her work on this – and also that of Saraceno (2011) – is that outcomes are brought about both by policy inactivity as well as activity (as the use of the label 'implicit' implies).

While the field has been characterized by lively debate on how to measure and operationalize the framework (see Lohmann and Zagel, 2016), there are problems with it as a concept. One is that it is open as regards underlying driving or causal factors, and, further, that is has been applied to mean very different things. Another problem is that it tends to reify family and treat it as a static category – the point being that the 'de' does not allow much leeway for an altered or changing family (Daly and Scheiwe, 2010). Thirdly, there is the problem – especially from our perspective – that it has no clear set of gender references. It may even be that the concept directs attention away from what happens within the family and that focusing on defamilialization has deflected the debate from gender equality.

Two attempts to redirect the focus are worthy of mention. Steven Saxonberg (2013) suggests that we use the continuum of genderization or degenderization, since in his view using familization/defamilization leads to ambiguity and obfuscation in identifying the gendered aspects of policies. With genderization he focuses on gender roles and the extent to which policies promote different gender roles for women and men. While he raises some important points and is correct to signpost the risks of marginalizing gender, Saxonberg may not fully appreciate the deeper and encompassing set of references contained in familialization/defamilialization in a feminist context. I believe he narrows equality too much to 'the elimination of gender roles'. Feminist analyses have always seen the problem to be both deeper and broader than gender roles, which renders Saxonberg's suggestions around the changes needed to degender somewhat delimited. But Saxonberg is right to remind us that the familialization/defamilializatiom framework has often led to an analysis of family policy without gender and is most comfortable at a depoliticized level of relationships among institutions.[3]

Recent work has argued for retaining the two. Mathieu (2016) wants to shift the weight of analysis from families to mothers agreeing that the focus has been too much on the institution of the family and that policies can affect the gender division of care labour without shifting it from the family (e.g. paternity leaves). She suggests integrating the motherization/demotherization perspective with that of familialization/defamilialization to produce a typology of forms of maternalism (defined as the way that policies strengthen the caring responsibilities of mothers) (Mathieu, 2016, p. 582). I can see substance to the point that it is changes in family policy in their own right and inter-institutional relationships that have benefited most from the application of the familialization/defamilialization framework and that we need to be more conscious and critical of how and whether gender is involved. Perhaps rather than sticking with the original starting point of gender inequality, we have allowed ourselves to be led by policy, which is increasingly using family policy to bring about changes in the lives of women, men and children without any reference to gender equality. Mathieu's (2016) point about focusing on the individual and agency level – for example on mothers – is also well taken and will inform the analyses that follow (in Chapters 3, 4 and 5 especially). Exploring

---

[3] See Calnitsky (2019) for a relevant development and application of the concept of 'genderlessness'.

maternalism – or in her phrasing 'motherization/demotherization' – seems to be gaining some traction, with Jane Jenson and Nora Nagels (2018) using it to understand the growth of conditional cash transfers in Latin America, and Dorota Szelewa (2019) applying it to trace developments around childcare in Poland. Some US scholars are strongly of the view that changing and broadening conceptions of maternalism underlie many of the recent changes in European welfare states – Myra Marx Ferree, for example, has described some of the changes around the expansion of paternity leave as expanding maternalism to encompass men in families (2009, p. 286).

2.3   CARE

As demonstrated in the last chapter, one of the great contributions of feminist work on social policy has been in uncovering an 'other world' of welfare, one taking place away from the spotlight in families and other 'private' contexts. Conceiving of this in terms of care has been another significant advance (although this is not above critique as will be discussed in the book's third section). Intuitively we associate care with health settings and activities connected with the care of young children and ill, disabled or frail adults. But the concept acquired an additional set of meanings once it came to be conceived of in relation to unpaid domestic work and interpersonal services more broadly. Interest was sparked especially by how such servicing and relations were constituted by the institutions of family, marriage and kinship. The early work here was probably more about caring than care as such. Conceived in the context of debate about domestic labour and the relations between production and social reproduction, the concept turned attention to the day-to-day reproductive work that goes on in households and families, including both the material activities involved and the ideological/normative processes which confirm women as (for the most part unpaid) carers and confine them to a home or family setting (Wærness, 1978; Finch and Groves, 1983; Graham, 1983; Lewis and Meredith, 1988). Over time, the concept and its application have been broadened. In the process, early 'theoretical unity' – which centred the work on majority practice in the high-income countries, focused on those who provide care rather than those who receive it and prioritized gender over other divisions – is beginning to be overturned (Graham, 1991). Hence, men are being included more and there is a better balance between the perspectives and interests of those who are 'cared for' and those who provide care as well as greater sensitivity to global processes and interests. In fact, one sees a tendency for care to be used as a general convening concept in a broad range of work.[4] In order to give a flavour of the scholarship, I offer a highly-summarized overview in the next paragraphs in terms of a number of main themes or trends.

One focus has been to both deepen and extend the understanding of care. Some of this work stayed within the original meaning of caring as unpaid labour, studying what is involved, how it is organized and experienced and its contributions (small and large) to personal life and economy and society. Thomas (1993), for example, identified seven dimensions to care. These pertain to the identity of the provider and recipient of care, the relationship between the two, the social content of the care, the economic character of the relationship and of the labour, and the social domain and institutional setting within which the care is provided. A further form of broadening is encapsulated by work that expanded the conception of care beyond the family. Graham (1991, 1993), for example, sought to include non-kin forms of home-based care. She makes the important point that defining the concept in terms of home-based care for family members has served to centre analysis around (white) women's reproductive work for kin while obscuring other forms of home-based work (paid domestic service for example) and relations of class and race. This kind of thinking also carried another risk: the conflation of the location of care in the sense of where the care is carried out with the social relations that determine who gives and who receives care. This critique continues to be present (see e.g. Duffy, 2005).

A second direction of travel combined notions of labour and 'love' to frame care in terms of relationality and interdependence, elaborating caring as a basic form of human interconnection and care as a vital human activity set within complex relations and moral commitments (Fisher and Tronto, 1990; Held, 2005). This moved care beyond the home. Indeed, in this perspective care's limits and foci are endless; it has application everywhere, from the environment and universe as much as to the persons we live with or beside. Fisher and Tronto's (1990) work is a classic here in defining caring as a species activity involving four phases: caring about, caring for, caregiving and care receiving. Drawing from moral theory, philosophy and legal theory, this approach elucidates a vision of how individuals can 'be' with each other and how an ethics of care could seed profound change at a local, national and especially global basis. As well as challenging the notion of the isolated individual of liberal and social contract theory, it emphasizes the intrinsic value of care and interdependence in opposition to individualism.

---

4   And in recent years two new journals in the field have appeared: *International Journal of Care and Caring* and *Journal of Long-term Care*.

Over time – and in another evolution – the domestic labour focus was developed by a consideration of wider notions regarding the connections of paid and unpaid care to the prevailing political economy. "Care is a route to the politics of welfare", wrote Carol Thomas in 1993 (p. 651). To what extent does care confer entitlement to public support? Actually the field and issues involved are very complex for social policy, involving challenges such as balancing the needs and situation of the person requiring care with those providing it, inter alia (Knijn and Kremer, 1997; Daly, 2002; Anttonen and Zechner, 2011; Williams, 2012a). The evolving story in the high-income countries is of increasing state purview and influence in the field of care, as governments find themselves needing to incentivize the provision of care (either within a family/home or a public services or a market context). This has led to a host of work undertaking rather fine-grained analysis of the policy packages (which, in the European countries anyway, typically combine interventions that provide time, financial assistance and/or services to support care givers and those in need of care). At its best this work excels at uncovering the architecture and different modalities of provision, whether cash benefits and/or services but also other policy modalities such as paid and unpaid leave, working time flexibility, part-time work, taxation provisions, vouchers for purchasing services, credits for pension and other benefits (Land, 1978; Gornick et al., 1997; Daly, 2002; Lister, 2002; Bettio and Plantenga, 2004; Saraceno and Keck, 2010).

There is no denying that the market is a key actor in care now, increasingly so as the concern to keep certain aspects of reproduction outside of commodification by locating them either in public services or the family seems to have weakened. Current trends are seeing the desire for both profit taking and state disengagement leading to a commodification of care and affective labour (Lutz, 2018). In this process, care is turned into a market commodity, one which is traded and on which a monetary value is placed. This, too, draws on long-standing feminist concerns about 'paying for care', a debate engaging with the moral and other implications of introducing state payments for the provision of care (Ungerson, 1995, 1997). The growth of payment and of markets – while not necessarily the same thing – is revealed to be associated especially with neoliberal restructuring of the state, the inter-connections between this and transnational capitalism and the growth of low-level servicing jobs. Under the spotlight here are questions about how care is carried out in different parts of the world and how an increasingly unstable care regime in the global North is leading to new inequalities and new care regimes in the global South (Parreñas, 2001; Aulenbacher et al., 2018; Peng, 2019).

With this focus, the work is frequently intersectional in perspective in tying together race and ethnicity, gender and class, as central to the story of care. It has been noted that the increased outsourcing of household/familial care responsibilities in a neoliberal market context has, rather than equalizing care responsibilities between genders, created increased social and economic polarization amongst women along socio-economic, racial/ethnic and citizenship lines (Peng, 2019). There are several ways in which such inequalities are being investigated and explained. Lutz (2018) suggests 'transnational social inequality' as a concept to pick up on key aspects, such as female care work as a social and gendered obligation across borders; the lack of social protection attaching to care work especially by migrants; and the race–migration nexus involved (the 'racialization' and 'gendered naturalization' of care work). Another leading idea is the concept of global care chains which focuses on the flow of care-providing labour across countries and regions and traces the implications for the providers (especially the individuals and their native countries) and the receivers (usually higher-income people and countries) (Hochschild, 2000; Parreñas, 2001; Yeates, 2011). Transnational family-making processes are also investigated (Baldassar and Merla, 2013). Another approach spotlights the role of states and national and international policy actors configurations (e.g. Mahon, 2018a). When it turns the lens on policy, there is an appeal in this work to think of the interconnections between economic, social, employment and migration policies (Michel and Peng, 2012; Williams, 2012b). The perspective is much larger than the classic conception of care as domestic labour or nurturance. The critical international political economy approach in particular crafts an explanation centred upon power relations and contestations among nations (in their own right and in regard to how these are institutionalized in policy) and the economic and political forces of global processes and imperialism in reproducing gender and other inequalities in various forms (Parreñas, 2001). The character of some care as non-relational is highlighted (Arat-Koç, 2018), thereby including a broader universe of workers as well as types of work (Duffy, 2005).

As a result, the conversations about care in our work are now more global than they used to be – crossing not just spheres but also continents and intersecting with issues of class, ethnicity, and country of origin, citizenship, employment law as well as gender. In the process, the nation state is somewhat decentred as the unit of analysis with analysis proceeding at different levels (although the national focus of much of the work is striking). Michel and Peng (2017) call for a multi-scalar approach – by which they mean a micro, meso and macro approach (see also Williams, 2018a). The original questions still resonate – who benefits and what are the underpinning relations of power? What are the fundamental elements of the care system? But these are now applied across borders or through analyses that connect to the global plane. Recognizing this starts to fill a gap in our understanding of how care is associated with complex inequalities in the context of international capitalism.

2.4 GENDER AND OTHER INEQUALITIES

The specific focus of much of the gender-oriented work has also been subjected to 'internal' criticism for its 'exclusivity', especially in regard to how it conceptualizes (if at all) the relationship between gender and other inequalities. Of the different possible sources of inequality, the relationship between class and gender has been foremost in the gender and welfare state literature (e.g. Crompton, 2006; Pettit and Hook, 2009; Cooke, 2011). This has been challenged and developed further by feminists and others working within an intersectionality perspective, which takes as its focal point complex inequalities with reference to both structural and cultural factors. An originating set of insights in this framework lies in the work by feminists of colour in the US and elsewhere, who showed how the forms of discrimination experienced by women of colour were not reducible to either their gender or their race but were of a different order – the product of multiple interlocking systems of oppression (Crenshaw, 1989; Hill Collins, 1990).[5] This unsettles the universalist orientation of feminism, opening up to question assumptions of shared identity and whether all women are similarly positioned in regard to institutions like nation, family, state and economy (Williams, 2018b, p. 38). Intersectionality is not a single theory. However, a unifying insight is about the complexity of identities and inequalities on the one hand and the existence of hierarchies among them on the other. The meaning and fluidity of the categories themselves – and especially the extent to which we can accept them without question or see them as untransformed by intersectional processes – are central concerns in intersectionality theory (Hancock, 2007). Contra single and/ or static categories, the notion of multiple positioning is suggested. While early work concentrated on understanding and exploring identity groups – e.g. women of colour, women subjected to violence – recent work has turned more to a structural exploration to focus on relationships of power. So in focus is not just who or what is the group/category, but the processes or struggles (such as 'racialization' or engendering) that are playing out (Ferree, 2010). All identities and social locations are shot through by

---

[5] See McCall (2005) for further contextualization of the approach, linking it to the postmodernist and poststructuralist critiques of modern Western philosophy, history and language.

intersections between gender, race, sexuality, class, nationality and age (for example) and these must be understood 'interactively' rather than studied as distinct axes of life or identity (Risman and Davis, 2013, p. 742). It is helpful for understanding the intersectionality perspective to consider it from both micro and macro levels. In the former regard, the development of the perspective is closely bound up with work on identity of individuals and groups, especially those who are excluded because they are defined by the cross-cutting of a number of intersections (e.g. age and ability and gender and/or ethnic background).[6] Studying these helps to investigate several things: the significance of identity markers, the standpoints and 'voice' of those who are so marginalized, questioning the utility of 'identity categories', investigating how they function to spearhead processes of marginalization. At a macro level, the perspective opens up the notion that stratification spills out beyond single institutions to produce complex and interacting inequalities and categories of identity, experience and resource access. Ferree (2010, p. 428) helpfully summarizes the fundamental characteristics of the intersectionality approach: "any perspective is today called intersectional if it takes multiple relations of inequality as the norm, sees them as processes that shape each other, and considers how they interactively define the identities and experiences – and thus analytic standpoints – of individuals and groups". The notions of 'synergy' and 'confluence' are powerful here (Fredman, 2016).

While it is well developed theoretically, intersectionality is less worked out as a distinct methodology (Phoenix and Pattynama, 2006; Few-Demo, 2014). Choo and Ferree (2010) identify three different approaches to applying intersectionality that have been used in sociological research: group-centred, process-centred, and system-centred. They suggest that the types be considered as tools that can be useful in different circumstances. The first centres on the perspectives of those who are 'multiply-marginalized', critiquing the exclusionary tendencies in early work which privileged the experiences and situations of white women and underlining the specific situations of differently-located people or groups, especially those who are positioned at points of intersection. This approach also underscores the

---

6 Fredman (2016) makes the important point that because of the way anti-discrimination law is constructed – and she is speaking especially of the EU context – it is difficult if not impossible to make a claim on more than one ground. This was Crenshaw's (1989) original point – that people at the intersection of different grounds are 'invisible' to the law. An added difficulty is that a comparator is essential to prove the case of discrimination given the underlying legal principle that likes should be treated alike (Fredman, 2016). In the context of intersectionality, this is particularly constraining as it requires one to determine from among the myriad of similarities and difference which should be the one to compare (Fredman, 2016, p. 36).

non-additive effects of multiple forms of oppression (Hill Collins, 1990). This commitment justified what McCall (2005) calls 'intracategorical' studies, focusing on the experiences of subgroups of people at neglected points of intersection. It risks, however, ignoring the role of the more powerful groups in these experiences (Walby et al., 2012). The second, process-centred, approach focuses on interactions and transformations that occur through such interactions. This moves above the level of the individual or group to consider locations and positionalities, and seeks to deconstruct and disrupt taken-for-granted categories. Dynamic forces rather than categories are the focus here – e.g. racialization rather than races, economic exploitation rather than classes (McCall, 2005, p. 134). This examines selected interaction effects among the various intersectional dimensions. McCall sees a potential weakness here of separating out primary from secondary effects and working with a hierarchical view of inequalities wherein one takes priority or is a master category (McCall, 2005, pp. 134–5). This gives pause for thought in the present context – given the focus on gender. The third, system-centred, practice of intersectionality works to disassociate specific inequalities from specific institutions (e.g. equating the economy with social class, or the family with gender) or processes and concentrates on how the systems themselves, or elements thereof, generate intersectional effects. The approach here is focused on interactions rather than main effects and systems rather than separate dimensions (McCall, 2005, p. 136).

The appeal of intersectionality is in many ways intuitive in a world where scholarship foregrounds the complexity of everyday life. "Intersectionality was greeted with hope and applause because of both its theoretical scope and its empirical inclusivity" (G. Lewis, 2013, p. 873). After all, as Phoenix and Pattynama (2006, p. 187) point out, the approach provides a concise shorthand for describing ideas that have come to be accepted in feminist thinking and women's studies scholarship. To some extent it was opening a door that was already ajar – Raewyn Connell's work has long seen people and systems as multiply positioned,[7] and in social policy as far back as 1989 Fiona Williams connected the gender critique to a critique of conventional social policy analysis as marginalizing race and associated issues. As she put it in a subsequent publication, the welfare state is built with the

---

[7] See Ferree (2015) for a thoughtful analysis of how Connell's earlier work – and especially the books *Gender* (2002) and *Gender and Power* (1987) – were intersectional in the way the former used social class to inform a sociological understanding of gender socialization and the latter in its focus on national variation and transnational organizing for gender equality.

bricks of the family, the mortar of national unity and the labour of women and minority ethnic workers (1993, p. 85).

That said, intersectionality – especially if understood in its full-blown complexity (as involving some combination of individual and group identity, lived experience, agency, representation, power structures and relations, institutions and processes) – has not yet moved from the academy to 'the streets'. Social policy and welfare state analysis is one of the areas where it has not been widely applied, mirroring a lack of attention in public policy more broadly (Hankivsky and Cormier, 2011).[8] My point here is not that studies have not contributed insights on intersectionalities but that it is not widely used as a theoretical or methodological departure point for much work in social policy. In other words, only a limited number of studies have consciously set out to apply an approach sensitive to intersecting inequalities to social policy. Some notable exceptions include the global care work and individual studies of gender and class (Pettit and Hook, 2009; Shalev, 2009; Cooke, 2011; Mandel, 2012; Korpi et al., 2013). Why has intersectionality not proved more popular? One reason is that the 'jump' from what we currently do to what is required is large, especially if we interpret intersectionality as requiring "severing the institutional anchors that tied gender to the institution of family, race to community-level institutions like education, and class to impersonal-seeming macro-models of the formal economy (capital formation, market relations, and national development)" (Ferree, 2015, p. 7). Site-specific factors are also at play. Conventional welfare state studies are in some ways the polar opposite of intersectionality: placing emphasis especially on characterizing welfare states as a set of class-based institutions and politics – in essence, fixing them. Even the gender work – which sought not so much to integrate gender into class-based analyses but to elucidate gender as its own strong line of division – is not necessarily receptive ground for intersectionality. Another important potential barrier to the use of intersectionality is around class as a form of inequality about which there is some ambivalence and even relative neglect in intersectionality theory (Walby et al., 2012). Since class is the mainstay of much welfare state research, this is another way in which an affinity to intersectionality is undermined. There is also the sheer complexity of the perspective – even its language tends to mystify rather than demystify.

For the present purposes, intersectionality shares some of the above sources of appeal as well as others: it directs analysis to people's everyday circumstances and experiences, and especially those of marginalized groups

---

[8]   However, see the new handbook edited by Hankivsky and Jordan-Zachery (2019).

or subjects. It also alerts us to layers of inequality and disadvantage, and is a superior perspective to identify systematic advantaging and disadvantaging. It also helps us better to see underpinning structures and explain developments such as the coincidence of some gender equality and soaring socio-economic and other inequalities (Watkins, 2018, p. 7). It also has significance from a policy perspective (Hankivsky and Cormier, 2011; Hankivsky and Jordan-Zachery, 2019). With its complex understanding of interactions, an intersectional approach particularly challenges the typical policy approach of starting with an identity category like gender or race and then, once other divisions are identified or challenged, placing them side by side or adding them in an aggregative approach. This latter approach has been used by the EU and some national governments, for example, where up to nine different grounds of discrimination are assembled, often in an additive logic and generally unthought-out fashion (Fredman, 2016). The question for the book, therefore, is not whether to be guided by intersectionality, but how.

2.5 CONCLUSION

In considering scholarship over the last three decades or so, this chapter has shown how the work proceeded in terms of developing and applying different lenses rather than following a unilateral approach and aiming for a grand theory. Theoretically and empirically, a comparative orientation and methodology have been defining features of the scholarship. As a result, much of what we know comes from juxtaposing different welfare state systems in the high-income parts of the world and identifying similarities and differences among them. This work makes clear that gender and other elements of welfare state/societal relations pattern across countries and that the study of such variations can be especially insightful.

Among other things, the work reviewed has underlined the significance of the differentiation made by social policy between the treatment of individuals versus that of collectivities. The connection to the family and the reliance on family as an agent of internal redistribution and labour management was and – as we shall see – remains a widely-used mechanism for governing access to public benefits and services. This has been highlighted as one of the main ways in which gender and other inequalities are perpetuated. European welfare states still struggle to get beyond familialistic orientations. This is part of the long continuity with the past whereby the state uses and shapes institutions like marriage, motherhood and fatherhood as means to effect preferred societal balances of power and resources.

One of the defining interests of feminist thinking that crystallized over the time period covered in this chapter centred around the question of what kind of overall gender model underlies policy and its reform (adult worker, male breadwinner or something else?). Work has also been led by an interest in identifying broader trends which shape the new or changing political economy of care and gender relations, such as marketization, commodification and globalization. The advent of care as a major focus of conceptual and empirical attention – nurtured by and in turn elucidating a broad-ranging set of intellectual, moral and practical concerns – reminds us of the connections between the micro level of bodies, personalities and emotional experiences and the macro level of cultures, institutions, econo-mies and societies (Ferree, 2015, p. 5). Studying care – and marketization more generally – has drawn attention especially to the interconnections between national and global processes and how their intersections and mutual dependencies involve a simultaneous marketization and 'migran-tization' of care. This has proven a challenge to much of the scholarship which has largely ignored processes associated with racialization and stayed within a national welfare state frame of analysis (and even compara-tive work does this).[9] The rise of intersectionality and its theorizations of multiple inequalities was highlighted as another important trend. While not without its problems and as of yet a rather limited application in social policy, its promise varies from uncovering the experiences and positioning of particular social groups (especially those at the intersections of different axes of division) to revealing the interconnections between systems of power at a more abstract level. Intersectionality underlines the necessity not just for more complex explanations but a multiplex theorization of inequality – which means recognizing that no single category – e.g. gender – is sufficient for understanding people's positioning, needs and experiences.

The next part of the book examines some important empirical trends following a short outline of the analytic approach to be followed.

---

[9] Fiona Williams's (1989) work is an exception here, as is that of Gail Lewis (2000). For the US the work of Mink (1990), Quadagno (1994) and Glenn (2002), among others, reveals the intersecting gender and racial fault-lines in the American welfare state. Mink (1990) is especially persuasive about how – in the decades following the turn of the twentieth century – policies for motherhood through mothers' pensions, wages and hours protection for working women and maternal infant care programmes (rather than for workers) were at root a means of managing racial divides and promoting a racial order in which whites were privileged. Her underlying point is that in the absence of a sense of common citizenship, selective citizen rights were given to women as mothers as the protectors of the race.

Intermezzo 1

Drawing upon insights from the preceding two chapters, I here set out the conceptual framework and methodological approach to be adopted for the analyses that follow in the next three chapters.

A central thread running through the critical social policy scholarship is women's chances of being financially independent. Economic welfare and financial autonomy are two leading concepts in this lexicon (Betti et al., 2015, p. 5). The former directs attention to relative finance/wealth levels and associated inequality and also to related risks of poverty and low income. Thinking in terms of financial autonomy is more complex. It draws on ideas of situated agency – Htun et al (2019) capture this sense when they define economic agency as the ability to make independent economic choices, based on both the disposition and capacity to do so. This emphasizes access to resources to enable choice and autonomy as per people's preferences (Orloff, 1993).[1] This has some commonality with Sen's capability framework approach although his is more open as regards outcomes. My focus, though, dovetails with Sen's interest in the means available to people for choice and, while I do not venture into the conversion processes whereby people utilize their resources to achieve their desired functionings, or indeed seek to explore choices, I do investigate the most important processes of resource accrual and use in the context of the physical realities of people's lives. Adopting a situated agency perspective also means a broader approach than economic participation or economic resource levels as it brings in people's agency and well-being in relation

[1] Note that Oxfam frames this in terms of women's economic empowerment. It conceives of this in terms of programmes focusing on women's ability to gain access and control over productive resources and to be recognized as fully participating economic actors (Oxfam, 2017).

to care and time. Jane Jenson's (2015) suggestion to conceive of the relationships and positioning involved as being shaped by the intersection of income, employment and unpaid work (time) seems very helpful. As a theoretical framework, this implies that the three are inextricably related and that real progress in gender equality depends on gains in all three in a relatively integrated manner.

As we have seen from Chapter 2, intersectionality is a major development in scholarship, training the spotlight on the interconnectedness of social categories and how the construction of categorizations serves to create overlapping, interdependent patterns of inclusion and exclusion, and inequality. It, too, suggests a view of agency as situated. One of the most convincing reasons to take an intersectional approach is because it lays bare broader underpinning structures and processes. It also provides a more accurate record of (a) where change has happened, (b) the potential limits of reform (for particular groups or processes) and (c) the ripple and other effects of change. Intersectionality helps us to pose an especially important question – who is being privileged here?

As mentioned, the issue for this book is not whether to integrate it, but how. A major matter to be considered is how an intersectionality approach fits with the book's aims or goals and the degree of primacy to give it. The book's guiding question centres on how gender inequality is approached as a social policy problem, the conditions under which this happens and the associated consequences. Hence, gender and its systemic elements will be foregrounded. The justification is that I want to investigate the distinctiveness of the inequality founded on gender and the welfare state's role in that. The risk, of course, is that what we think of as, and assume to be, gender-related processes may have their origins and motor of development in more than one 'system' – or in another system altogether – and are transformed by intersections (Hancock, 2007). This enjoins me, at the minimum, to disaggregate gender categories and also to consider other categories and axes of known inequality, especially social class, family status, age and race/ethnic origin.

I adopt a two-tier intersectional approach. First, the analytic foci are selected because they are intersectional and cross spheres – that is, access to income, employment and time. These cut across most typologies and categorizations and move us beyond sphere-based differentiations while adhering to the recognition that these are the core sets of resources from an inequality perspective. This kind of connected perspective is also sensitive to the point that it is systems of relations and policies – conceived as consisting of connected policy packages – rather than individual policies that people respond to and operate within. Admittedly, the orientation is towards material factors which means that identity aspects or categories

are not considered specifically. This reflects the structural as against cultural orientation of the book (and the study of social policy more broadly).

A second element of the intersectional approach adopted is to actively
search out differences among groups of women and men. Hence, we accept
the categories as units of analysis but do not treat them as homogeneous
or uniform. There are real limits to how many and which intersections
one can examine at any one time though, especially when one is relying on
secondary data as I am here. The constraints limit us to consideration of
mainly socio-economic, family status and age-related differences, and to
a lesser extent ethnic status. Not just the number but the depth to which
we can explore categories is another constraining factor. For example, to
measure ethnic background we have to rely on migration status (and there
are many cases where this data breakdown is not available).

The chapters, then, rest on an analytic framework which pins change (or
lack of movement towards gender inequality) to social location (understood intersectionally in terms of gender, socio-economic position, family
status, age, and, where evidence allows, ethnic background). It must be
said, though, that it is the co-existence or simultaneity of different axes or
categories of inequality that I identify rather than their deeper causal roots.

The two key empirical lines of analysis in each chapter centre on: What
is the status quo and what is the direction of change over time? The empirical strategy followed is to focus, first, on key elements of people's lives, to
examine what gender inequalities obtain, how these disaggregate into more
precise differences, and what has been the pattern of development over the
last decade or so. This period coincides with the 2008 recession – which
may have distorted developments and has certainly brought restructuring.
However, I try where possible to start the evidence examination at least a
few years before the onset of recession. The canvas is the EU-28 member
states and the evidence base is drawn mainly from Eurostat sources. Given
space constraints, I concentrate on the global EU picture, although I also
look at national developments as appropriate. While the identification of
regimes or typologies is not a primary objective, country groupings are
sometimes used as an analytical device, as they are a useful shorthand
to link developments to policy sets, although no causal relationship is
inferred.

To set some of the backdrop here, we might bear in mind that different regimes or welfare state types face particular challenges in regard to
gender. For example, in the Nordic countries the challenge has been to
enable women's progress and equality in the labour market, especially in
the private sector, while at the same time making for equality and quality
in family life. The uppermost challenge in the Continental European countries, where family has value as a political and moral entity and is promoted

as a way of life and a force for social integration, is to enable widespread female labour market participation and develop a model of gender equality that draws less from maternalism and more from sameness. In the liberal and Mediterranean countries, the provision of services and supports necessary for greater female participation in the labour market is a major challenge. In both country sets, supportive services are under-developed with the added complication in the Mediterranean countries of a national philosophy that conceives of the family as a private institution of welfare. In the Central Eastern European and Baltic countries, the fading of the command economy and state provision has led to struggling labour markets and has given oxygen to the (re)emergence of traditional gender patterns while the entrance of these countries into the EU has imposed upon them a commitment to formal gender equality.

3. Income, wealth and poverty

This chapter focuses on money and financial well-being as a domain of economic inequality. The chapter first considers the evidence yielded by the overview index of financial inequality by gender compiled on behalf of the EU to assess progress on gender equality. Next, inequalities in women's and men's financial resources are examined in greater depth, looking first at wealth before going on to consider financial (in)security through the lens of poverty rates. The latter is an established tradition in gender and welfare state research (see e.g. Glendinning and Millar, 1987; Chant, 2010; Bennett and Daly, 2014). Gender inequality in access to pensions is also considered. A tension that underpins much of the relevant discussion here centres on how we assess and theorize people's individual resource holding as against collectivizing resources for the living unit as a whole. Using both the individual and collective units of analysis where possible, I signpost rather than resolve that tension which most income data collection exercises overlook, attributing unproblematically to individuals an equal share of the resources of their households or families, and more or less completely ignoring that sharing income and other resources is usually subject to negotiation and even power relations.

Having examined the relative distribution of economic resources and related income risks in the first parts of the chapter, I then go on to identify how access to welfare state benefits is associated with the identified income-related outcomes. Pensions are taken as a case study here. The research question underlying the chapter as a whole enquires about the 'progress' that women are making in relative financial well-being and economic agency vis-à-vis men with the gauge set on the last decade or so. As with the other chapters in this section, the intent is to identify the status quo as well as signature trends and situate these in considerations regarding the prevailing social policy. I underline again that measurement and data (availability) issues seriously constrain the breadth and depth of analysis. The constraints are such that in some cases I have to piece together a picture from diverse sources. In particular, there is no available information comparable across EU countries on gender inequalities in access to welfare-state benefits other than pensions.[1]

3.1 FINANCIAL EQUALITY

The European Institute for Gender Equality, an autonomous organization of the EU, compiles each year a Gender Equality Index to measure a series of gaps between women and men.[2] Six main dimensions are included – work, knowledge, money, time, health and power – along with a number of satellite dimensions, in particular violence as well as, since 2017, intersecting inequalities.[3] The six domains, comprising 31 indicators, are tabulated individually as well as combined into a global index. While this is arguably the best available index, we have to be mindful of its limitations, not least its reduction of inequality to a gap and its treatment of women and men as binary categories. Bearing such considerations in mind, we can avail ourselves of the index, mindful of its merits, not least that it is based on comparable information across member states.

Here I use the evidence from the money index from 2015 to set the scene in regard to financial resources. The money index is based on two component sub-indices. The first – access to resources – measures gaps in both mean monthly earnings and mean, equivalized by household size, net income (which includes earnings, pensions, investments, benefits and any other source of income). The second sub-domain – economic situation – encapsulates women's and men's differential risk of poverty (the gap is computed on the proportion of women and men not at risk of poverty) and inequality in income distribution amongst women and men (the ratio of the bottom and top quintiles by sex). Note that these are mainly calculated on collective rather than individual income or risk and that all monies are equally split between the adult female and male members of couple households.

---

[1] It is interesting to note that data on gender inequalities in access to benefits is not widely available. The OECD Gender Initiative examines existing barriers to gender equality in education, employment, and entrepreneurship. This website monitors the progress made by governments to promote gender equality in these areas in both OECD and non-OECD countries and provides 'good practices' based on analytical tools and reliable data, but it does not include access to social security and means-tested benefits in its evidence (see http://www.oecd.org/gender/). The same is true for the EU's Gender Equality Index which considers income from all sources rather than itemizing it.

[2] See http://eige.europa.eu/gender-equality-index/about.

[3] The intersecting inequalities include age, (dis)ability, migrant background (measured by country of birth) and family composition. According to the Institute's justification, the satellite domains are treated as such because they measure what is considered an 'illustrative phenomenon' – that is, a phenomenon that only applies to a selected group of the population. This occurs when considering issues that are related to women only, for instance in the case of violence against women, or when examining gender gaps among specific population groups (people with a disability, lone parents, and so forth) (European Institute for Gender Equality, 2017a).

Table 3.1   Money gender equality index in the EU-28 countries 2005 and 2015

Overall gender equality index	2005	2015
Money	73.9	79.6
Financial resources	60.9	73.0
Economic situation	89.7	86.7

Source: European Institute for Gender Equality (2017a).

Table 3.1 shows the comparisons for 2005 and 2015 (European Institute for Gender Equality, 2017a). The messages are mixed. Revealed, first, is the existence of a significant gender gap – of some 20 percentage points in 2015 – and, second, a considerable improvement over the ten-year period. In fact, money was the second fastest improving domain of all six (behind power – which is not included in this book[4] – but has the lowest gender equality scores (48.5) of any of the six domains). As can be seen from the disaggregation in Table 3.1, the improvement is driven by the first indicator – level of financial resources – which narrowed significantly between 2005 and 2015, indicating an improvement of the income gap in earnings, pensions, investment and so forth between women and men. The background documentation shows that most of the improvement happened between 2005 and 2010 (that is, the period before the worst of the recession kicked in).[5] Rising female income through earnings was in the driving seat here, with male earnings stagnating or growing more slowly. In contrast though, the evidence on the second indicator of economic situation (gender gaps in poverty and income inequality) shows a worsening gender gap, although the decline in gender equality is small (in itself and compared to the degree of improvement in the level of the gap in financial resources). This sub-indicator (as measured by male/female gaps in poverty and inequality) is one of the smallest gaps in the index as a whole (being only around 13 percentage points in 2015 in comparison to 34 points for the overall inequality index).

It is clear that the two indicators are picking up somewhat different

---

[4]   Divided into social, economic and political areas, the indicators are as follows: women's share of ministries, in national parliaments and in regional assemblies; women's share of board membership in largest quoted companies, on the boards of the central bank; women's share of membership of boards of research funding organizations, public broadcasting organizations and on the highest decision-making level of the national Olympics sports organizations.

[5]   See European Institute for Gender Equality (2017a).

trends, though, and that the improvement in gender inequality in the European Institute's money index as a whole is not translating into a lowered incidence of financial risk of poverty for women vis-à-vis men or indeed gender gaps in income inequality among women and men. In fact, they are going in different directions. The differences by country/region are insightful here, especially if we focus on the divergence between the two sub-indicators. This shows, for example, that a strong divergence between the two characterizes the Central Eastern European, Baltic and some Mediterranean states. The nature of the divergence is such that large gender gaps exist in levels of financial resources but these do not translate into gender gaps in poverty or inequality. The most plausible interpretation of this is that in these countries household factors are intervening to keep measured gaps in poverty rates low and that income inequality is low overall. There are, of course, likely to be sub-group differences here but these are impossible to ascertain in sufficient detail across countries given the global nature of much of the data.

When the figures for the index as a whole are broken down by demographic and other elements of background situation, age group and education level stand out as factors making for variation (more so than country of origin which is taken as an (admittedly rough) gauge of migration status) or family type. The gender gap increases with rising age – the gender gap in earnings, for example, rises from 87 per cent for those aged between 15/16 and 24 years, to 51 per cent for those aged 65 and over (based on 2015 figures). The evidence for education level shows that the gap between women and men with low education is around the same – at two-thirds – as it is for the higher-educated sectors. This suggests that gender – rather than socio-economic status as indicated by education level – is a dominant line of division in this relationship.

Country variations abound – with the overall gender money gap varying from 10 per cent in Luxembourg to 40 per cent in Romania. In terms of national patterns, the gender gaps in money are smallest in the Nordic and Continental European countries (Austria, France, Luxembourg and the Netherlands) and largest in the Central Eastern European and Baltic nations. This cross-national patterning should be noted, for it is quite robust across the different dimensions considered in this chapter.

In terms of change over time, all EU countries except Greece saw an improvement in the overall gender gap in money in the ten years between 2005 and 2015. There is an indication that this change was generated by a catch-up in the countries that were initially low, such as the three Baltic nations which recorded over the ten-year period an improvement above the EU average, as did Malta, Poland and Slovakia (all of which joined the EU in 2004). However, these are all still below the EU average and they are, as we have seen above, the countries where it looks like gender gaps in poverty and income inequality are somewhat independent of gaps in financial resources. It is important to note that the high-performing countries – the Nordic nations as well as the Continental European countries mentioned above – continued to make progress. This made for relative stasis in the ranking at the top, with the listing of the top-ranked countries almost unchanged between the two survey dates. In terms of component elements, the gender gap in the economic situation (measured by poverty and inequality) widened in the ten years between 2005 and 2015 in around one-half of the member states. Sweden, Germany and Denmark saw increases in the gap but, to put this in its relative context, the gap was only 2 percentage points in Sweden in 2005 (by 2015 it had 'fallen' to 6.9). These remain countries with low gaps in both poverty and average income inequality by gender.

These results suggest complexity and also perhaps polarization in that greater labour market entry/participation is not only not synonymous with a reduction in money-related inequality between women and men, but actually also co-exists with an increase in economic inequality. That said, we need to treat these figures with caution for there are real questions about their veracity in measuring gender gaps, especially in the empirical analyses. One major factor is that all data except the earnings data are based on household income. The procedure used is to calculate an individual income on the basis of dividing the household income equally among all household members. This is an inherent weakness in income distribution analysis. The dilemma is that we know that almost all people living together have different levels of own income and enjoy economies of scale in sharing costs (such as housing, electricity, and so forth). However, the classic practice of resolving this dilemma – by assuming full and equal sharing – ignores known differences in women's access to income (Bennett, 2013; Daly, 2018). The index follows the accepted convention of using household and individual income computed on the above basis, and so we must read it with caution. We will encounter this again in the analyses later in this chapter.

In response to the overall question of whether we can see much change, the answer is: some. Notably, gender gaps in level of financial resources are narrowing everywhere (except Greece). This a very robust trend, although its relationship to gender gaps in poverty and inequality is not straightforward, either within or across countries. The likelihood is for trade-offs and intersectional inequalities.

Access to other assets apart from income is also an important component of financial well-being. Data on wealth is extremely hard to obtain, in general and in regard to individuals (and women especially). I am able to piece together some of the wealth story though, and so can reveal the status quo for some countries, although I could not obtain any data showing change over time.

3.2 WEALTH INEQUALITIES

Based on data from the 2010/11 European Central Bank Household Finance and Consumption Survey for Euro-area countries in 2010[6] and also using households as the unit of analysis, Sierminska (2017) reports for the Eurozone countries as a whole that women have 62 per cent of the wealth of men at the median and 73 per cent at the mean.[7] This research also shows that the gender-related differences in wealth are quite varied across the Eurozone countries, although nowhere are they in women's favour. The largest differences in female and male wealth measured by the ratios of their medians and means are found for the Netherlands and France (0.28 and 0.49, respectively, at the median, and 0.51 and 0.64, respectively, at the mean). A wide gap is also present in Austria and Germany. The narrowest gender wealth gap is found in Slovakia, Greece and Luxembourg – a motley group of countries for which it is difficult to make sense of as having a similar outcome, especially from a welfare state perspective. Again though, the general caution regarding the measurement of wealth at household level prevails (although it is not obvious to me how this would affect the country comparisons). Sierminska (2017, p. 16) cites work for Germany which measures individual wealth holding by women and men in couple households to show that in such German households women hold 37 per cent of the couple's mean wealth and in only 29 per cent of cases is women's mean wealth share greater than that of men.

Intersections are also to be found here, although we need to be mindful of limitations posed by households as the unit of analysis. That said, there is a clear age and marital status effect. Among single people, the ratio of women's to men's average wealth levels is 0.84. The gap gets larger with age (and more complicated family situations) and is largest amongst the oldest age group. Sierminska attributes this either to cohort effects, or to differential mortality rates among richer and poorer households, as well as such differences between women and men.

When the gender wealth gap was decomposed in each country, over 50

---

[6] Austria, Belgium, Cyprus, Estonia, Finland, France, Germany, Greece, Ireland, Italy, Luxembourg, Malta, the Netherlands, Portugal, Slovakia, Slovenia and Spain.

[7] Net wealth is defined as total household assets, excluding public and occupational pension wealth, minus total outstanding liabilities.

per cent of the gap at country level can be explained by the differences in socio-demographic characteristics – particularly in Austria, Germany and Greece. Italy is an exception here in that even if Italian women and men were equally educated and their other characteristics were similar, the predictions are that women would still have lower wealth levels. Overall, the research identifies the largest contributing factors to the wealth gap as education and income differences between women and men. Employment status also has a significant effect on the gender wealth gap, but in fewer cases than income and education. One of the recommendations this report makes is that wealth data should be collected at the individual level in order to monitor the distribution of wealth within the household. I would add to that the qualifier that the data should be 'robust and disaggregated to individual level'.

Another piece of the puzzle is provided by research by Atkinson et al. (2016) which focuses on those at the top of the income distribution (on the basis of income tax returns) in eight countries (Australia, Canada, Denmark, Italy, New Zealand, Norway, Spain and the UK).[8] Their results show strong similarities between these countries in the patterning of gender inequality in income. The regularity is very striking. On average, women account for between a fifth and a third of those in the top 10 per cent of income holders and between 14 and 22 per cent of the top 1 per cent. In most of the countries, the proportion of women in the top 0.1 per cent is half or less than the proportion in the top 10 per cent, showing a tightening of opportunities at the highest level. However, the presence of women in the high-income categories has generally increased from the 1990s in all the countries except Australia, with Denmark recording the most significant increase. The rise has been smaller at the very top and the under-representation of women (between 2010 and 2014) increased more sharply for the top 1 per cent as compared with the top decile. In the case of Canada, Denmark, Norway and New Zealand, there appears to have been a reversal over time, with the slope of the upper tail having been steeper for women in the past. The authors undertake analyses that show that at the end of the period women disappear faster than men as one moves up the income scale in all countries. This leads them to suggest that a 'wealth glass ceiling' exists for women.

The patterns in regard to wealth holding while showing some variation and small change over time suggest entrenched gender inequalities. What do we know about causal factors?

This and other research highlights the importance of labour market

---

8   These were chosen because they have individual taxation systems and hence the data allowed individual-level comparison between women and men.

situation for gender-based wealth inequalities. Schneebaum et al. (2014) underscore the significance of what they call 'work autonomy' (which in their study design mostly captures self-employment and higher-ranking employed work), the ratio of full-time work to age, and household earnings, for the statistically significant relationship with net wealth in the Eurozone countries in 2010 and especially lower levels of wealth in female households. These authors suggest that the gender wealth gap appears to be a result of either unexplained higher wealth of male households, or of the lower wealth of households that include a woman (i.e. female-headed or couple households). They say that they are not in a position to attribute a causal relationship here. We will discuss this in more detail in Chapter 4 but it is relevant in this context to underline how much and how often women are still secondary earners, especially in light of the findings on the significance of the labour market situation for wealth inequalities and resource holding. There is some evidence that allows us to look somewhat more closely at this.

Working with Luxembourg Income Study[9] data for 46 countries – 18 of which are in the EU – between 2000 and 2013,[10] Nieuwenhuis et al. (2018) identify whether women aged between 25 and 54 years have personal income from employment (including short-term, insurance-based income replacement) and the proportion of this income relative to the household income as a whole. Reproducing their results for the 18 EU member states underlines huge variation (Table 3.2).

As one might expect, women in the Nordic countries are most likely to have a personal income (only around 5 per cent of Finnish women report no personal income, for example – the lowest of any of the countries). At the other extreme are Greece and Italy, where, respectively, 43 per cent and 38 per cent of women of working age report no income from employment-related activity. The Continental European and also the Central Eastern European states resemble each other with the upper threshold of women reporting no personal income at around a fifth. Ireland and the UK perform relatively poorly with about a quarter of women with no labour income of their own. The latter are also the countries reporting the largest social class-related differences among women (see second data column in

---

[9]   This is a public-access archive of micro datasets that are harmonized into a common template. The LIS Database includes repeated cross-sections from participating countries, with datasets available for up to 12 points in time depending on the country. The Database includes income, labour market and demographic indicators. See https://www.lisdatacenter.org/.

[10]   National variations for the exact data points notwithstanding, their analysis generally covers the period beginning in 2000 and ending in 2012/13. For most countries they have evidence spanning at least ten years.

Table 3.2   *Proportion of women (aged between 25 and 54 years) with no income from employment in 2010–13 in a range of countries and gaps between those in the top and bottom income quintiles*

Country	Percentage of women with no own income	Difference between the proportion of women with no own income in the top and bottom income quintiles
Austria	11.6	23.4
Czech Republic	15.6	26.8
Denmark	7.9	22.0
Estonia	10.5	20.5
Finland	4.7	14.0
France	14.5	51.1
Germany	11.3	27.4
Greece	42.8	52.7
Hungary	21.3	23.3
Ireland	27.3	59.2
Italy	37.8	54.0
Luxembourg	16.8	27.9
Poland	32.0	46.4
The Netherlands	11.9	24.6
Slovakia	18.1	42.6
Slovenia	14.2	33.2
Spain	22.6	37.6
UK	24.7	54.2

Source: Calculated from Nieuwenhuis et al. (2018, Table 4.1).

Table 3.2). For example, there is a gap of over 50 percentage points in the UK (and in Ireland nearly 60 percentage points) between women in the lowest and highest income quintiles in regard to whether they have any earned income. Gaps of a similar magnitude also exist in France, Italy and Greece. So the indications are that the intersection between gender and socio-economic status is strongest in these countries in regard to involvement in employment (assuming that personal income can be read from labour market participation). Finland is again the country with the smallest gap by top/bottom quintile comparison (14 percentage points) unlike Denmark where the gap is 22 percentage points (but this is below average overall). Gaps of similar magnitude characterize the Continental European countries (apart from France) and Central Eastern European countries (apart from Slovakia and Poland where much higher gaps exist). All told, this evidence is very convincing about the presence of socio-

Table 3.3 *Proportion of women's (aged between 25 and 54) income as a percentage of couple's income in 2010–13 in a range of countries, and percentage change between 1999–2000 and 2010–2013**

Country	Women's income as percentage of couple's income	Change from 1999/2000 to 2010/13 (in percentage points)
Austria	30.3	+3.6
Czech Republic	34.1	−1.2
Denmark	42.5	−3.3
Estonia	37.9	−0.2
Finland	42.1	+0.6
France	37.3	+5.6
Germany	31.7	+3.9
Greece	27.6	+7.2
Hungary	39.7	−0.3
Ireland	38.9	+13.3
Italy	26.8	+4.2
Luxembourg	35.6	+11.6
The Netherlands	25.6	+0.4
Slovakia	36.5	−5.9
Slovenia	45.1	+1.6
Spain	34.6	+13.6
UK	35.4	+5.4

Source: Calculated from Nieuwenhuis et al. (2018, Table 4.2).

Note: * Actual year varies by country but in most cases is 1990/2000 and 2010/13.

economic factors in whether women have personal income and polarization among women in this regard in some countries. This also indicates that dual-income households are a near prerequisite in most countries to be in the top income quintile, as Nieuwenhuis et al. point out (2018, p. 14).

When it comes to the share/contribution of women's income in couple households (using the same data and countries), great variation in the midst of some familiar patterning is again a pronounced finding (Table 3.3).[11] The Scandinavian countries of Denmark and Finland almost approach parity (with 'parity' at around 42 per cent), but they are preceded by Slovenia (45.1 per cent) which has the smallest gap of any of the countries. On this measure Ireland and the UK are close to the Continental

---

11   See also the work of Rastrigina and Verashchagina (2015).

European countries and also Spain with women's employment-related incomes equivalent to between a quarter and a third of the couple's income. Women's contribution is something that is generally increasing over time (as the second data column on changes in the decade to 2010/13 in Table 3.3 shows). Countries reporting significant positive change since 2000 include Ireland, Spain, Greece and Luxembourg. This kind of development, together with a general upward move, is attributed to a stronger presence of women in the labour market alongside a weakening of men's labour market positioning due to the economic crisis (Bettio, 2017). Especially in the countries hit hard by the recession – including Greece, Ireland and Spain – the effect could be produced by falling male incomes and rising male unemployment, as Sánchez-Mira and O'Reilly (2018) report.

Although not evident in the Nieuwenhuis et al. data, Klesment and Van Bavel (2017) indicate that, across countries, women's income is larger than that of men in at least a fifth of households.[12] The countries with larger proportions of female breadwinner households are Latvia, Lithuania and Slovenia (and not the Nordic countries as one might expect).

Overall, the picture is one of improvement and reducing inequality regarding income and financial position (especially as that is associated with greater presence in the labour market). The wide variation across countries is notable (how can one speak of the EU in the singular?). But there is some patterning – the Nordic nations conform to expectation with both high numbers of women having income of their own and small gender difference in intra-household income contribution (although this appears to have plateaued out). So too do the Mediterranean countries where there are significant proportions of women not earning and large gender gaps in household earnings contribution. The UK and Ireland have similar levels of women with no earnings as do Italy and Spain (and also socio-economic differences therein), although women's earnings constitute a higher proportion of the overall income in Ireland and the UK. The Central Eastern European nations provide another pattern in that, while having own income is relatively widespread among women (although in Hungary and Poland to a lesser extent), the socio-economic differences are less and women's income constitutes a significant share of the couple's income. These countries join Denmark and Finland with smaller polarization as compared to the others. Greece is an outlier.

---

[12]   Their analysis was based on nearly 100,000 couple households (in which the woman was aged between 25 and 45 years) and where at least one partner had income from employment using EU-SILC (EU Survey on Income and Living Conditions) data for the years 2006 or 2010 in 25 EU member states as well as Iceland and Norway.

Poverty gives us an alternative lens through which to view income-related disadvantages.

3.3 POVERTY

3.3.1 Poverty Rates and Trends

On statistics for 2017, 17.6 per cent of women and 16.3 per cent of men over the age of 16 were identified as being at risk of poverty in the EU.[13] If we add social exclusion (measured by indicators of enforced deprivation)[14] and low work intensity to the relative income poverty figures, the poverty rate shoots up but the gender ratio remains more or less the same: the rate in 2017 on this triple-sided measure for women was 23.3 per cent, while that for men was 21.6 per cent in the EU (Table 3.4). The overall gender gap in poverty or social exclusion was 1.7 percentage points in 2017.

There were only two countries with negative gender gaps: Denmark and very marginally Slovakia. The countries with the highest gender gaps (all in women's disfavour) in 2017 were the Baltic states of Latvia (a gap of some 6.2 percentage points, the highest of any country), Estonia (a gap of 4.6 percentage points) and Lithuania (a gap of 3.8 percentage points) as well as the Central Eastern European countries of Bulgaria and the Czech Republic (of around 3 percentage points).

In terms of trends over time, between 2009 and 2017 the share of both men and women at risk of poverty or social exclusion followed a similar path as the poverty trends overall. That is, the overall trend was generally

---

[13] The data are from the Eurostat EU-SILC (EU Survey on Income and Living Conditions) database and were downloaded from https://ec.europa.eu/eurostat/web/income-and-living-conditions/data/main-tables. At risk of poverty is measured on the basis of 60 per cent of median, equivalized income after social transfers.

[14] Note that the definition of poverty and social exclusion I take is from the EU Survey on Income and Living Conditions (EU-SILC). Note that this is known in EU parlance as 'people at risk of poverty or social exclusion' which is the official EU definition. This is a three-composition measure. The first consists of relative income poverty or in the EU's parlance 'at risk of poverty', which is calculated as the share of people with an equivalized disposable income (after social transfers) below a threshold of 60 per cent of the national median equivalized disposable income after social transfers. The second component consists of severe material deprivation which is defined as the enforced inability to pay for or afford at least four of nine items considered to be desirable or necessary to lead an adequate life (including unexpected expenses, a one-week annual holiday away from home, a meal involving meat, chicken or fish every second day, adequate heating of a dwelling, and durable goods like a washing machine, colour television, telephone or car). The third element relates to employment, in particular low household work intensity which is defined as the number of persons living in a household where the members of working age worked less than 20 per cent of their total potential gainful employment during the previous 12 months.

Gender inequality and welfare states in Europe

Table 3.4   Female poverty or social exclusion rates in 2017, gender gaps in 2017 and percentage point change in gender gap between 2009 and 2017 in the EU-28 countries

	Female poverty or social exclusion rate 2017	Gender gap 2017 (men's minus women's rate)	Gender gap 2009–17
EU-28	23.3	+1.7	−0.8
Austria	19.3	+ 2.5	−0.4
Belgium	21.4	+2.3	−1.0
Bulgaria	40.4	+3.1	−0.9
Croatia	27.2	+2.2	+0.2
Cyprus	26.4	+2.4	−2.7
Czech Republic	13.9	+3.4	0.0
Denmark	16.6	−1.2	0.0
Estonia	25.6	+4.6	+0.2
Finland	15.7	+0.1	−−2.2
France	17.6	+1.0	−1.6
Germany	20.3	+2.7	+0.3
Greece	35.7	+1.8	−1.1
Hungary	26.1	+1.2	+0.3
Ireland	23.5	+1.7	+0.3
Italy	29.8	+2.0	−1.8
Latvia	31.1	+6.2	+2.8
Lithuania	31.3	+3.8	−0.1
Luxembourg	22.8	+1.5	−2.1
Malta	20.2	+1.7	−0.8
The Netherlands	17.3	+0.6	−1.0
Poland	19.6	+0.3	−1.3
Portugal	24.0	+1.5	−0.3
Romania	36.5	+1.6	−1.0
Slovakia	16.2	−0.1	−3.2
Slovenia	18.3	+2.5	−1.5
Spain	27.1	+1.1	−0.7
Sweden	18.3	+1.3	−1.1
UK	23.0	+2.0	+0.3

Source: Table ilc_peps01 at https://appsso.eurostat.ec.europa.eu/nui/show.do?dataset=ilc_peps01&lang=en.

downward in the EU between 2005 and 2009, after which it went up quite sharply until 2015 when it started to fall again. After 2012, however, the poverty or social exclusion rate decreased more for women than it did for men, thereby reducing the gender gap by nearly a half. Taking the period as a whole, the gender gap narrowed in almost all EU countries between 2009 and 2017, except for Latvia which saw a most significant increase (see Table 3.4). There is another strong hint here that the situation of men worsened relative to that of women, or, put otherwise, that men's income situation was more adversely affected by the recession than that of women. Perrons (2015, p. 48) confirms this, showing that between 2005 and 2013 in the EU the numbers of women at risk of poverty and social exclusion increased by 1.4 million compared to a 3.6 million rise for men. These changes – especially if they indicate long-term trends – hint that men may be becoming less financially secure and therefore potentially more reliant on women's incomes. Corsi et al. (2016), working on evidence for the period between 2007 and 2013 on individual data for women and men across the EU, noted such a trend, not just from data on male poverty but also for men's financial dependency between 2007 and 2012.

Notwithstanding a rise in male poverty, it is important to bear in mind that a gender gap is the norm across the EU and that women's greater risk of poverty compared to that of men is a relatively constant feature of the EU, although it is small (see Table 3.4).

What is the nature of these differences and who are the poor women and men?

3.3.2 Factors Associated with the Gender Distribution of Poverty

Women's and men's risk of poverty is affected by a range of intersecting inequalities (European Institute for Gender Equality, 2016). Some of these intersections are demographic – with age as one such factor. Poverty is in Europe concentrated among the young – those aged 18 to 24 years are the most likely to be at risk of poverty or social exclusion of any age group and they are followed in this by 'children' (those aged between 0 and 17 years). To put this into figures, almost a third of young people were at such risk in 2015 and for those aged 17 or less the rate was 26.9 per cent (European Institute for Gender Equality, 2016). The situation of young people aged 18 to 24 has deteriorated the most compared to other age groups since 2010. Gender differences among the 18–24 age group generally reflect those of the population as a whole. Older people – those aged 65 or over – present two contrasts as compared to the younger cohorts. First, they have the lowest risk of poverty or social exclusion, at 17.4 per cent on 2015 figures, and their poverty risk steadily declined between 2010 and 2014. Second, this is the age group with the highest gender imbalance in poverty. In fact, from the age of 65 on, men's poverty rate remains more or less static while that of women increases consistently and significantly with age. Incorporating older people into poverty figures, then, generally increases gender differences (Brady and Kall, 2008). It is also important to note that this age group is one for which we can best measure gender differences given that it is the period of life when women are most likely to be heads of households (and hence methodological comparability is improved). Although there is much cross-national variation, women over 65 are on average over one-and-a-half times more likely to live in poverty than men of similar ages in Organisation for Economic Co-operation and Development (OECD) countries overall (OECD, 2012). The general explanation for high levels of old-age poverty for women is a lifetime pay penalty, which as well as lowering earnings also leads to low or no pensions (which we will investigate further below). In 2017, the gender gap in pensions for those aged 65 and over stood at 34.8 per cent (European Commission, 2019, p. 69). The 2018 gender equality report from the European Commission underlined the divergence in the pension gap among EU countries, varying from 47 per cent in Cyprus to 2 per cent in Estonia (European Commission, 2018). There is no simple patterning by region or welfare state type in the size of the gaps other than that they are smallest in the Baltic states, large in the Continental European (especially Austria and Germany) and Mediterranean countries and moderate in the Nordic nations (apart from Denmark where the gap was only 8 per cent in 2016). While the gap is increasing in a minority of member states and there is some indication that it is shrinking in others, there was only minimal improvement at aggregate level in the EU between 2013 and 2016 (European Commission, 2018, p. 24).

But intersecting inequalities are also a part of the patterning. The groups showing the highest risks of poverty (above the EU28 average), apart from the life course-related factor which renders the young and the old vulnerable, include single people, those who are foreign born, lone parents, those with low educational levels and people with disabilities. Among these groups, lone parents stand out. Approximately one in three lone mothers is at risk of poverty in the EU, compared to one in five of lone fathers (European Commission, 2018, p. 26). This is double the average and higher than for any other household type. Single mothers run a particularly high poverty risk in Greece (57 per cent), Luxembourg (51 per cent), Malta (47 per cent), Lithuania (46 per cent), Germany (43 per cent), Latvia (42 per cent), Italy (41 per cent), and Bulgaria (40 per cent) (Van Lancker 2015, using data for 2012).[15] Obviously, this is a mixed grouping of countries in terms of social policy model and so not just is there no particular patterning by country or policy regime type but the indications are that this

---

[15]   See also Nieuwenhuis et al., 2018.

phenomenon is widespread although less prevalent in the Nordic countries. However, Nieuwenhuis et al. (2018, p. 23) point out that this is related to the proportion of women with an income of their own and that poverty rates in general are lower in countries where more women have a personal income. This relationship between poverty rate and earnings' status applies for women in low-income as well as high-income households.

In official EU parlance, these kinds of differences are attributed to the 'low work intensity' of lone-mother households. This is a descriptive rather than a causal analysis though. The fact that women's economic status and income standing is highly sensitive to their partnership status (unpartnered, widowed, divorced or separated), or the arrival or departure of a family member (including having a baby) (Bould et al., 2012), should be a clue to structural underpinnings (or in another guise – impoverishing processes), and in particular the significance of the distribution of caring responsibilities in this regard (to be considered in the following chapters). Leaving employment on entering lone parenthood (Paull, 2007), and falling income for women following marital splits (Jenkins, 2008), are both significant routes into poverty (although declining in influence). In the UK and elsewhere, repartnering is the main way for single divorced mothers to escape (household) poverty (Price, 2009).

In terms of male poverty, Dermott and Pantazis (2014) shed light on those male groups for whom the risk of poverty has increased in the UK. They highlight especially the poverty risk of men who live alone. These men – in the UK context anyway – are not whom we might expect – younger men who experience educational and labour market disadvantages. They are, rather, a mix of older, widowed and retired men, those who have retired from the labour market prematurely for reasons of ill-health, and middle-aged fathers who do not live with their children.

The evidence also makes clear that ethnicity is a major factor in poverty risk along with gender and age. Women and men born outside the EU are twice as likely to be at risk of poverty (36 per cent for women and 38 per cent for men) than people born in the country where they live, highlighting how migration affects the possibility for women and men to achieve economic independence and financial well-being (European Institute for Gender Equality, 2016). Countries with the highest risk of poverty for migrant women in 2012 were Greece (52 per cent), Spain (47 per cent), Belgium (39 per cent), Luxembourg (35 per cent) and France (35 per cent) (Van Lancker, 2015). The gap between migrant and native-born women was largest in these countries also: 30 percentage points in Greece, 29 in Belgium, 24 in Spain, 23 in Luxembourg and 21 in France. Although the poverty risk of migrant women is below average in Sweden (28 per cent) and Finland (27 per cent), the 20 percentage point gap between native and migrant women in these countries is significant (Van Lancker, 2015). However, the gender gaps within the migrant (that is, non-native born) population are not any larger than those of the EU-born population sector (European Institute for Gender Equality, 2016, p. 78) – both migrant women and men are at a roughly similarly high risk of poverty, given their exposure to economic inactivity or part-time work, among a number of other risk factors.

Viewed through a long lens and connecting family-related exigencies and positioning to income, the long-term effects of life patterns are thrown into sharp relief by the poverty statistics. There are several points to note here. Out of all women identified as in poverty or social exclusion in the EU in 2014, 20 per cent were engaged in unpaid domestic work as their main form of activity, a further fifth were retired or had finished their business activity (retired entrepreneurs), and 15 per cent were unemployed (European Institute for Gender Equality, 2016, p. 43). The data show large gender differences in so-called 'inactivity' due to domestic tasks among those who are poor, although the proportions of women in this situation differ significantly by country (European Institute for Gender Equality, 2016, p. 43).[16] Another factor to note is that women tend to become 'inactive' at an earlier age than men and, in addition, their economic inactivity increases sharply before retirement age (the inactivity rate of women aged 55–64 is 52 per cent, while for men in this age group it is 36 per cent) (European Institute for Gender Equality, 2016, p. 72). Such reduced employment intensity among women (both single and married) as their lives progress becomes especially apparent and consequential in old age. For, as emphasized, although women were more likely to be at risk of poverty or social exclusion than men in all age groups in 2015, the largest differences were to be seen in the oldest group (65 or over).

Gender inequality in the overall poverty statistics is quite static.

3.3.3 Underlying Patterns

On the face of it then, the EU poverty figures suggest that gender inequality or disadvantage is not so large. It would be erroneous to accept this at face value, however. The truth is that we do not know the female/male relativities here, mainly because of the convention of measuring income and poverty at collective unit level. There is a real possibility that such

---

[16]   In particular, while the average is 20 per cent for women in the EU as a whole, in Malta for example such women constitute over 60 per cent of those in poverty. Other countries reporting higher than average EU rates include Greece, Ireland, Italy, Luxembourg, Romania and Spain (European Institute for Gender Equality, 2016, p. 43).

measurement conventions mean that gender differences – and especially women's poverty levels – are under-reported. What we are referring to here is the practice of European Union Statistics on Income and Living Conditions (EU-SILC)[17] as well as other major income surveys to measure income and other resources at the household level and then calculate the income of individuals by assuming that households with more than one member share their income equally. Since all women within households are therefore attributed an income equal to all other adults in that household, they can only be counted as poor if the total income is below the poverty line. This has two main implications. First, it means that the gender poverty differentials are a result of comparisons only between a subset of households containing women – essentially, single-person households and lone-parent households (representing a small proportion of women over-all). Second, since most women are not heads of households and since it is men who usually earn the majority of household income (and therefore have arguably greater control over it), the income and poverty situation of women is not well covered by these income data.[18] Moreover, the assumption of equal sharing is rendered counterfactual by evidence from other studies that only 71 per cent of households in the EU treat all income as a common resource (European Institute for Gender Equality, 2016, p. 47) and that this is as low as 53 per cent in Finland for example.

Keeping open the possibility that these numbers underestimate female poverty and hence gender differences, some research has undertaken to calculate poverty rates on the basis of individual income from labour, social transfers and other sources. Using a measure of financial dependency – based on women's and men's personal income levels – and comparing it to a household-based measure adjusted for the attribution of the individual income to women and men, Corsi et al. (2016) find that from a global EU analysis in the period between 2007 and 2012 the gender gaps in income jump from 4–6 per cent when the latter is used to 47–55 per cent when the former is used. In terms of poverty rates (measured as below the threshold of 60 per cent of the national median equivalized income), the jump for women is from around 16 per cent to 42 per cent and for men the jump is

---

[17] The origins of EU-SILC are in the European Community Household Panel (ECHP) in which a sample of households and persons was interviewed year after year for the purpose of ascertaining income and living standards. The ECHP ran for eight years, from 1994 to 2001 (eight waves). It was succeeded by the EU-SILC survey from 2003/04 which is run annually and covers all the member states. See https://ec.europa.eu/eurostat/web/microdata/european-union-statistics-on-income-and-living-conditions.

[18] Research on the then EU-27 member states – using a special module of the 2010 EU Survey on Income and Living Conditions (EU-SILC) – found that some 30 per cent of couple households do not fully pool their income, with 22 per cent partially pooling and 7 per cent not pooling (Ponthieux, 2013, p. 17).

from around 14 per cent to 21 per cent. All told, the gender gap in poverty jumps from around 2 percentage points to 21 percentage points. It is salutary to bear in mind, then, that existing knowledge of gender differences of poverty, income and wealth is effectively based on a rather small sector of the population: a comparison of households headed by women and men. This means that rather than gender gaps in poverty among the whole population it is gaps between single female households, mainly mother-only households with dependent children but also those of older women (who are more likely to live alone than men of a similar age), and all those headed by a man that are the differences being signposted.

Another piece of the picture is provided by research on the chances of avoiding poverty without the income of one's partner (assumed to be shared). If the husband/father were to lose his income and the family had to rely on the mother's income and benefits, the proportion of couple families with children in poverty in the EU-28 on the basis of 2014 data would rise from 15 per cent to 69 per cent (European Institute for Gender Equality, 2016, p. 52). By comparison, the poverty rate would double to 34 per cent were the family to lose the mother's income. Countries in which couple families with children have the greatest dependence on the male income to avoid poverty are the Central Eastern European nations, but also Austria, Germany, Italy and the UK. These are also the countries which have the largest gender gap in regard to dependence on one partner's income to avoid poverty. In this context, it is interesting to remind ourselves that Ann Orloff (1993) identified the capacity to maintain an autonomous household as one indicator of the relationship between gender inequality and social rights, and the degree of progressivity therein.

These patterns have deep roots – the concept of feminization of poverty has been invoked in the past to explain this. Lewis and Piachaud (1992) demonstrated for the UK that throughout the twentieth century women in poverty had always outnumbered men. Glennerster et al. (2004) put numbers on this: in 1899, women made up about 60 per cent of all adults in poverty, and by 2001/02 they made up 54 per cent of those aged 16 and over living in poverty.

3.4   UNDERPINNING FACTORS: ACCESS TO BENEFITS

The significance of transfer payments for the reduction of gender-specific differences in poverty (indeed all poverty rates) is confirmed by research. Moreover, it is also well known that, as compared with men, women tend to receive a higher proportion of their income from welfare benefits.

This seems to be the European way. In a summary of two decades of comparative research using Luxembourg Income Study data, for example, Gornick (2004, pp. 213, 224) underlines how cross-national differences in tax and transfer policies explain a large share of the variation in poverty between women and men in different countries. Gornick and Jantti (2010) confirm the role of public income transfers in reducing poverty disparities between women and men of prime age (25–54 year olds) in 26 countries,[19] although as we have seen in most countries women have a higher risk of poverty than men. The underlying point is that the country one lives in and its social policies matter hugely, especially in terms of the actual rates of poverty both before and after transfers.

Avram et al. (2016) confirm this, looking at the effects of the changes in tax-benefit policies on disposable income over the period between 2008 and 2014 separately for women and men in a mixed set of 18 EU countries.[20] They investigate three alternative scenarios regarding income sharing within the household – favouring the primary earner, favouring the secondary earner and equal pooling. Overall, they find that the policy changes led to a substantial increase in mean income in five countries (Belgium, Bulgaria, Denmark, Poland and Sweden), a decrease in seven countries (Estonia, France, Hungary, Ireland, Italy, Latvia and Spain) and little change in the Czech Republic, Finland, Germany, Luxembourg, the Netherlands and Romania. Pensions played a major role in increasing incomes whereas increases in taxes were the main cause of falls in those countries where incomes fell. Lone-mother families were especially affected in those countries where incomes fell (except France). When it comes to broader comparisons between women and men (using the three ways to attribute collective income to individuals as outlined above – an analysis they undertake for Belgium, Czech Republic, Finland, France, Romania and Spain), Avram et al. (2016) find that, under all assumptions, the effects of policy changes on the disposable income and estimated poverty rate are either the same or improved for men whereas the income and poverty risks for women worsen on all measures. Moreover, the effects vary hugely by household type, suggesting social policies' complex engagement with gender and household type.

Pensions are hugely significant in all of this and they are worthy of

---

[19] All EU member states, except Australia, Brazil, Canada, Columbia, Guatemala, Mexico, Peru, the US and Uruguay.

[20] Belgium, Bulgaria, Czech Republic, Denmark, Estonia, Finland, France, Germany, Hungary, Ireland, Italy, Latvia, Luxembourg, the Netherlands, Poland, Romania, Spain and Sweden.

some consideration for not only do they affect the current generation of pensioners but they exert an impact that spans the entire lifecycle.

Defining a pensioners' gender gap as the difference in average pensions between men and women over 65 years, calculated in terms of pensions pre taxes and using 2011 EU-SILC data, Betti et al. (2015) find for the (then) EU-27 countries (apart from Croatia) that men on average were entitled to pensions greater than those of women by 39 per cent. This is similar to the rate quoted above for the EU-28 for 2016. They also show that pension gaps are larger than gender pay gaps (this is mainly because the former reflect inter-generational patterns as compared with the more current pay gaps). When gender gaps in pension coverage (including people who have zero pensions) are included in the computation along with gender gaps in pension income, the overall gap is somewhat higher at 43 per cent. When they split their sample into younger and older pensioners (those aged between 65 and 80, and those over 80, respectively) – in order to address the question of change over time – they find a definite tendency for gender gaps to be higher for the younger group and to appear to fall with age. For example, the average gender pension gap for the younger group is 41 per cent, whereas for the older group it is 9 percentage points lower, at 32 per cent. This – together with the suggestion of a trend for the gap to widen over time (comparing 2005–11) – contradicts the expectation that things are getting better. There are some points to note though. One is that historical factors are exerting a strong effect here as are longevity factors which mean that the most disadvantaged are likely to be concentrated among the younger (as against the older) cohort. In the older age group it is survivor pensions that are the main source of support so one is not talking about personal pensions in the same way as one is for the younger generations. But there is a significance to note here in that doing away with survivor pensions will actually have a negative effect on pension equalization (Betti et al., 2015, p. 138).

These gaps and inequalities are the result of *longue-durée* processes. Earlier in their lives women incur pension entitlement and other income gaps mainly due to childcare-related gaps in their employment history and patterns of employment with low pension coverage. The gaps also are a further clue to the significance of family organization in that single (never-married) women in general face lower gender gaps in pensions, as do widows and divorced women. Having said that, it is significant that among those who are single, gender gaps in pensions remain sizeable (the EU average being around 29 per cent). In all cases, married women have the widest gaps (EU average 50 per cent). In many national settings, this gap even exceeds 60 per cent: in Luxembourg it is 67 per cent, for example, in Germany 62 per cent, and the Netherlands 58 per cent (Betti et al., 2015).

When looking at the value of pensions and gender inequalities in that regard, Betti et al. find that for the EU-27 average, 63 per cent of women are 'squeezed' into a pension range that holds the poorest third of men (which could be expressed as saying that there are 1.9 times as many pension-poor women as pension-poor men; or for every pension-poor man there are 1.9 poor equivalent women) (Betti et al., 2015, p. 60). Among high-income pensioners, women are correspondingly under-represented — only 12 per cent of women reach the pension enjoyed by the richest third of men (for every three pension-rich men there is about one pension-rich woman). The countries that perform badly in terms of both a higher incidence of lower pensions among women and a lower incidence of women earning top pensions are the classic male breadwinner states of Austria, Germany and Luxembourg, together with Bulgaria and Spain.

Looking at reform and change over time, Betti et al. (2015, p. 8) identify two trends in pension systems that have special significance for gender inequalities. The first is the switch in emphasis from first pillar (usually provided by the state and based on societal solidarity and pay-as-you-go funding) to second pillar pension provision (provided collectively on the basis of occupational solidarity and prefunded). The second trend is the increasing emphasis on longer employment lives, which is a core component of the EU's policy for example. The authors make the important point that women are not protected by the internal operational logic of either pension system, new or old. Hence, women may be more at risk than men as recipients: "their rights on social insurance are often 'derived rights' (survivors' pensions, married people's supplements); in those systems where a second pillar is taking hold, women are more likely to rely on state systems, or to be more affected by gaps in contributions and broken careers; finally, in many countries, they persist in the role of carers (for children or aged parents) even as unpaid work is receiving less recognition" (Betti et al., 2015, p. 9).

One might add a third trend: the long-term move to individualize pensions. This at face value looks like – and in some respects is – a pro-gender equality move but removing derived rights and derived benefits without other structural changes often means less income for women. 'Derived' benefits obtained either as a dependant of their partner, or following his death, are still important for women, in particular for pensioners and widows (Price, 2008). This may also be true in some situations for divorcees. In this way, marriage lives on as a determinant of income levels by family status (Daly and Scheiwe, 2010), at a time when cohabitation is on the increase. This status has been extended in the UK recently to same sex partners in civil partnerships. However, with the new single-tier state pension, derived and inherited rights to pension entitlements will be abolished.

3.5 CONCLUSION

The global evidence on the comparable financial situation of women and men – as measured by the European Institute for Gender Equality's money index – suggests some improvement since 2005 in women's level of financial resources, although an overall gap in the money inequality index of the order of some 20 percentage points indicates persisting gender inequalities. The degree of recorded change from 2005 to 2015 was of the order of a 6 percentage point improvement. There are very large variations among countries, with the Nordic and Continental European countries showing the least significant gaps in 2015 and the Central Eastern European and Baltic nations the most. The patterns of change over time indicate that improvements in the Nordic nations may have plateaued out and that the main improvements took place in countries where gaps had formerly been large (as in some of the Baltic and Central Eastern European nations). There is likely to be a laggard effect here. Notably in the countries most affected by the recession – especially Greece – gender gaps have grown as incomes have fallen overall.

When access to income and wealth was examined in greater detail, the evidence confirms large gaps between women and men. The evidence on wealth (which is rather weak data so needs to be treated with care) shows that such gaps increase with age and family living situation (with the lowest gaps between single women and men). The evidence points to structural differences: women's households in general and those which contain a woman have less wealth than male households. Research comparing women's and men's individual incomes shows that part of the inequality is attributable to significant numbers of women in most countries having no personal income. This is changing only slowly in most countries (with some exceptions such as Luxembourg, Ireland and Spain which have seen rapid change in this regard).

The chapter has also considered differences in poverty, and showed that across countries the prevalence of poverty is greater among women as compared with men, although men's situation looks to have worsened as a result of the recession. Overall, gender gaps are not changing much though. One can again identify structural factors exerting an influence: the types of household that women tend to head (e.g. elderly and lone parent); women's lower labour market participation vis-à-vis that of men; the effect of women's family situation on their risk of poverty (with lone mothers especially vulnerable). Intersectional inequalities were also revealed with older women, lone parents, and foreign-born people more exposed than their counterparts. When pensions were taken as a case study of how welfare state benefits are implicated in the results, the findings confirm the significance of pensions for gender-based income inequalities (with men across countries in receipt of pensions that are greater than those received by women by 39 per cent on average). The evidence reviewed also contradicts the expectation that things are getting better.

In terms of cross-national variations, the patterning across the range of indicators used is not that strong. However, the Nordic nations tend to have the lowest gender gaps in income and women there are least likely to have no income from employment. The poverty risk for women was also relatively low in these countries as was the gender gap in poverty. The Baltic and Central Eastern European nations also tend to cluster together (with some exceptions) with relatively large gender gaps in money and poverty risk, although women's income from employment constitutes a relatively high proportion of the overall household income. Change is afoot in these countries though, with evidence of movement to smaller gender gaps in money. The patterning that can be observed for the Continental European countries is one of a middle way – in these countries the gender gaps in money and poverty risk are smaller than in the Baltic and Eastern European nations but larger than the Nordic countries. Moreover, there is a strong seam of traditional dependence on male incomes, judging by the average proportion of couple income contributed by the female partner. It is important not to over-interpret the similarities though.

We are obliged to note that a lot of the findings regarding income comparisons between women and men come with a 'health warning' in that they rely on collective income and assumptions about equal sharing of the collective (household or family) income between women and men. In a context where the collective unit continues to be taken as the unit of measurement for both income access and poverty, the truth is that we do not know the reality with certainty because of standard data and research practice that fails to problematize internal household or family processes regarding income sharing.

4.   Access to employment

Access to employment is one of the most important dimensions of economic status, income level and financial well-being. This is for several reasons but its importance is notably increased by the policy turn towards social investment which has shifted the focus more closely towards labour market and employment as sources of income. It almost appears as if we are in the midst of a great experiment – to reveal how good the market is at supporting people and redistributing the 'goods' that are considered 'progressive' while downgrading the redistributive role and purview of our welfare states. The EU has sought especially to elevate women's rate of labour market participation, targeting it as part of the overall 75 per cent employment rate to be achieved through its Europe 2020 programme (European Commission, 2010a). High female employment participation is construed as a good in itself, the assumption being that it brings all kinds of benefits – especially utility maximization – and is the mark of an economic and social model fit for the twenty-first century. The idealized model for women is, by and large, full-time employment in the male mould, with some 'softening' introduced by the appeal to 'work–life balance' which legitimizes and resources short-term exit from the labour market for childbirth and early child-rearing purposes (the actual policies involved will be considered in later chapters). The thinking goes – and it is not clear whether this is intent or rationalization – that for women more employment would confer greater independence and career development. This draws especially from the Swedish model which promotes working life as the arena where gender equality is most expected to be realized (de los Reyes, 2016). While there is a sense of gender equality in increasing women's labour market participation, it can be rather shallow. A deeper version, for example, might take account of women's needs, the conditions or quality of employment and other goals such as social justice or redistribution (Watkins, 2018, p. 14). There is another reason also to take some critical distance to the goal of high female labour market participation rates as an end in itself – it rests on a very specific model of the heterosexual couple responding to the needs of the labour market (Mulinari, 2016, p. 139).

This chapter looks at the empirical reality of employment for women vis-à-vis men to identify the patterning of gender and other forms of inequality in relation to labour market engagement and working conditions. Again the key questions are: What is the status quo? What are the signature trends? Is the situation improving in regard to gender equality? We should bear in mind here the strong suggestion in some of the literature of trade-offs in regard to labour market inclusion/exclusion on the basis of gender and class intersections (e.g. Pettit and Hook, 2009; Cooke, 2011; Budig et al., 2016). The chapter is organized into three main sections. The first considers employment rates. The second section examines a range of sources of labour market-related inequality, especially in regard to structural matters (for example, duration of paid work, sectoral location, pay levels). The third section provides an overview of the factors that have been identified by existing research as explanations for gender inequality in relation to employment rates and pay inequality.

4.1 EMPLOYMENT PARTICIPATION: RATES AND CONDITIONS

4.1.1 Access to Employment

According to the EU, women contributed more than two-thirds of the overall change in the labour force in the past 20 years in the EU-15 member countries, and more than three-quarters if only the prime-age population is considered (Eurofound, 2016, p. 5).[1] While there is vibrancy in female employment patterns, the meaningfulness of this kind of statement has to be probed. First, it conceals different trends over time. The period prior to the recession – that is the 10–15 years up to the mid-2000s – was a high point of female integration into the European labour market (Karamessini and Rubery, 2014), but this movement has since stalled. Second, when a more differentiated analysis – in terms of time and place – is conducted, robust gender gaps reveal themselves as do progressive patterns disrupted by the recession in almost all member states and the EU as a whole.

As Table 4.1 shows, the female employment rate in the EU as a whole increased between 2010 and 2017 (from 62.1 to 66.6 per cent) with women's employment rate growing more than that of men. However, there are limits to both female growth and movement towards parity; the gender gap in economic activity has stagnated for the last few years at around 11–12 percentage points and is actually more than 18 percentage points when

---

[1] That is, the countries that constituted the EU before the expansion in 2004. These are Austria, Belgium, Denmark, Finland, France, Germany, Greece, Ireland, Italy, Luxembourg, the Netherlands, Portugal, Spain, Sweden and the UK.

Table 4.1   *Various indicators of gender differences in relation to employment in the EU-28 countries, 2005/10–2015/17*

EU 28	2010	2017
Employment rate*		
Women	62.1	66.6
Men	75.1	78.1
Part-time employment rate**		
Women	31.3	31.7
Men	7.8	8.9
Gender pay gap*	16.4	16.2 (2016)
Gender segregation in occupations* [2]	24.9	24.1 (2016)
Gender segregation in sectors*	19.1	19.0 (2016)
Gender gap in pensions 65+*	38.2 (2013)	36.6 (2016)
European Institute for Gender Equality employment gender equality index***	70.0 (2005)	71.5 (2015)
Participation	77.5 (2005)	79.8 (2015)
Segregation and quality of work	63.3 (2005)	64.0 (2015)

Sources: * European Commission (2018); ** Labour Force Survey Eurostat, Table LFSA_EPPGA; *** European Institute for Gender Equality (2017a).

Note: Unless otherwise stated the data is for 2017.

full-time equivalent employment is the basis of the calculation (European Commission, 2018). This scale of gender employment gap – defined by Eurostat as the difference between the employment rates of men and women aged 20–64 years – is equivalent to some 17 million women. Given this pattern, Bettio (2017, p. 20) estimates that it will be 2037 before women's rate of employment reaches the 75 per cent level in the EU as a whole (assuming that it would grow at the average pace recorded between 2002 and 2014).

There is a considerable degree of variation across the EU member states in this (as in other employment-related matters), however, so much so that generalization is difficult and rather risky (Castellano and Rocca, 2017). With female employment participation rates ranging between 55 per cent

[2]   These indices reflect the proportion of the employed population that would need to change occupation/sector in order to bring about an even distribution of men and women across occupations or sectors. The index varies between 0 (no segregation) and 50 (complete segregation).

and 77.6 per cent, the EU contains both classically low female employment countries such as Greece, Italy and Malta, and traditionally high ones which include the more northern countries such as Finland and Sweden and, increasingly so, Latvia and Lithuania. Such country differences look to be entrenched as there has been no significant catch-up in the gender employment participation gap between low- and high-performing member states over the last decade (European Commission, 2018, p. 10). This and other evidence suggest the persistence of strong regional inequalities, although there has been an upward surge in female employment rates in some individual countries (e.g. in the Baltic states).

The recession of 2008 may have hindered the upward movement of women's employment rate. Looking at the effects of the recession up to the period 2010/2012, Bettio and Verashchagina (2014, p. 76) comment that one of its most serious repercussions is going unnoticed: the widening of geographical disparities within the EU and the emerging threat of a two-tier country system. Employment in the EU has shifted from south to north, with Germany and the UK accounting for most of the new jobs (net of jobs lost) created in the EU between 2008 and 2016, while most of the jobs lost in Greece and Spain in this period have not (yet) been recovered (Eurofound, 2018a, p. 24). The concept of a two-speed Europe applies also from a gender perspective.

In terms of further explicating national variations and inequalities, Karamessini and Rubery (2014, p. 18) point out that it is variations in labour-market participation rates among the less educated and the youngest and oldest cohorts that are at the root of much cross-national variation. In 2014 in the EU-28, only 43 per cent of women (aged 20–64) with low levels of qualifications were employed and as many as 17 per cent had never been employed (European Institute for Gender Equality, 2017c, p. 9). But the behaviour of the middle cohort is also vital, especially that of mothers. Within and across countries, the employment gap is especially high for mothers and women with caring responsibilities. In 2016 more than 19 per cent of the so-called 'inactive' women in the EU were of this status because they were looking after children or adults. On average, the employment rate of women with a child under 6 years is 9 percentage points less than the employment rate of women without children, and in some countries this difference is over 30 percentage points (Czech Republic, Hungary and Slovakia) (EU Commission, 2018, p. 10). This has been identified and studied (together with wage rates) as the 'motherhood penalty' (see e.g. Budig et al., 2012, 2016).

To see how this effect plays out, Stier et al. (2018) – in a study of 19 countries between 1994 and 2012 – classified mothers' work attachment as strong, moderate and weak (depending on the hours worked when their children were under and over school age).[3] Their results are very interesting. While there is considerable change over the 20-year period with mothers of young children generally tending to increase their labour force participation over time, the majority of countries in 2012 still had as their dominant pattern moderate maternal attachment to the labour market. This set of countries includes the EU member states of Austria, Germany, Ireland, Sweden and the UK. The Central Eastern European countries stand out for the degree to which mothers there have strong labour market attachment although the strength of such attachment is declining in these countries (which may explain the points above regarding the high gaps in the Czech Republic, Hungary and Slovakia). Other notable trends over time are increases in mothers' attachment in Ireland and Sweden. To the extent that there is change in the Continental European countries (with Austria, Germany and the Netherlands the relevant included countries), it appears that the main route to strengthening mothers' employment is through part-time employment (hence the 'moderate' route). The situation is similar for the UK. This evidence indicates no real patterning as might be expected from regime-type thinking.

The effect of low qualifications on labour market involvement varies for women and men. Across the EU as a whole, women with low qualifications are significantly more likely than equivalent men to be out of the labour market (59 per cent as against 42 per cent). This is actually where the largest gap is – the labour market participation rate becomes more similar as we move up the qualification spectrum, to the point where the differential falls to 7 per cent for those with high qualifications (European Institute for Gender Equality, 2017c, p. 19).

4.1.2   Part-time Employment

It is almost impossible to speak of women's labour market participation in the EU region without considering part-time employment. Indeed, the EU and OECD are of the opinion that 'gender sorting' into part-time work is an important factor keeping women attached to the labour market (or not), especially after they become mothers (EU Commission, 2018, p. 11; OECD, 2017). Some scholars identify it as a signature European route to gender equality (e.g. Ferree, 2009; Pettit and Hook, 2009). This seems to be widespread (see Table 4.2). In the EU-28 countries taken as a whole, nearly

---

[3]   The countries studied were: Austria, Australia, Bulgaria, Canada, Czech Republic, Germany, Hungary, Ireland, Israel, Japan, the Netherlands, Norway, Philippines, Poland, Russia, Slovenia, Sweden, the UK and the US.

Table 4.2 *Proportion of women in part-time employment 2005–16 and absolute change over the period in the EU-28 countries*

	2005	2016	Change
Austria	30.7	34.7	+4.0
Belgium	33.1	30.0	−3.1
Bulgaria	2.7	2.0	−0.7
Croatia	9.0	6.0	−2.9
Cyprus	12.0	13.9	+1.9
Czech Republic	5.5	8.0	+2.5
Denmark	23.9	26.7	+2.8
Estonia	9.5	11.9	+2.4
Finland	14.8	17.7	+2.9
France	22.6	22.0	−0.6
Germany	38.8	36.9	−1.9
Greece	11.4	16.1	+4.7
Hungary	5.3	5.5	+0.2
Ireland	34.6	34.8	+0.2
Italy	28.8	32.6	+3.8
Latvia	9.4	9.7	+0.3
Lithuania	11.3	9.3	−2.0
Luxembourg	30.7	24.1	−6.6
Malta	19.1	18.4	−0.7
The Netherlands	60.7	59.8	−0.9
Poland	17.4	9.0	−8.4
Portugal	14.1	11.5	−2.6
Romania	6.0	4.6	−1.4
Slovakia	3.7	7.6	+3.9
Slovenia	9.3	11.1	+1.8
Spain	21.0	22.3	+1.3
Sweden	19.0	17.8	−1.2
UK	38.5	37.5	−1.0

Source: OECD Employment Database, Chart LMF1.6.C, https://www.oecd.org/els/soc/ LMF_1_6_Gender_differences_in_employment_outcomes.pdf.

Note: The figures present part-time employment as a proportion of total employment. 'Part-time' refers to persons who usually work less than 30 hours per week in their main job.

every third woman works part-time (30 per cent) compared to one out of every ten men (8 per cent).

In terms of identifying the status quo, the Netherlands stands out among member states for very high proportions of female part-time employment (and also for (very large) gender gaps therein – of the order of over 50 percentage points in 2017) (European Commission, 2018, p. 11). Austria, Belgium, Denmark, Germany, Ireland, Italy and the UK are the countries with the next largest proportions of part-time female employment. It does appear, then, that these Western European countries are the 'gender equality by part-time work countries'. The Central Eastern European and Baltic countries present a contrasting path of much smaller proportions of part-time employment among women (and also smaller gender gaps therein – data not shown) (Table 4.2 and European Commission, 2018).

When we look for change over time, we can see from Table 4.2 that between 2005 and 2016 the changes were relatively minor and for the EU as a whole tended to balance each other out making for a status quo over the period. Looking at the individual member states, significant growth of part-time employment occurred in Austria, Greece, Italy and Slovakia, whereas Luxembourg and Poland saw noticeable falls. There is no real patterning by regime type here either. Part-time employment among men is growing more than it is for women – a 2.2 percentage point increase between 2005 and 2016 (compared to an increase of 0.3 percentage points among women for the OECD area as a whole, figures driven by growth in non-EU member states).[4] Overall then, the evidence supports two claims: both part-time work and the strong unequal gender ratio in it are stable, although there are significant country differences; part-time work is growing somewhat in the EU as a whole, associated especially with the growth of the services sector (which accounts for upwards of 70 per cent of employment in the EU today) (Eurofound, 2018a, p. 5).

There are known negative factors associated with part-time work that need to be highlighted. Involuntary part-time workers are the group of workers at highest risk of in-work poverty in the EU (Eurofound, 2018b, pp. 8–9), for example. Furthermore, we know also – and will see further below – that part-time work is one of the key factors contributing to the gender pay gap, thereby hampering progress towards equal economic independence. There is also a longer-term, life course effect associated with low wages which renders women's incomes low and/or inadequate in old age. As Table 4.1 shows, the gender gap in pensions in 2016 was of the order of 36 per cent.

In broader comparison, in member states where the culture or availability of part-time employment is scarce, such as for instance Croatia, Hungary, Portugal and Romania, it is predominantly women with high-earning potential who are in the labour market. The low availability of part-time work seems to have a double effect: it lowers the chances of

---

[4]   See https://www.oecd.org/els/soc/LMF_1_6_Gender_differences_in_employment_out-comes.pdf.

low-income women's employment and it acts to lower female employment rates overall (in cases where the national rate is below the EU average) (see also Pettit and Hook, 2009). The obverse cases are those countries with a more widespread culture of flexible working arrangements in terms of part-time employment, such as Denmark, the Netherlands and the UK, where female employment rates above the EU average are largely driven by the wide prevalence and use of part-time work opportunities and where social class effects in female employment are less entrenched. On the basis of their comparative study of 19 countries between 1994 and 2012,[5] Stier et al. (2018) report that mothers are more likely to have a moderate rather than a strong labour market attachment when part-time work is available. This leads these authors to the opinion that part-time work can be viewed as a way to discourage a stronger attachment to the labour force on the part of women. This is a key element of the European gender settlement, one of the trade-offs highlighted by Pettit and Hook (2009).

Caring responsibilities are an important consideration here. The EU has calculated that such responsibilities mean that up to 10 per cent of all women of working age, compared to 0.5 per cent of equivalent men, either do not work in gainful employment at all or do so on a part-time basis (European Institute for Gender Equality, 2017a, pp. 40–41). This seems a conservative estimate. It is, though, clear evidence of women not having the same opportunities as men, although it may be that there are elements of choice involved here.

4.1.3 Pay-related Inequalities and Employment Conditions

A further very important element of gender inequality is labour market segregation. Table 4.1 presents a composite measure of both occupational and sectoral segregation in the EU as a whole, showing the gap in the former to be wider than that in the latter (24.1 per cent, compared with 19.0 per cent). The table also shows that there was no significant improvement in either type of segregation between 2010 and 2017. To take an example, over the past ten years men's share of employment in the education, health and social work sector has remained at around 8 per cent while that of women – which is in the range of 30 per cent – increased (European Institute for Gender Equality, 2017a, p. 19). The gender gaps in the STEM fields (science, technology, engineering and mathematics) remain unchanged. For example, of vocational graduates only some 10 per cent of women compared to 41 per cent of men work in STEM occupations;

---

[5]   See note 3.

at tertiary level, the figures are one-third of female STEM graduates working in STEM occupations, compared to one in two men (European Commission, 2018, p. 21).

All of these factors contribute to a further form of inequality – gender gaps in pay (defined by Eurostat as the difference between average gross hourly earnings of male and female paid employees, expressed as a percentage of the former).[6] These are robust also with women on average earning 16.1 per cent less per hour than men across the EU in 2016 (European Commission, 2018, p. 17). Considered over time, the gap is hardly moving (0.2 per cent in six years). In fact, there has hardly been any improvement since the early 1990s (Bettio, 2017). The EU has estimated that at the current rate of change it would take another century to close the overall gender earnings gap (European Commission, 2017b, p. 25).

The global figures mask some differential movement among countries, however, although in none is the gender pay gap changing rapidly and in some pay rates are moving in a direction that disfavours women, especially Malta, Portugal and Slovenia. The countries seeing the greatest improvement over the last decade are Lithuania, Luxembourg, Poland and Romania (European Commission, 2017b, p. 56). In general, the grouping of the Central Eastern European countries (with the exception of the Czech Republic and Slovakia) is the regional grouping with the lowest gender wage inequalities. But these are also countries with low levels of pay in general. So this suggests another clear trade-off.

Familial context makes a great difference to the gender gap in pay inequalities. This can be appreciated from the following overview facts (European Institute for Gender Equality, 2019). In the EU as a whole, a single man earns 14 per cent more per month than a single woman. This is the gender gap at its smallest. The gap increases to 30 per cent among people in a couple without dependent children, to 38 per cent for those in a couple with children and to 40 per cent for lone parents. It is also the case that family formation means higher monthly earnings for men and the opposite for women (European Institute for Gender Equality, 2019). The former is true even when men raise children as a lone father (and in fact lone fathers' earnings are the highest among any group). If we keep the comparison among women, single women are the highest earners of all women. Women living in a couple with no children earn on average 91 per cent of the earnings of single women. The proportion falls to 82 per cent for women with children and 85 per cent for lone mothers (European Institute for Gender Equality, 2019).

---

[6]   See https://ec.europa.eu/eurostat/statistics-explained/index.php/Gender_pay_gap_statis tics.

Looking across countries three trade-offs for women can be seen: in the labour market or outside of it with a heightened risk of poverty for the latter; in the labour market on a part-time basis with lower career opportunities and poorer pay; in full-time employment in some of the low-wage countries (Baltic and Central Eastern European regions).

Another relevant indicator of inequality in labour markets is flexibility in employment times and conditions. There is a general trend in this regard (Plantenga and Remery, 2013). As with other aspects, when viewed cross-nationally there is both convergence and variation. The countries where flexible working time arrangements are most widespread are Denmark, the Netherlands and Sweden, with at least 50 per cent of men and women having access to flexible working time schedules according to these authors. Finland also scores relatively highly, with almost half of male and more than 40 per cent of female employees working with some kind of flexibility in their working hours. Low flexibility is most widespread in the Southern and Central Eastern European member states. Overall, the most widespread flexible working time arrangement is the possibility to adapt working hours within certain limits, followed by the choice between several fixed time schemes. In most countries, only a small minority of employees can entirely determine their working hours themselves. The highest share is found in Denmark, the Netherlands and Sweden, where about 15 per cent of male employees and 10 per cent of female employees have this option. Other evidence also suggests that in most countries gender differences in access to flexible working conditions are rather small (Eurofound, 2017a).

Job precariousness is another important indicator of employment quality. A recent study (European Institute for Gender Equality, 2017c) shows that out of all employees aged 15–64 years, 27 per cent of women and 15 per cent of men across the EU work in precarious jobs (understood as jobs with very low pay, very short hours and low job security). Of the latter defining characteristics, the largest gender differences are in pay. Amongst employees, almost every fifth woman and every twelfth man receives very low pay.

In-work poverty is also a significant risk. Eurostat figures estimate that 10 per cent of workers are at risk of poverty (Eurofound, 2018a, p. 9) (equivalent to 20 million people – Peña-Casas et al., 2019). In-work poverty increased during the financial crisis – 8 per cent of workers were estimated to be at risk in 2007, 2 percentage points lower than in 2014. In-work poverty is strongly associated with being in part-time work and/ or temporary contracts of employment. This contributes to its gender specific character. Young women aged between 18 and 24 have the highest in-work poverty rate of any age or gender group – some 15 per cent were in poverty in 2014 (European Institute for Gender Equality, 2017b, p. 57). Depressed wages, cuts in working hours and job loss penalty among earners in a household all exacerbated financial hardship. But the dynamics are complex, which makes it difficult to establish the extent to which workers' living standards have changed (European Institute for Gender Equality, 2017b, p. 57).

4.1.4   Overview

The European Institute for Gender Equality Index for employment – measured on the basis of participation rate and segregation – is presented in Table 4.1 above (last row).[7] It confirms a generally stationary picture, with improvement of only 1.5 percentage points between 2005 and 2015. When one looks at patterns within and across countries, they generally reflect the global trend of relative stasis, apart from Cyprus, Luxembourg, Malta, Spain and Sweden, which have managed a significant improvement on the employment participation score (which, recall, measures gender gaps). The evidence for the sub-indicators shows that it is employment participation that is responsible for any improvement (rather than, for example, improving segregation or quality of employment). Hence women are entering labour markets which continue to be segregated structurally with risks for the quality of work and the chances of a good career. It seems that while the economic crisis increased the share of female employees it may well have worsened women's working conditions (Castellano and Rocca, 2017). The Nordic countries score best in terms of overall gender employment equality but so also do the part-time female employment countries of Austria, the Netherlands and the UK. It is notable that the trends for both dimensions are generally in the same direction on this indicator (as distinct from the money indicator considered in Chapter 3). Also notable is the fact that the highest-ranked countries have not generally improved on the level of gender segregation and quality of work, suggesting the existence of a ceiling or 'improvement to limits' (again something we encountered also in Chapter 3).

Intersectional inequalities are widespread. These include socio-economic differences – for example, of people with the lowest education, 36 per cent

---

[7]   The five sub-indicators consist of full-time equivalent employment rate, duration of working life, employed in education, health and social work, ability to take an hour or two off during working time for personal or family matters and career prospects index (the latter is measured in terms of continuity of employment, defined in relation to type of employment contract, job security (the possibility of losing a job in the next six months), career advancement prospects and development of the workplace in terms of the number of employees – downsizing).

of women and 16 per cent of men receive the lowest income (European Institute for Gender Equality, 2017c). Family situation is another major factor, with differences and inequalities manifesting between mothers and non-mothers especially. Thirdly, although we did not consider it (mainly because of data limitations) country of birth is an important factor, especially in regard to experiencing precarious working conditions. Nearly one in three non-EU-born women (35 per cent) and one in four such men (24 per cent) work in precarious jobs (European Institute for Gender Equality, 2017c, 2019).

4.2 UNDERPINNING FACTORS

In the search for explanations for gender inequality in employment, research has identified a range of factors. Among these, four lines of explanation predominate: personal and situational factors, labour market factors, culture/public opinion, and policy. It is possible to take either a micro- or macro-level explanatory focus, although newer work suggests the importance of interaction effects between levels (Thévenon, 2016). As we have seen, inequality is multi-dimensional and intricate. When considering the evidence for the purposes of explanation therefore, it is important to be clear about what is being explained, and in particular to distinguish between work that seeks to explain either gender gaps and disadvantages in employment rate or pay and/or other inequalities in the labour market. In what follows I consider both.

4.2.1 Explaining Women's Employment Behaviour

In regard to women's employment rates, one of the most widely used theoretical approaches is the micro-economic model which conceptualizes women's employment-related behaviour as at least in part a utility maximizing response to the costs and benefits of employment vis-à-vis other activities (Becker, 1981; Steiber and Haas, 2012). In this theorization, opportunity costs of employment loom large with human capital theory especially suggesting varying rationalities regarding participation in paid work on the part of women with different levels of education. Another micro-level theory is social psychological in orientation, underlining how women's dispositions and preferences affect their labour market participation. In this vein, Catherine Hakim (2000) has suggested the significance of mothers' preferences regarding work–family orientations for their labour market participation. Both orientations have fed a strand of scholarship that investigates especially the relationship between women's attitudes towards gender roles and family responsibilities and their employment-related behaviour.

The consensus of research seems to be that these factors have some effect amidst a broader set of causal factors. Uunk (2015), for example, in a study of gender culture more broadly as well as the attitudes of individual women, reports a substantial positive and independent effect of a country's egalitarian gender-role attitudes on individual women's odds of being active in the labour market (his analysis covered 33 countries and was based on European Social Survey data from 2008[8]). When the causal effects are broken down, Uunk attributes one quarter of the effect to that of individual-level attitudes and one tenth to institutional support for women working – the remaining majority effect he attributes to national gender role attitudes. He suggests that the latter may take effect through normative sanctioning of women who are seen to break with the national norms. To think through how this might happen, the work of Boeckmann et al. (2015) is helpful in elaborating conceptions of motherhood as an axis of stratification.[9] Their findings, from some 19 countries (mainly EU but also Australia, Russia and the US), indicate that greater acceptance of mothers' (full-time) employment is associated with smaller motherhood gaps in employment probabilities and working hours. They view this effect as potentially occurring through the easing of work–family conflict for mothers and a weakening of attitudes viewing motherhood and employment as incompatible.

One should not forget the matter of need in all of this – as Sánchez-Mira and O'Reilly (2018, p. 3) say, work–family arrangements must be understood as an expression of both need and opportunity rather than one of abstract choice. Complexity is therefore to be expected. In this regard, there is evidence that women are not bound by their own values and attitudes with recent research reporting considerable dissonance between the attitudes women hold and their labour market engagement (García-Faroldi, 2018). García-Faroldi measures dissonance in terms of gaps between what mothers say they believe to be the best employment arrangement (full-time, part-time or no employment) when their children are pre-school or at school and their actual employment arrangement. She undertakes such analysis for 12 countries (all EU except Japan, Norway and the US), between 1994 and 2012. García-Faroldi shows, first, that no country has achieved absolute coherence between what mothers consider

---

[8]   Mainly EU member states, together with Iceland, Macedonia, Montenegro, Norway, Russia, Switzerland and Ukraine.
[9]   Monique Kremer (2007) is on similar territory with her leading concept of 'ideals of care'. See also the work of Birgit Pfau-Effinger (2004).

desirable and their actual practice, suggesting constraints everywhere. The Nordic countries and especially Sweden are the nations where mothers can most easily pursue their preferences, as is the case also in the US; by contrast, less coherence is found in the ex-socialist countries and the least in the Mediterranean nations. Secondly, comparison indicates that when two countries have similar levels of 'coherence', this does not mean that the combination of work and family will be the same. Hence the importance of national context and of other factors apart from attitudes or culture is indicated. Thirdly, level of education exerts a significant effect – across countries women with lower education compared to those with tertiary education are most likely to feel their choices are coherent when staying at home and are less likely to work full-time (indicating a generic patterning of more traditional attitudes and practices). The availability of part-time employment seems to be extremely important in enabling coherence.

A different approach to investigating causation is employed by Hook and Paek (2018) who undertook an analysis to decompose the change in women's labour force participation in 12 countries between 1988 and 2015.[10] They find that much of the change is attributable to compositional factors (primarily shifts to higher levels of educational attainment). However, behavioural change is also very important and in this the labour market behaviour of partnered mothers with lower levels of education was both the largest behavioural component and showed the greatest variation across countries. These authors, therefore, underline that to understand change in women's labour force participation the patterns of low-educated women need to be a central focus (especially given that labour market participation rates of more highly-educated women appear to have 'topped out'). This finding has resonance with much labour market research underlining how women with lower levels of education are more sensitive to variations in context (England, 2010; Korpi et al., 2013; Steiber et al., 2016).

When more macro-level factors are theorized, the focus, rightly, tends to be on the labour market on the one hand and policy packages (either on their own or together with cultural factors) on the other. In regard to the former, McDowell (2014) points to the rise of what she calls 'poor work', arguing that contrasting patterns of female/male employment over the life course can no longer be taken for granted. The service sector is crucial here and is of increasing significance in employment. According to the European Commission (2017b), the highest rates of job creation are found in information and communication, administrative and support services

---

[10] Austria, Canada, Czech Republic, Denmark, France, Germany, Greece, Italy, Luxembourg, the Netherlands, Norway and the US.

and professional, scientific and technical activities. Between 2005 and 2017 in the EU-27 (that is, minus the UK), there was a 13 per cent growth in employment in the private sector and 11 per cent in the public sector compared with a fall of 8 per cent in the manufacturing sector and 12 per cent in construction (European Commission, 2017b, p. 11). Most of these new jobs were created in small- and medium-sized businesses. McDowell points out how a greater female presence in the labour market has coincided with a general deterioration of jobs and prospects in employment (highlighted by Rubery, 2015, p. 516, among others). One might also add that paid care-related work has contributed hugely here – speaking of the US, for example, Rachel Dwyer (2013) has argued that the growth of such work is an important causal factor in job polarization there. 'Feminization' has therefore a double meaning: more women in the labour market but also more jobs typically associated with women being insecure and precarious. Rubery (2015, p. 517) calls this the 'destandardization of work'. Karamessini and Rubery (2014, p. 28) provide further detail, pointing to contradictions and stress points in the labour market and jobs' structure following the recession and austerity policies. A primary tendency they identify is a hollowing out of the labour market in middle-level jobs in some European countries (Fernandez-Macias et al., 2012). This especially has negative prospects for lower-educated women and men in that it reduces their chances of escaping from low-paid or precarious employment.

We should not forget the impact of workplace norms and other aspects of employment culture. Joan Williams (2010), focusing on the US, sees working conditions that are so unfriendly to family life that many employees are, as she puts it, only one sick child away from being fired. Her insightful analysis reveals a gender bias in a whole range of workplace-related norms and practices in that country – from the naming of jobs to judgements about the type of worker needed to carry out certain jobs (not just in terms of skill but also disposition and orientation). Williams is interested especially in deconstructing 'femininity' and 'masculinity' as they are embedded in workplace culture and investigating how masculine norms not only create gender bias against women (leading to such phenomena as a maternal wall, glass ceiling and gender wars) but place huge pressure on men to perform as 'ideal workers'. One of her strong messages is how workers are constantly forced to take risks – in the case of women this is often for reasons of exigency such as a sick child or a lack of child-care; for men it is rooted in norms around masculinity on the one hand and a wish to continue in the breadwinner role on the other. An important part of the context here is the lack of public service infrastructure and parental entitlements in the US. There is another aspect to organizational culture as well – this is that firms and organizations are the contexts within which statutory and other policies are played out. 'Entitlement' often has to be negotiated or at least worked out contextually and hence firms and other workplace organizations play a crucial role in mediating work–family policies in practice (Stainback et al., 2010; Mun and Jung, 2018). Note that there is a sense of self-tailoring in the whole work–family balance debate (in line with what Catherine Rottenberg, 2018, says of much of the debate of self-proclaimed elite feminism in the US). Much of this is a way of managing or avoiding the contradictions – 'contradiction dodging'.

From a gender perspective, the most obvious explanation is how women and men are placed vis-à-vis family commitments and care. Social policy scholars frame this in terms of how policy seeks to affect these relationships/situations as a core research concern. Here too there is much research. As a backdrop it is generally important to recognize that the amount and type of support provided to working parents with young children varies cross-nationally (Daly and Ferragina, 2018; Ferragina, 2019). Thévenon (2016) differentiates the English-speaking countries (also called the 'liberal welfare states') from other country sets by virtue of how little in-time and in-kind support they provide to working parents with young children (as adjudged by their spending on paid leave, birth grants and childcare services for the under-3s for example). In these countries, women's labour force participation depends heavily on their possibilities to leave and return quickly to the labour market, which means that female labour market status and hours worked are highly stratified by family composition (especially number of children and partner's employment status) (Thévenon, 2016, p. 476). The Nordic countries make up the opposing pole, providing comprehensive support to working parents with young children. In between are the Continental and Southern European states which are organized to ensure the stability of men's employment and to protect family income in the case of unemployment.

In the research on policy impact, the two sets of social policy measures that are highlighted as having greatest effect are paid maternity and parental leave on the one hand and childcare services on the other (Paull and Taylor, 2002; Jaumotte, 2003; Sanchez-Mangas and Sanchez-Marcos, 2008; Del Boca et al., 2009; Pettit and Hook, 2009; Cipollone et al., 2014; Budig et al., 2016). In terms of maternity leave, for example, it is now taken for granted that such leave helps mothers to combine work and family, with some provisos around its length and some dispute in regard to its impact on women's labour market participation (Pettit and Hook, 2009; Nieuwenhuis et al., 2017; Brady et al., 2018). A recent analysis reports that, in countries with short periods of childcare leave, the motherhood employment gap is smaller than in those with no childcare leave, while in countries with long periods of childcare leave the motherhood-employment gap is bigger than in countries with short periods of leave. There is also evidence, however, to indicate that the effect of maternity leave has weakened among mothers, especially in countries that provide long periods of leave (Stier et al., 2018; see also Brady et al., 2018). Again here though, we should note a social class/education effect in that different groups of women appear to react differently to the availability of support for maternal employment. Findings by Stier et al. (2018) show that extending the generosity of maternity leave reduces educational differences regarding the choice of whether to maintain continuous full-time employment when children are young or to combine full- and part-time involvement in paid employment. It also reduces educational disparities in the decision as against staying out of the labour force, by allowing less-educated women to work on a full- or part-time basis, thereby serving to equalize the opportunity costs for women with different levels of human capital. It is also well known that childcare services play a key role in enabling women to be employed and also to work for longer hours. Indeed, there is evidence to suggest that, of the different policy measures, it is policies that foster greater enrolment in childcare (as against parental leave, for example) that have the more robust effect on women's labour market participation (Thévenon, 2016). Moreover, access to formal rather than informal childcare is more strongly associated with maternal employment (de Wachter et al., 2016). Here again educational background makes a difference in that across the EU it tends to be the highly-educated mothers who are more likely to make use of childcare (de Wachter et al., 2016). However, key aspects of the background and interactive effects also remain unknown.

4.2.2 Explaining Pay Inequalities

When it comes to explaining pay gaps, as with the work researching variations in women's labour market participation, the most penetrating research assesses both personal characteristics and those relating to the job and the structure and context of employment such as horizontal and vertical segregation, hours of work and discrimination. The EU's (European Commission, 2018, p. 21) analyses suggest that almost a third of the wage gap is explained by industrial or sectoral affiliation. This is a familiar story: essentially women are over-represented in industries with low pay levels, and under-represented in well-paid industries. There is some indication that this might have increased during and after the recession of 2008 (Périvier, 2014; Castellano and Rocca, 2017). Many jobs are still commonly considered as 'women's jobs' or 'men's jobs'. In the 2016 European Working Conditions Survey, 58 per cent of men and 54 per cent of women stated that their 'co-workers with the same job title' are mostly of the same sex. Only 19 per cent of men and 22 per cent of women stated that there were an equal number of men and women working in a similar position at their place of work (Eurofound, 2017b, p. 27). This suggests an interaction between structural and cultural factors.

There is, however, also evidence suggesting that a large part of the pay gap – about two-thirds of the 16 per cent gap (or around 10 per cent of wage difference) – cannot be resolved by any of the main explanatory factors (European Commission, 2018, p. 18). Moreover, looking at individual countries, this 'unexplained' part is never lower than 5 per cent (except for Belgium) (European Commission, 2018, p. 18). To put this more specifically, the wage gap cannot be attributed to differences in average characteristics of working men and women such as age, education, occupation, industry affiliation, part-time or temporary employment, job tenure, firm size, or employment in private versus public sector. It has been said (European Commission, 2018, p. 19) that women taking career breaks following childbirth may be a strong contributory factor to wage inequality. The 'unexplained' gender pay gap is also likely to include discrimination in hiring, career progression and opportunities. Claudia Goldin (2014) adds further insight here with her point about flexibility not as a characteristic of supply but of demand, and how jobs are structured and remunerated to reward and enhance temporal flexibility. Her underlying point is that hours of work in many occupations are worth more when given at particular times and when the hours are more continuous, and when employees demonstrate a willingness to work long hours at a stretch. "The gender gap in pay would be considerably reduced and might vanish altogether if firms did not have an incentive to disproportionately reward individuals who labored long hours and worked particular hours" (Goldin, 2014, p. 1091). This is her main recommendation for improving the situation.

Tying into a broader welfare state analysis, research by Mandel and Semyonov (2005) has suggested that, if and when one adjusts for the wage structure, welfare state interventions and especially long periods of paid maternity leave increase the wage gap between women and men. This has been subject to considerable criticism, however, on several grounds (see Brady et al., 2018). Korpi et al. (2013) confirm the positive effect of generous employment-oriented family policies for mothers with low educational attainment and report a finding of no major negative effect for women with tertiary education. Recent research (Halldén et al., 2016) confirms this line of thinking, suggesting that both the length of maternity leave and the proportion of small children in publicly-funded childcare are associated with a reduction in the motherhood wage penalty regardless of skill (or education) level across countries. That said, in cross-national research these associations seem to be driven by the Nordic countries and there is a need for research on other policy models.

In a more composite analysis, the EU statistics agency Eurostat has attempted to generalize the gaps to the total population (whether employed or not) and then isolate the contribution of different elements of employment to assess and explain the overall earnings gaps on the basis of data for 2014. They use three main types of employment-related inequality: employment rate, level or depth of engagement, and remuneration levels. A very complex picture is revealed (European Commission, 2017a). First, the overall gap – at 40 per cent – is much higher than that found for comparisons of workers. This was down from 41.1 per cent in 2010 and 44.2 per cent in 2006. Even in the most equal countries (Lithuania, Slovenia, Bulgaria, Latvia and Finland), the overall gender gap in earnings stood at 20 per cent or so, while it reached 45 per cent or more in Germany, Greece, Malta, the Netherlands, Austria and the UK. The variation is immense. This, together with the varied impact of each of the three elements, confirms a complex picture. In terms of constituent elements, the gaps in pay contribute somewhat more than the other two elements. It is almost impossible to draw any general conclusions beyond this. For example, if we take the two highest gap countries – the Netherlands and Malta – they are almost polar opposites in terms of the causal factors; in the former the main contributor by far is gender variation in the number of hours worked whereas in the latter it is variations between male and female employment rates. Equally, the contributory factors are different for the two countries with least inequality – Lithuania and Slovenia. A key question is whether the welfare state types or models hold up – in this regard the Nordic countries look similar in level although they vary somewhat in regard to the contributory factors. The Continental European countries tend to divide between France, Belgium and Luxembourg (which have lower overall levels of inequality) and Germany, Austria and the Netherlands (which are all at the upper end). There is little patterning either among the Mediterranean or the Central Eastern European nations.

In all of this it seems hard to avoid the conclusion drawn by Pettit and Hook (2009, p. 22) that gender inequality is institutionalized through households and within the labour market. They see two general types of institutional effects: those that foster women's labour market inclusion/exclusion and those that influence inequality among workers. These lead to tensions and trade-offs between inclusion/exclusion and equality/inequality. This suggests that it is the interconnections (especially between the domestic division of labour and the allocation of workplace access and rewards) that have to be configured into an explanation.

4.3 CONCLUSION

This chapter has sought to uncover the details of women's engagement with the labour market and underlying patterns of inequality in that regard. The balance sheet is mixed. Women's employment rate – which is heavily promoted and idealized by EU and national social policy – is rising across the EU, albeit with some downward movement or stalling impact occasioned by the 2008 recession which has made both for greater intra-EU variations and also in some cases diminishing gender inequalities as men's labour market position was affected by the recession even more negatively than that of women. So in reply to the status quo question, the trend is one of 'improvement'. But the real question is not how many women work but under what conditions. The evidence here suggests that any progress is limited and that high levels of female labour market participation tend to be associated with the availability of part-time work which is known to be less rewarding and less likely to play host to coherent and progressive career trajectories. This pattern is especially characteristic of mothers. For this and other reasons, gender gaps in pay are significant and progress seems to have stalled, leading to, inter alia, a heightened risk of in-work poverty (especially for young and lower-educated women). Segregation across occupations and sectors is entrenched and hardly changing and this means that there are differential effects for women from different socio-economic backgrounds. Mothers with low levels of education are considerably less likely in most countries to be in employment than their better-educated counterparts and when they are in work they tend to experience jobs with low pay and other poor working conditions.

Two questions emerge as hugely important: Which factors make the differences and how can policy affect the behaviour of lower-educated women? We do not have a definitive answer to either of these questions but there are some insights available. When thinking causally, it is important to underscore that it is the labour-market engagement of mothers that makes the most difference and that this varies by socio-economic background. That said, in fact, across the EU, the majority of countries still had as their dominant pattern moderate maternal attachment to the labour market in 2012. The situation is therefore one of growth to limits. The Central Eastern European and Baltic countries stand out as an exception for the degree to which mothers there have strong labour market attachment and women as a whole have high full-time participation rates. This is characteristic also of Portugal. The Central Eastern European countries are an interesting example of women's participation in the labour market not being associated with divided labour markets in terms of pay and segregation or female participation patterns divided by class (as Pettit and Hook,

2009, suggest is more generally the case). This is one model. A second – very prominent one – is of part-time work as the segue into (remaining in) employment. This pattern conjoins some of the Continental European countries (Austria, Germany and the Netherlands) with Denmark, Ireland and the UK. Thirdly, there is a pattern of in or out for women – to be seen in Italy, Malta and Cyprus for example. In this pattern, highly-educated women are in the labour market whereas women from other education backgrounds tend to be home-based. As Pettit and Hook (2009) point out, education bifurcates female employment patterns in many countries.

In regard to the matter of causality, the structure of the labour market and prevailing supply of employment are especially important. In particular, the growth of the service sector with its tendency towards poor and changeable work conditions and low pay plays a strong causal role. Associated with this have been processes of privatization and a decrease of the size of and investment in the public sector which, for all its problems, has been historically progressive for women on a global basis (Watkins, 2018, pp. 54–5). Cultural factors continue to be hugely important. That said, there is evidence that many women/mothers live with significant levels of dissonance between their beliefs about the appropriate role of mothers and the conduct of family life and their own (labour-market) behaviour when they are employed. Hence, women's (and men's) employment engagement emerges as being an expression of both need and opportunity rather than one of 'abstract choice' around employment and care (Sánchez-Mira and O'Reilly, 2018, p. 3).

5. Inequalities of time use and life satisfaction

As a follow-on from Chapters 3 and 4, we might note two points: first, that employment of women or men is an imperfect predictor of women's access to resources; second, that female employment is heavily conditioned by family situation (among other factors). This chapter, in reflecting further on the roots and consequences of these practices, turns to the third resource – time – and reviews how paid and unpaid work are distributed and organized, both collectively and individually. The chapter also considers some of the concomitants and consequences associated with the distribution of time, especially in regard to the attitudes that people hold about the appropriate gender distribution of family-related tasks and responsibilities, and also systematic variations in life satisfaction by gender and other factors. The chapter is guided by two main research questions: What is the nature of the gender divide in paid and unpaid time and how has this changed? How are these patterns related to attitudes and culture? As with the two preceding chapters, the focus is on explicating the status quo and identifying patterns over time. The factors and dimensions considered move us away from a one-dimensional interpretation of familialization/defamilialization as the outcome of a dynamic between the state and the market which has been criticized for insufficient attention to the division of labour within the family setting (Ciccia and Bleijenberg, 2014, p. 54). I also give more attention to cultural factors than is customary in the field.

From a feminist perspective the material covered in this chapter helps to reveal the sphere of social reproduction, that is, the social provisioning that underpins individual and societal functioning and also the power-related elements associated with arrangements (Kofman, 2012; Davis and Greenstein, 2013; Verschuur, 2013). In this, unpaid work is extremely important. As well as material aspects, it speaks, inter alia, to gender role specialization and it can also reveal aspects of identity. Housework, for example, has been analysed as a form of gender display through which women affirm their identity (Geist and Ruppanner, 2018) and men's reaction to childcare has also been highlighted as a symbolic expression of their masculinity (Brandth and Kvande, 1998). But more than this, scholars of social reproduction make the important point that it is part of a different type of economy (the domestic economy), operating to an unpaid logic and particular set of social and power relations (Verschuur, 2013).

This chapter also takes up the question of what has replaced the male breadwinner model or indeed whether it is appropriate to even speak of a male breadwinner successor. I start in this chapter therefore with the structure of households with children and the prevalence of different types of household/family arrangement regarding paid employment. The chapter then moves on to consider the distribution of paid and unpaid labour and time. Later sections of the chapter review the prevailing attitudinal consensus around the appropriate division of responsibility between women and men regarding family tasks and how contemporary configurations are associated with life satisfaction.

5.1   WORK–FAMILY FORMS AND ARRANGEMENTS

As mentioned in earlier chapters, the family or household form has been a pivotal consideration in analyses of the relationship between gender and social policy. Whether conceived in terms of models (male breadwinner versus adult worker) or processes (familialization versus individualization or defamilialization), the organizational form of family life is taken as a vital clue to and determinant of the gender distribution of resources and the state of gender (unequal) relations more broadly. There is a large literature on the connection between household labour and gender inequality (e.g. Fuwa, 2004; Hook, 2010) as well as on the sociology and political economy of housework (e.g. Treas and Drobnič, 2010). Much has been written also on household and family as a site of constructing gender – Sara Berk (1985) likened the household to a gender factory, for example. But from a social policy perspective, a smaller field has been carved out, with the matter of unpaid work conceived and investigated in two main ways: in terms of the prevailing economic arrangement of household or family, and unequal patterning in the execution of unpaid (care) and paid work.

What kind of arrangements prevail? Information about households in terms of demographic composition – size and relationship among adults – is regularly collected by statistical offices at national and international level in Europe. This data tells us, for example, that the most common type of household in the EU in 2017 was one composed of a single person, accounting for one-third of the total number of households.[1] This living

---

[1]   Eurostat Household Composition Statistics at http://ec.europa.eu/eurostat/statistics-explained/index.php/Household_composition_statistics#Household_size.

arrangement is also the fastest growing type, spearheading a trend towards smaller households. Almost two-thirds of all households in the EU-28 countries were composed of one or two persons in 2017 and the number of larger households continues to decline. It is relevant here to note that women are more likely to live in single-person households than men (associated with the demography and sociology of ageing). The statistics also tell us that just around 30 per cent of EU households had child members and that 15 per cent of all households in the EU in 2017 were headed by a lone parent. While usefully indicating that significant structural change is underway, this type of information gives us only vague clues about how people and families organize their lives and their resources.

Table 5.1 presents information from the OECD for 2014 on couple households with a child or children aged under 14 years, using the OECD's five-fold classification of the employment-related status of the two partners. This population sector – couples with children – is the key sector to tell us about breadwinning arrangements. We should note that the upper age cut-off for children is 14 years.

If we look at the EU average first, it is clear that the dual, full-time earner household (hereafter: dual breadwinner households) is the single most common type of arrangement prevailing. Almost a half of couples with children aged under 14 years organize themselves thus, compared to 28 per cent with a single-breadwinner pattern (the second most widespread arrangement). To complete the picture, around 14 per cent of the families operate a one-and-a-half earner arrangement, and in 6 per cent of cases neither of the partners works, with a further 5 per cent described as 'working other'. These figures suggest a polarization between the two main types.

There is, as we might expect, great cross-national variation. The Nordic countries of Denmark and Sweden together with Slovenia (which is frequently a regional outsider) are most likely to have dual breadwinner arrangements and the counterpole comprises the Netherlands (an outlier on the opposing end) together with Germany, Austria, Ireland, Italy and the UK which have the lowest prevalence of dual breadwinning households. It is not the case, though, that the latter countries utilize a single breadwinner model – in fact it is the Mediterranean nations of Greece, Italy, Malta and Spain, together with some of the Central Eastern European countries (Czech Republic, Hungary, Poland and Slovakia), where the single breadwinner arrangement prevails most widely among couples with children. In the Continental European countries of Austria, Belgium and the Netherlands as well as the UK, the one-and-a-half earner model is most widespread. The Netherlands is an outlier here with over half of all couples with children having a one-and-a-half earner arrangement. So, in

Table 5.1 *Distribution of household employment patterns in couples with at least one child aged 0–14 years in the EU-28 countries in 2014*

	Dual earner	One-and-a-half earner	Sole breadwinner	Both partners not working	Other
Austria	31	40	21	4	4
Belgium	47	22	20	6	5
Bulgaria	54	1	25	11	9
Croatia	57	3	31	8	1
Cyprus	52	10	27	7	4
Czech Republic	54	6	36	3	1
Denmark	68	11	16	3	2
Estonia	50	8	37	3	2
Finland	56	7	26	4	7
France	50	15	24	6	5
Germany	25	40	27	4	4
Greece	36	8	42	10	5
Hungary	44	4	36	7	9
Ireland	32	22	28	9	9
Italy	30	18	37	9	6
Latvia	55	7	32	4	2
Lithuania	59	9	23	5	4
Luxembourg	41	22	27	3	7
Malta	40	18	37	3	2
The Netherlands	21	51	20	3	5
Poland	55	7	33	4	1
Portugal	59	5	24	4	8
Romania	56	4	29	8	3
Slovakia	47	3	39	6	5
Slovenia	67	8	21	3	1
Spain	34	12	34	10	9
Sweden	68	10	14	4	4
UK	31	32	24	5	8
EU Average	47	14	28	6	5

Source: OECD Family Database (Chart LMF2.2.A).

Note: Figures rounded to nearest decimal point. Data for Denmark, Finland and Sweden refer to 2012, and for Germany the reference year is 2013.

addition to polarization, the second descriptor suggested by the data is of diversity.

There is cross-national patterning by intersectionality as well, confirmed by existing research although data availability restricts consideration to social class factors. Jennifer Hook's work (2015) helps to analyse this set of relationships, providing a detailed picture of work–family arrangements cross-nationally in 16 countries (all in the EU except Japan, Switzerland and the US) in the mid-2000s. She finds three groupings of countries. The first comprises the Nordic states where not only are most women employed but they tend to work on a full-time basis (making for a strong prevalence of the dual earner model overall, as we have seen above). This model holds among families across the social class spectrum in these countries. In Hook's second grouping of countries the one-and-a-half earner model predominates – the Continental European countries are firmly in this category and here, too, the model is prevalent across classes. The third country set she labels as 'polarized' – France, Greece, Italy, Spain and the US – in that it contains both countries where the male breadwinner model is the predominant form (the Mediterranean countries) and those where dual earning families (with a considerable number of the women working part-time) predominate (the US and France). When the patterns in these countries are examined by social class (operationalized in terms of the mother's education level), this latter grouping of countries emerges as strongly differentiated by social class. That is, in France and the Mediterranean nations as well as the US, highly-educated women tend to be in dual-earner families whereas the sole-earner form is the norm for low-income families. This, as Hook says, consolidates and reinforces social class divisions. The OECD data also allow us to identify trends over time (see Table 5.2).

Three trends are noteworthy. First, there is a move away from the sole breadwinner household, with only two countries – Slovakia and Slovenia – bucking that trend by recording an increase over the nine-year period. The countries which see the biggest trend away from sole breadwinning are those in the Continental European heartland, that is, Austria, Germany and Luxembourg, together with Spain and Ireland (both of which were strongly affected by the recession). Secondly, there is a move towards dual earner arrangements, with 14 out of the 23 countries for which information is available showing a trend in this direction. The strongest increases of this arrangement have taken place in Belgium, Bulgaria, Luxembourg, the Netherlands and Poland. Where there has been a move away from dual earning, it has occurred most robustly in Cyprus, Greece and Slovenia. Thirdly, there has been no clear trend regarding the one-and-a-half earner model, except for Austria where the scale of the increase in such a household arrangement is equivalent to the decline of sole breadwinner ones.

Gender inequality and welfare states in Europe

Table 5.2   *Percentage point change in the distribution of household employment patterns in couples with at least one child aged 0–14 years in the EU-28 countries between 2004 and 2014*

	Dual earner	One-and-a-half earner	Sole breadwinner	Both partners not working	Other
Austria	−1.1	+7.3	−7.7	+0.3	+1.1
Belgium	+9.6	−1.3	−2.8	+1.0	−6.4
Bulgaria	+8.9	−0.1	−5.4	−1.8	−1.5
Croatia	–	–	–	–	–
Cyprus	−4.9	+1.0	−5.2	+5.7	+3.4
Czech Republic	+1.7	+2.5	−2.5	−1.4	−0.3
Denmark	–	–	–	–	–
Estonia	+2.1	−0.1	−0.7	−2.9	+1.6
Finland	–	–	–	–	–
France	+4.8	−2.1	−4.9	+1.0	+1.2
Germany	+6.9	+1.8	−6.3	−2.1	−0.2
Greece	−9.2	+1.2	−2.0	+6.8	+3.3
Hungary	−1.1	+1.0	−5.3	−2.6	+7.9
Ireland	+3.3	−4.4	−6.3	+3.4	+4.0
Italy	−0.3	+0.1	−4.2	+3.9	+0.5
Latvia	+2.0	−0.9	−1.0	+0.5	−0.7
Lithuania	+4.1	−1.8	−3.2	+1.5	−0.5
Luxembourg	+12.8	−4.3	−14.8	+1.1	+5.2
Malta	–	–	–	–	–
The Netherlands	+9.3	−4.8	−4.5	−0.3	+0.2
Poland	+10.0	−3.0	−3.6	−2.3	−1.1
Portugal	−5.3	−1.3	−1.7	+2.1	+6.0
Romania	+1.6	−0.6	−1.0	−1.0	+0.8
Slovakia	−3.8	+1.1	+3.2	−3.1	+2.7
Slovenia	−10.7	+4.0	+5.4	+0.8	+0.6
Spain	−3.8	+2.3	−11.9	+5.3	+8.1
Sweden	–	–	–	–	–
UK	+5.3	−5.8	−0.8	−0.8	+2.2

Source: OECD Family Database (Chart LMF2.2.B).

There are some countries where hardly any change has taken place over the nine-year period – Czech Republic, the Baltic states, Romania and Slovakia. The Continental European countries (apart from France and Belgium) as well as the countries which experienced significant recession – Greece, Ireland and Spain – are those which saw most change, suggesting adaptation among households. There is also a notable increase in both partners not working in the latter countries, as well as in Cyprus. Notably there is no data available for any of the three Nordic member states (or Malta).

There is some work available which helps us understand the effects of the economic crisis more closely and to reflect on its gender dimensions. Looking at a narrower sample of countries but in an analysis focused on change, Dotti Sani (2018), in a study of patterns in six European countries between 2005 and 2012,[2] confirms that the recent recession has occasioned significant change in household arrangements, especially in the countries most affected. In the two countries in her sample where the recession had the deepest impact – Greece and Spain – she finds that dual earner households have decreased over the years and those with no earner increased. The reduction of dual earning households occurred across the socio-economic spectrum. These patterns are mirrored by increases in female main-earner households in Greece and Spain at all levels of education but mostly among the highly-educated. Similar patterns are found by recent work on Great Britain which examined the working lives of British couple families across the first decade of the millennium using EU Labour Force Survey data (2001–13) (Connolly et al., 2016). The authors interpret the evidence as indicating both convergence and greater diversity in economic provisioning within parent-couple households. Household employment patterns, they say, continue to be strongly associated with maternal education and family size although they are becoming less sensitive to the age of the youngest child. They draw the conclusion that the dual, full-time earner model is growing in significance for British parents of young children but that a new gender egalitarian equilibrium has not yet been reached.

Another lens on change – and a very important issue from the present perspective – relates to female breadwinner households. There are different conceptions of this as a phenomenon, as well as varying estimations of its extent. Vitali and Arpino (2016) help us by virtue of their study of the factors associated with the likely prevalence of female breadwinner, male breadwinner or equal-income couples based on data from individuals reporting their household model. The evidence base consists of data from the European Social Survey of 2010–11 and Eurostat for 12,822 respondents spread across 26 countries (mainly EU and mainly analysed on a regional basis).[3] Their results suggest a prevalence of around a tenth

---

[2]   France, Germany, Greece, Spain, Sweden and the UK.
[3]   Their sample consisted of individuals who are currently co-residing with a heterosexual spouse or partner (with or without children), with both partners aged between 25 and 54 years (prime earning age), and with none of the partners being disabled, in education, military service, retired, or 'other'.

of female breadwinner household types. However, it should be noted that the categorization is based on responses to a question asking 'Around how large a proportion of the family income do you provide yourself?' when the female (or male) respondent answered 'over a half', 'very large' or 'all' (or 'none', 'very small' or 'under a half'). Cross-national variation is quite widespread. While their results confirm high prevalence of the male breadwinner family arrangement in the Mediterranean countries and some of the Central Eastern European nations (Czech Republic, Hungary, Poland and Slovakia), the female breadwinner arrangement is more likely in countries and regions in Spain, Ireland, other regions of Central Eastern Europe and Greece, and the UK. On average, male respondents were less likely than female respondents to report being in an equal income or female breadwinner couple (as opposed to a male breadwinner couple). Of the two contextual factors that they examined, male unemployment rates were more closely associated with the prevalence of female breadwinner couples than attitudes to gender equality. This suggests that the female breadwinner form may not necessarily be associated with high-income sectors of the population and that it may be a functional arrangement rather than one driven by values and ideology. However, gender egalitarian attitudes do matter – increasing the probability of being in an equal income or female breadwinner couple. The likelihood of the female breadwinner model also increases with age and decreases with the number of children. Again an intersectional effect is confirmed in that both equal-income and female breadwinner couple types are more likely to exist when the woman is older and when she is equally or better educated than her partner. The prevalence of male breadwinner families is associated with both a low male unemployment rate and low gender egalitarian attitudes. Taken as a whole their analyses suggest a complex patterning within and across countries in regard to couple or household economies and how gender factors affect these.

We now move on to consider patterns within the household or family by examining the distribution of time devoted to paid and unpaid work by women and men.

5.2 THE VOLUME AND DISTRIBUTION OF PAID AND UNPAID WORK

Information about paid and unpaid work is mainly collected at an individual level and typically consists of individual estimates of the time expended on paid and unpaid activities in an average period.[4] This provides an indication of the total labour expended in a household or family setting and about the relative distribution of such labour between women and men.

We should note in advance that existing research indicates that there are no countries where men are known to do more domestic work than women and historical estimations suggest that women do around two-thirds of all the domestic work in the world (Knudsen and Wærness, 2008). We should also note the significance of unpaid caring-oriented work. At a European level, an evaluation of the size and value of unpaid family household activities has shown that their total value ranges between 27.7 per cent and 36.8 per cent of the EU GDP, depending on the methodology applied (Giannelli et al., 2012; Francavilla et al., 2013).[5] Globally, it has been estimated that unpaid work undertaken by women amounts to as much as US$10 trillion of output per year, equivalent to 13 per cent of global GDP (McKinsey Global Institute, 2015).

In terms of the gender distribution of time expenditure, recent EU evidence indicates that across the EU men estimate that they spend 39 hours on paid work in an average week, whereas the comparable outlay estimated by women is 33 hours (European Commission, 2017b). An important part of the background here is that the overall number of hours in paid work is not changing – between 2005 and 2015 average usual weekly working hours declined by only 0.8 hours for men and 0.1 for women (Eurofound, 2017a, p. 3). The increase in part-time work – identified by said report as the most consistent trend in European labour markets in recent decades – plays a significant causal role in keeping the hours worked to existing thresholds (which are already high by EU standards).

The gender pattern is reversed when it comes to unpaid work: employed women report spending 22 hours per week on unpaid work of caring and maintaining the household or family, while working men spend fewer than 10 (European Commission, 2017b, p. 12). The men who say they provide care are more likely to be in full-time employment than the women. When the time spent on unpaid work is added to the hours spent on paid work, women expend 55 hours weekly compared to men's 49 hours. It should be noted that gaps in the dimension of time (effectively gaps between

---

4   Note that there is no EU-wide survey of time use. The closest is the Harmonised European Time Use Surveys (HETUS), an initiative spearheaded and overseen by Eurostat in the 1990s. This covers only 15 member states, however. Two waves have already been completed (2000 and 2010). The 15 countries are: Belgium, Bulgaria, Estonia, Finland, France, Germany, Italy, Latvia, Lithuania, Norway, Poland, Slovenia, Spain, Sweden and the UK. The OECD has some overview data for its member countries at https://stats.oecd.org/Index. aspx?datasetcode=TIME_USE.

5   Considerable endeavour has concentrated on counting unpaid care and lodging it into national accounts (Budlender, 2010). See also Waring, 1988.

women and men in the proportion of time invested in leisure and unpaid family-related work) reversed between 2005 and 2015, a drop in the score of 3.2 percentage points (European Institute for Gender Equality, 2017a). This means that, compared to ten years ago, the way in which women and men organize their time has become more unequal. Regression or stasis happened across a range of countries, with disimprovements in the following especially notable: Belgium, Bulgaria, Finland, Hungary, Luxembourg and Slovakia.

When the life course dimensions of hours of paid work are examined, we observe a close correspondence between the gender gap and age (which can be taken as a proxy for stage in the family life cycle). Women's hours in paid work decline in the parenting phase and those of men increase slightly. Only the Nordic and some of the Central Eastern European countries avoid a strong effect of gender during this life phase. Across countries a gender gap opens up again in later years – from age 50 upwards. In this life phase, the gender gap is associated with women's greater involvement in care of disabled or ill family members or friends.

On average, then, women put in about double the amount of time in unpaid work that men do.

There are marked country and regional differences, though. This is true in regard to both the overall volume of unpaid care and its gender distribution. In regard to the former, it is people in the Continental European countries of Belgium and France (although not Austria, Germany or the Netherlands) who most report being a carer for people with a disability or infirmity and it is in the Nordic and aforementioned Continental countries where the least prevalence of such caring is reported. In terms of the gender distribution across countries, the division of housework and care between women and men is more equal in the Nordic countries, although there is still a gap of about a third or more between women's and men's reported unpaid time inputs in these countries on average. This pales in comparison to countries like Cyprus, Greece and Romania, however, where men do only about a fifth of the unpaid work of women. The countries with the smallest gender gap in unpaid work are those with the highest female employment rates (OECD, 2012), suggesting a virtuous egalitarian cycle.

Familiar, time-worn patterns mean that gender inequality resides not just in the time investment but also in the distribution of tasks and activities. What the research, within and across countries, shows is that women tend to perform more of the routine, labour-intensive and rigidly-scheduled tasks, in rapid alternation or even simultaneously (European Commission, 2017b, p. 12). When the unpaid work input is broken down by type of care/identity of recipient, it is the care of children which consumes the lion's share of men's unpaid work (indicating a preference on their part perhaps). Yet their contribution here remains significantly lower than that of women. Men in the EU estimate their childcare involvement, on average, at 21 hours a week compared with an estimation of 39 hours by women (Eurofound, 2017c, p. 43). A similar pattern of greater frequency/volume/spread of engagement by women is found for care for disabled or infirm relatives/friends: twice as many women as men say they provide this care every day (Eurofound, 2017c, p. 43). A gender preference/bias is also found for domestic tasks; only 34 per cent of men report engaging in cooking and housework on a daily basis for at least an hour in comparison to 79 per cent of women (European Institute for Gender Equality, 2017a, p. 41). The widest gender gap in relation to domestic work is found among couples with children. This is notably the case when women become mothers, but is also present in the care of elderly or disabled relatives. In the latter case, women tend to be more involved when and if care becomes more intensive and regular: among 18–64-year-olds, 20 per cent of women and 18 per cent of men were informal caregivers, of which 7 per cent of women provided care on a daily basis compared to 4 per cent of men. Moreover, women spend more time on multiple and overlapping activities, such as care for children, elderly and ill people, cooking and cleaning, and they are more likely than men to combine paid and unpaid work (often simultaneously).

There is also evidence of variation by social class, with two elements (at least) to consider here. First, the analyses by Francavilla et al. (2013) report that gender gaps in market and domestic work tend to decrease in all countries as education increases. Second, and at variance with time investment in other unpaid activities, there is considerable evidence suggesting that gender gaps in childcare increase by education level (to the detriment of lower-income sectors of the population). This is found across the EU – except France where it does not vary, Italy and Poland where it decreases by a few hours, and Estonia where it shows a drastic decrease – and also other high-income countries (Gauthier et al., 2004; Bianchi, 2011; Francavilla et al., 2013). Somewhat against expectation given the higher opportunity costs of child-related time for higher-income parents (especially in dual-earner families), these figures indicate a positive relationship between time spent in childcare and level of education; it confirms other work that speaks of greater time investment in their children by upper-class or highly-educated parents. The phenomenon is known as 'intensive parenting' (Hays, 1996; Lareau, 2003) and dovetails with increasing public attention on parental behaviour and ideologies promoting good parenting as a set of behaviours and orientations (Ramaekers and Suissa, 2012) and childhood as a phase of life to be cultivated. Culture-related (drawing from more sociological rather than economic insights) explanations are invoked here, with social class-based ideals of good parenting – and specifically a perspective among high-income, high-achieving parents of child-development activities as a form of investment – especially highlighted (Sayer et al., 2004). The research by Dotti Sani and Treas (2016) suggests that greater time investment in their children characterizes both highly-educated fathers and mothers. One prominent explanation invokes changing images and ideals of fatherhood – some speak of 'good fatherhood' (Henwood and Procter, 2003) or 'new fatherhood' (Hook and Wolfe, 2012).

What about fathers specifically? Altintas and Sullivan (2017) use Multinational Time Use Study data to study patterns of fathers' time investments in housework and childcare in 15 countries (all EU countries except Australia, Canada, Israel and the US) between 1971 and 2010.[6] They are especially interested in patterning by welfare state regime type. They confirm that Nordic fathers continue to set the bar in terms of the degree of their participation in childcare but that this has been relatively static for at least a decade now, whereas fathers in other regime types – especially the liberal and Southern welfare states – have been increasing theirs. The results are quite different for housework though – fathers' involvement in that is significantly less than in childcare and has even dropped over the period in the liberal countries examined, although the time investment of fathers in the Southern countries increased during the 2000s. Level of education is a major factor here again, and is closely associated especially with greater father involvement in childcare but also engagement in housework. Sullivan et al. (2014) in a study of 13 countries report increased involvement of younger, more highly-educated fathers both in childcare and also domestic work.[7] We know that inequalities are somewhat independent of the available time (measured in terms of hours worked). One interpretation of this by Treas (2010, p. 6) is that men who fall short as dominant breadwinners can reassert their masculinity by avoiding 'women's work' around the house.

---

[6]   This dataset, located at the University of Oxford, brings together more than a million diary days from over 70 randomly sampled, national-scale surveys, into a single standardized format. At its most extensive the evidence covers some 55 years and 30 countries. See https://www.timeuse.org/mtus.

[7]   Canada, Denmark, Finland, France, Germany, Italy, the Netherlands, Norway, Slovenia, Spain, Sweden, the UK and the US.

5.3   CHANGES IN TIME USE

One way of assessing change over time is through summary indicators comparing for different years the evidence compiled for the EU Gender Equality Index which includes time (as one of six dimensions). In that index, time equality is measured in terms of the gender division of caring- and household-related labour on the one hand and time spent in social activities on the other. The former measures gender gaps in the involvement of women and men in caring work related to educating and caring for their children or grandchildren and/or older and disabled people, as well as their involvement in cooking and housework. Social participation measures gender gaps in women's and men's engagement in sport, cultural or leisure activities outside of their home, as well as their engagement in voluntary and charitable activities.

Table 5.3   Time gender equality index in the EU-28 countries between 2005 and 2015

	2005	2015
Overall gender equality index time	66.7	65.7
Care activities	69.9	70.0
Social activities	63.6	61.6

Source: European Institute for Gender Equality (2017a).

Conceived and measured thus, the latest evidence suggests poor and declining gender equality, especially in regard to the social and leisure sub-domain (see Table 5.3). The time dimension has the third lowest score in the overall Gender Equality Index. The score in 2015 was 1 percentage point lower than in 2005 and some 3.2 points lower than that of 2012. To put numbers on it, in 2015 some 38 per cent of women in the EU were engaged in care for children, grandchildren, older people and/or people with disabilities on a daily basis for at least an hour compared to 25 per cent of men. Significant gender differences are found for every life course and demographic category, including parents of young children. There are two groups showing very significant differences. One is people born outside the EU (taken to indicate ethnic difference). Close to a half of such women – compared to 28 per cent of men – have caring responsibilities. These women also tend to have lower employment rates, pointing to more traditional patterns along gender lines. These differences are not just due to cultural factors but reflect also differences in life situation and socio-demographic positioning (age composition and fertility). The second group is lone parents – of the different family types considered for the purposes of analysing the time deficits, the gap among female and male lone parents is the highest of all. The European Institute for Gender Equality (2017a, p. 40) attributes this in part to the fact that lone fathers are caring for older children as compared with lone mothers.

When broken down into constituent elements, it is the leisure time score that accounts for negative outcomes with a score of 60.1 compared to 70.0 for the sharing of domestic work in 2015. This relativity holds true also in terms of change over time (although it should be said that the scores in the distribution of unpaid work show no improvement). As well as indicating stasis or slow improvement, the evidence shows that changes in the organization of time between women and men are not linear (European Institute for Gender Equality 2017a, p. 38).

Once again we find, unsurprisingly, significant variation across countries, both in regard to the gendered distribution and change over time. The overall story regarding the comparison between member states in 2015 confirms the highest equality for the Nordic nations together with Estonia, Ireland, the Netherlands and the UK, with Sweden having by far the smallest gap (90.1 points). The countries with the largest gender gaps are in the Central Eastern European region together with Portugal and Greece. In regard to change over time, this is the only domain where as many as 12 member states saw a decline in their score, while only eight member states had some increase. The biggest drop in the score took place in Slovakia (−9.1 points), followed by Belgium (−9 points) and Bulgaria (−8.3 points) whereas Latvia (+6.7 points), the Czech Republic and Spain (+ 6 points) made most improvement in terms of progress towards gender equality in time expenditure on care- and home-related and social activities.

When it comes to change, we must also note changes in preferences for time investment rather than assuming a static set of preferences or practices. Preferences in regard to childcare investment by parents appear to have changed (Sullivan et al., 2018). Research tracing patterns from the 1960s to the 1990s/2000s – in 11 high-income countries[8] – confirms the point made above that both mothers and fathers have increased the time they spend on childcare (with the exception of France) (Dotti Sani and Treas, 2016). Mothers' mean daily time investment on childcare across the 11 countries almost doubled from around 54 minutes in 1965 to a predicted 104 minutes by 2012. For fathers the estimates increased even more: from 16 minutes daily in 1965 to 59 minutes in 2012. There is evidence also of other adjustments – as women's time in the labour market increases they

---

[8]   Canada, Denmark, Germany, France, Italy, the Netherlands, Norway, Slovenia, Spain, the UK and the US.

tend to reduce the amount of time they allocate to domestic work, making greater use of technology for example, and also employing help when this is possible (Fagan and Norman, 2013).

Patterns such as these have a longer and deeper significance. Gershuny and Kan (2012) argue that household dynamics leading to gender specialization, combined with a high rate of marital break-up, are associated with gendered differences in life course prospects for financial well-being, in that men take enhanced human capital away from the relationship, while women take the child/ren, and reduced human capital because of domestic work. There is an important point here, for, instead of women's resulting poverty being seen as caused by unequal responsibility for unpaid care – as well as inadequate income support and/or labour market disadvantages – it may instead be framed as a problem of women's 'economic inactivity' (Ingold and Hetherington, 2013).

Some have interpreted these trends as indicative of a stalled revolution (England, 2010) but this interpretation has been questioned by Sullivan et al. (2018) who suggest that we should understand and analyse developments in terms of a model of lagged generational change, whereby the factors within which these practices are embedded – gender ideologies, public discourses, welfare and legal systems – change but slowly. Hence, the division of paid and especially unpaid labour is embedded in long-term processes that tend to result in slow change. Rather than a stall, therefore, they see a continuing, if uneven, long-term trend in the direction of greater gender equality. They make an important point here regarding our expectations about change and over what is a reasonable time horizon for change to happen.

5.4 THE ROLE OF ATTITUDES

We have seen in Chapter 4 that considerable attention is devoted to cultural factors in explaining the nature and persistence of gender inequalities, with the argument that a strong (if tacit) belief in gender essentialism – in England's (2010, p. 150) words, "the notion that men and women are innately and fundamentally different in interests and skills" – is acting to stall progress. We will look at how people feel in regard to this matter.

Some essentialist attitudes continue, as attested to by the opinions expressed in an EU Special Eurobarometer survey of some 28,000 EU citizens on the subject of gender equality undertaken in 2017 (European Commission, 2017c). More than four in ten (44 per cent) of those responding generally agreed with the statement that the most important role of a woman is to take care of her home and family, with 17 per cent in total agreement. There was no notable difference between the opinions of men and women in this regard. A similarly high minority (43 per cent) generally believe that the most important role of a man is to earn money, with 16 per cent in total agreement with this statement. Men are, however, more likely to think this way than women (47 per cent versus 41 per cent). Opinions are keenly regionally differentiated, however, especially on an east/west gradient. For example, agreement with the women's role-related statement ranges from 81 per cent in Bulgaria, 78 per cent in Hungary and 77 per cent in Poland and the Czech Republic to 11 per cent in Sweden, 14 per cent in Denmark and 15 per cent in the Netherlands. Overall, there are 15 member states where a majority agree with this statement (most to the East and the South). A similar geographical split prevails for the statement about men's role but opinions are generally less clear-cut on this. These kinds of findings are important as cultural indicators in their own right. But for the present purpose they have an added significance given that research is increasingly pinpointing gender essentialism and the significance of prevailing attitudes about the respective roles of women and men in conditioning people's time outlay as well as their use of extra-familial childcare and employment leaves (Budig et al., 2012).

5.5   QUALITY OF LIFE

The consequences of long hours of paid and unpaid work are ominous. In the latest European Quality of Life Survey of 2016 (Eurofound, 2017c), women reported experiencing tiredness due to work more than men, and particularly young women between the ages of 18 and 34 years. In fact, two-thirds of women under 34 years claim to be too tired from work to do household jobs at least several times a month (up 15 percentage points compared with 51 per cent in 2007) (Eurofound, 2017c, p. 39). With regard to difficulties in fulfilling family responsibilities because of time spent at work, 41 per cent of women under 34 years reported this as an experience in 2016 (up 11 percentage points compared with 30 per cent in 2007). Among men, it is those in the 35–49-year age group who experience the greatest difficulties with work–life balance: 61 per cent reported being too tired to carry out household duties after work while 42 per cent said they had difficulties in fulfilling family responsibilities because of time spent at work. The reconciliation problems recede for both women and men at age 50 and beyond.

The countries where respondents most often claim to be too tired from paid work to do household jobs are Bulgaria and Romania (67 per cent of respondents) and the UK and Ireland (66 per cent). The lowest proportion of respondents reporting difficulty at least several times a month in doing household duties after work is found in the Nordic and Continental country clusters (53 per cent and 55 per cent, respectively) (Eurofound, 2017c, pp. 40–41). Differences across occupational classes are also substantial. Blue-collar workers have the greatest difficulties doing household chores after work, with 64 per cent experiencing this several times a month, compared to managers/professionals and white-collar workers whose score of difficulty is 5–7 percentage points less (Eurofound, 2017c, p. 42).

In terms of change over time in self-reported work–life balance, the trend in the EU is downward. A summary indicator shows a decrease between 2011 and 2016 of feelings of work–life balance for the EU as a whole from 6.2 to 5.8 per cent (Eurofound, 2017c, p. 42). The summary indicator reveals that, overall, Croatia (mean = 3.7) had the lowest level of work–life balance in 2016 and the Netherlands had the highest (mean = 6.6). Croatia was also the country that experienced the greatest decline in work–life balance (from 5.1 to 3.7) between 2007 and 2016. While the overall level of work–life balance satisfaction fell slightly in the Continental EU countries, it remained more or less stable in the Nordic countries as well as the Baltic states and Ireland and the UK. The Mediterranean nations – especially those which experienced a deep economic recession – showed the greatest drop.

Note also that in response to a general question of whether they have autonomy over their lives, there are no differences between women and men (except for Lithuania where 82 per cent of men and 72 per cent of women felt they were free to decide how to live their life). In general, approximately three-quarters of Europeans (76 per cent) believe that they have autonomy over their life (similar to 2011, 75 per cent) (Eurofound, 2017c, p. 20). However, over one-third (36 per cent) of people in the EU feel that they seldom have time to do things they enjoy (the same as in 2011) (Eurofound, 2017c, p. 20). No significant differences are reported here by gender.

5.6 THE ROLE OF SUPPORTIVE SERVICES

Despite some moves toward the dual earner (or in other words, universal breadwinner) model in practice, an unequal division of paid and unpaid time between women and men is reflected in the organization of childcare services. In the majority of EU countries, these remain embedded in traditional gender norms according to the analyses of key features and different ideal type models of childcare provision provided by Ciccia and Bleijenberg (2014). Austria, Czech Republic, Germany, Greece, Latvia,

Poland and Slovakia are designated as 'male breadwinner countries' in that they provide limited alternatives to home-based childcare both in the form and timing of service availability and public financial support. A second grouping of countries also rests on traditional patterns – known as the 'caregiver parity model' (following Fraser, 1994). These are Bulgaria, Estonia, Finland, Hungary, Lithuania, Luxembourg, Romania and Slovenia, which promote a traditional gender division of labour and strengthen women's role as mothers and the provision of care within the home. According to Ciccia and Bleijenberg (2014), this model goes further than the male breadwinner in levelling opportunities for mothers across different socio-economic backgrounds to stay at home with their children. These countries differ though in terms of the emphasis on and acceptability of public investment in childcare – in Finland and Hungary such investment is among the highest in Europe but in Finland especially cash for care encourages and enables parents to care for their children at home also (Grönlund et al, 2017).

Interestingly, Ciccia and Bleijenberg's analysis suggests that there is no general tendency in Europe except in the UK context towards a one-and-a-half breadwinner model (note here that the Netherlands did not conform to any ideal type). The remaining countries are designated as dual breadwinner. But these vary in terms of whether this is intentional or not. Cyprus, France, Ireland, Italy, Malta, Portugal and Spain are said to come close to a market-liberal type mode in that they do not openly promote separate gender roles for men and women, but the scarceness of affordable childcare tends to perpetuate gender traditionalism owing to the dominance of cultural norms that place primary responsibility for childcare with mothers. Class inequalities in access are deeply rooted here. Only in Sweden, Denmark and Iceland – which the authors designate as a 'supported universal breadwinner model' – is the focus on maternal employment accompanied by the provision of largely accessible, high-quality and affordable childcare services.

We should also note here the growing private outsourcing of care-related services, conceptualized by Estévez-Abe and Hobson (2015) as a process by which both the state and family increase their reliance on private markets to carry out both care and non-care domestic work. The evidence is not that widespread, particularly cross-national comparative evidence, but there are some indications that the phenomenon of outsourcing is significant but varying in extent. Estimates suggest that up to 8 million people in the EU may be involved in the provision of such services (Morel, 2015; Manoudi et al., 2018). These numbers need to be treated with care, however, for the sector is characterized by a high level of undeclared work (up to 70 per cent in some countries)

(Manoudi et al., 2018). It is also a sector that is changing rapidly, with the growth of, for example, online platforms which offer the service of matching the needs of 'employers' and workers (Manoudi et al., 2018). However, there is some systematic patterning. For one, across countries it is highly-educated women who are more likely to outsource domestic services, even when household income is controlled for (Estévez-Abe, 2015). Another systematic variation is associated with the availability of low-skilled, immigrant labour – when this is available countries are likely to have higher levels of outsourcing (Estévez-Abe, 2015). The latter has meant less outsourcing in the Nordic countries as compared to elsewhere, although this is changing and governments there have introduced policies incentivizing outsourcing (through service vouchers for care for older people for example, or tax incentives for the purchase of domestic services) so the degree to which the Nordic welfare states crowd out the market in this regard is lessening. Outsourcing is rare in the Central Eastern European and Baltic countries and also in Greece, Ireland and Portugal (Manoudi et al., 2018). Other welfare state models are also seeing the growth of policies to support outsourcing, for example Belgium, France, Germany and the Netherlands, and the EU is strongly supporting the growth of what it calls the 'personal and household services' sector, as a source of job growth and also in the name of work–life balance (Morel, 2015).

5.7 CONCLUSION

We may conclude, therefore, that there is considerable movement and dynamism in how couples with children organize their family and working lives. It also appears, though, that there is strong resilience in regard to traditional roles in the majority of European countries and that any movement away from the male breadwinner model is gradual and incomplete. Female breadwinner households are, for example, sufficiently rare to constitute an exception. That said, more couples in more countries are moving towards a dual earner model – the EU average for this type of arrangement for couple families with children aged between 0 and 14 years in 2014 was 47 per cent, making it the most common family–work arrangement (among this sector of the population). These patterns are marked by national variations and within that social class variations. In the former regard, the dual earner family is most common in the Nordic and Central Eastern European nations (with some exceptions in the latter) and least common in Continental European member states as well as Ireland and the UK and the Mediterranean countries (apart from Portugal). In regard to social class differences, it tends to be the arrangements of the higher-educated women that most conform to the dual earner model. Moreover, the patterning by socio-economic status and gender is least in the Nordic countries and most pronounced in the liberal and Mediterranean countries. These latter countries have been described as 'polarized' (Hook, 2015). We still await detailed data on and study of how the recent recession affected these patterns and cross-national variations.

The chapter has also revealed some of the constituent elements of the different models of family life, especially in terms of the division of time and labour. Women across countries put in about double the time in unpaid work as compared with men. Moreover, change is slow, in terms both of male time investment and the actual type of activities undertaken by women and men (with a persistence of stratification by type of task such that the tasks that most closely resemble care giving are completed predominantly by women). Time investment is one domain where progress towards gender equality reversed in the EU between 2008 and 2015 and the gender gap in this at the latter date was of the order of 34 percentage points. Social class and age differences are widespread in regard to this aspect of family life also, with young and higher-educated fathers (and couples) displaying the least gendered differences and the most time investment of any fathers in their children. This demographic and educational pattern is also found for women. There is evidence of variation by welfare state type in this though, although these tend to be differences of degree rather than kind. Gender divisions are least in the Nordic countries but these still record a male–female gap in time input on unpaid work of the order of 30 per cent or more.

There is an underlying point to be made here about the complexity of work–family and economic arrangements and the difficulty of reading off such arrangements from the structure and composition of the household alone. This is a point with particular resonance from a comparative perspective, especially if the prevailing attitudes to gender roles and responsibilities and how these are reflected in the volume and type of support services are taken into account. The extent and influence of 'traditionalist' attitudes and public policies that reflect these should not be underestimated.

Intermezzo 2

Having examined what is happening in practice, the remaining section of the book – and especially the next two chapters – turns to examine the focus of policy and undertakes analysis of the main thrust of developments in regard to how policy has approached (problematized) the issues. Here we might remind ourselves of the key questions underlying the book: How do women's and men's situations compare, and what role does social policy play in affecting these and shaping both women's lives and gender patterns? The task now is to pinpoint the policy filaments that contribute to the situations we found in Chapters 3, 4 and 5. The particular emphasis is on the degree of policy engagement with gender inequality and policy's understanding of 'the problem'.

There are two challenges in regard to examining policy for these purposes. The first is that there is no adequate label or rubric to capture the domains of relevant policy; the second is that some areas of policy are more pertinent than others. Hence I undertake the analysis in two chapters. The first focuses on EU equality policy and the second on social policy more broadly (and across the member states rather than just at EU level). The second is more selective than the first as the potential policy field is much broader. The logic of the analysis is as follows. I start with generic gender inequality policy and then move on to consider relevant social policy from a broader perspective. The latter takes us especially into the realm of family-oriented policy, in terms, for example, of measures oriented to parents and children. It also means looking at social policies directed towards the care of older people. Theoretically, we might think of the approach as differentiating between explicit and implicit gender-oriented social policy. The focus is as much on guiding visions as it is on taking a reading of the actual policies introduced and the goal throughout is to set the general context rather than trace particular outcomes. Hence, I am not positing any direct relationship between policy and these outcomes; rather what I seek to do is to identify broad trends and movements and juxtapose different policy approaches, and through such exercises to take a reading on likely future directions.

6. The EU, equality and social policy

The key questions that run throughout this chapter centre upon how equality has been conceived and addressed as a policy goal by the EU and what progress has been made in prioritizing gender. We focus on the EU not just because it provides the broad transnational policy backdrop to the developments reported in earlier chapters but also because it was one of the first major institutions in the world to seek to ensure equal treatment for women and men (Rees, 1998, p. 48). Thematizing and detailing the general EU approach to gender equality also helps set the scene for Chapter 7 which looks at the current state of play in regard to relevant domains of social policy mainly at national level. This chapter especially homes in on the social policy-related dimensions of EU equality policy. Its core interest in the problematization of gender equality leads the chapter to examine the different approaches that have been deployed at different stages, sometimes requiring us to reach back 30 to 40 years. Historical depth is important to reveal the lineage and contextual setting within which developments took place.

Both theoretical and methodological clarity are called for at the outset. Philosophically, equality is a multi-layered idea(l) and its application in policy is quite diverse. One robust differentiation of approaches from a policy perspective is that between equality of access and of outcome. The former centres upon the absence of legal and institutional barriers to entry or participation whereas equality of outcome refers to the distribution of economic and other resources and benefits and therefore is more about tangible results. Equality of opportunity, embracing the capacity and the resources to participate, falls somewhere between the two. I have suggested elsewhere (Daly, 1996) the idea of an 'equality order' to capture the notion of different levels and types of equality from a policy perspective. Each stage is cumulative and inter-related to the others. We will discuss this further towards the end of this chapter.

Methodologically, the exercise involved in this chapter is to identify the underlying paradigm as well as the policy measures or programmes that comprise it. Carol Bacchi's (1999) 'construction of the problem approach' is useful here as it seeks to identify both the angle that is taken on the 'problem', recognizing that all problems are constructions or interpretations, and the underlying assumptions. It is a route to identifying philosophical orientation and reminds us also to look for what is not problematized. But the questions to be asked cannot be negative only. Other potentially useful questions – drawing from the literature and especially Jenson (2015) and Watkins (2018) include: To what extent are measures such as women's engagement (e.g. in employment) an end in themselves or are they promoted for broader purposes relating to gender equality? Is women's empowerment (as against employment participation alone, for example) part of the aim? These questions help us to recognize and differentiate between different policy visions.

The chapter generally follows a chronological line of analysis. This serves to reveal the thinking (problematization) prevailing at different points in time as well as the cumulation of different approaches and their institutionalization. I start with the legal approach adopted in the 1970s and then move on to consider how, in the context of wavering faith in this view, gender mainstreaming was adopted as the favoured approach. Note that I do not cover the influential decisions of the European Court of Justice (see Burri and Prechal, 2013; Leibfried, 2015), but I do recognize that the Court at various stages has been influential in pushing a social interpretation of EU Treaty articles.

6.1   LEGAL APPROACHES TO EQUALITY

There are different versions of the history of gender equality in the EU and of the associated policy vision or goal. It is generally agreed though, following Rees (1998), that the EU has utilized three different types of policy approach over time. One operates with a goal of equality of rights between women and men; a second is oriented to countering women's disadvantaged positioning as compared with men; and a third is focused on addressing gender inequality. The first – equality of rights or equal treatment – was pursued through legal or legislative means. Rooted in the idea that women should not be discriminated against vis-à-vis men, this was a prominent approach in the EU in the 1970s. The second, positive action, approach to reduce women's disadvantage mandates a role for policy in improving the conditions and opportunities available to women by positively favouring them, if necessary. In the EU context, this approach has often taken the form of action programmes accompanying legislation that provide funding for such activities as capacity building, support networks, piloting innovations and service improvements. The EU's third approach has generally problematized gender inequality through the method of gender mainstreaming which turns attention towards the systems, processes and norms that generate gender inequalities (Rees, 1998) and to some extent away from individuals and their rights (equal treatment), or women's disadvantageous position (positive action). These are not mutually exclusive or necessarily contradictory approaches. I will proceed to analyse these further bearing these differences in mind but also noting the importance of not 'freezing' the different approaches for (a) they are not always understood or applied in a manner that is consistent with their philosophical foundations and (b) they evolve and interact over time and hence change.

Gender was the only equality issue on the legal agenda of the EU from its establishment in 1958 (MISSOC Secretariat, 2012, p. 11). It took the form of the principle of equal pay for equal work. Hence it was inspired not by the expansive view of equality but an economic perspective – instituted because some member states (especially France which had already introduced legislation on equal pay) did not want their social rights (wage regulation, benefit generosity) to distort their economic competitiveness. As the EU developed – and especially from the 1970s on – it broadened its approach and became an important protagonist for an economic understanding of gender equality. But this was not without opposition or at times hesitation – for part of the long thread in the EU's development is that social policy matters have always had a hard fight within what is essentially a market-oriented endeavour (Falkner, 2013; Anderson, 2015). This is to some extent a matter of political philosophy or political position but there are also issues of legal capacity in play since EU powers and remit are heavily circumscribed and derive essentially from law around the four freedoms (of goods, services, money and people) as elaborated in the Treaties (Armstrong, 2011).

With a legislative approach prevailing in the first period, between 1975 and 1996, the Council of Ministers of the EU adopted a series of legal directives that dealt either directly or indirectly with gender inequality. These tended – given the originating interest – to be focused on employment conditions. The first (in 1975) covered the topic of equal pay, outlawing sex-based discrimination in all constituents and conditions of pay for the same work or work of equal value. The second in the following year – Directive 76/207 – introduced the principle of equal treatment for women and men in access to employment, vocational training and promotion, and working conditions. The legislation explicitly affirmed the existence of indirect discrimination although it did not specifically define it (Jacquot, 2015, p. 32). A third relevant Directive (79/7) focused on the progressive implementation of the principle of equal treatment in matters of social security. As one of the few directives addressed at a social security or welfare-relevant framing of gender equality, this Directive is extremely important for the present purpose (and is therefore given some space and discussion below). A further relevant (sister) Directive is 86/378 which extended the equality principle to professional social security schemes. Directive 86/613 covered the application of equal treatment to women and men in independent professions (including agriculture) and the protection of self-employed women during pregnancy. This was directed towards protecting women whose professional status is unclear, including wives who work in family enterprises. There was also a pregnant workers safety Directive of 1992 (92/85), and a 1996 directive on parental leave (96/34).[1] Other important Directives include the Equal Treatment Directive of 2006 (2006/54)[2] (on the implementation of the principle of equal opportunities and equal treatment of men and women in matters of employment and occupation) and the Goods and Services Directive (2004/113/EC) which addressed gender equality beyond the labour market (and included race/ ethnicity as a ground of inequality as well).[3]

These Directives did not sit alone. As became customary practice in this and other fields, the EU accompanied the legal measures with a set of programmatic activities and incentives oriented to fostering and embedding change in practice. These Medium-term Community Action Programmes – the first of which was in 1982 and the last ending in 2000 – sought to finance and resource positive action strategies – often at micro level – in member states.[4] Although they are usually term-limited they can be very important. Basically their purpose was to establish a framework – of ideas, funding and actions – within which the legislation and Directives could be enacted and embedded (Rees, 1998, p. 45). They were usually focused on key spheres of action or target groups – the second one (1986–90), for example, initiated social policy projects in three areas: childcare, maternity protection and sexual harassment. These were intended as both practical interventions and also to pioneer innovations. The funding was often

---

[1]   Repealed by Directive 2010/118.

[2]   This so-called 'recast Directive' modernized and simplified existing provision and from August 2009 on replaced some of the previous directives, in particular 75/117 (on equal pay), 76/207 (on equal treatment in employment) and 86/378 (on equal treatment in occupational social security schemes), inter alia (Burri and Prechal, 2013, pp. 1–2).

[3]   Note also the Framework Directive on Parental Leave (Directive 2010/18/EU) from 2010 which laid out as the EU norm four months of parental leave for each parent, one month of which is non-transferable, and in the broader human rights field Directive 2011/36/EU on the prevention and fight against human trafficking and Directive 2012/29/EU on minimum norms on rights, support and protection for victims of crime.

[4]   The general idea of a supportive infrastructure for policy co-ordination at member state level was continued in subsequent years under a different rubric in The Framework Strategy for Equality between Women and Men (2001–05) and Roadmap for Equality between Women and Men (2006–10).

directed at pilot projects and the creation of networks to facilitate the flow of information and measure progress towards equal opportunities. Knowledge development and exchange therefore figured prominently in these 'demonstration projects'.

However, it was the legislative equal treatment approach that predominated throughout the 1970s and 1980s and even into the 1990s. The first relevant and most influential Directive from a social policy perspective was that of 79/7. This seemed like an answer to some feminist demands as, adhering to an individual rights approach, the driving idea behind it was equal treatment (Luckhaus, 1990).[5] Focused on a number of extant social security schemes, the Directive drilled down into their DNA, including their scope and conditions of access, the contribution conditions and obligations, the calculation of contributions and benefits and the conditions governing the duration and retention of entitlement (many of the issues highlighted by feminist analysis). As defined in the Directive, equal treatment meant no discrimination on grounds of sex either directly or indirectly (for the latter express reference is made to marital or family status). 'Direct discrimination' was defined to inhere in rules or conduct which are overtly sexist in character while 'indirect discrimination' was deemed to occur when the effects of rules or conduct which appear non-sexist act to disadvantage one sex relative to the other. The latter – more gender-oriented perspective – was not limited to discrimination on the grounds of marital or family status but was considered to occur whenever a rule, prima facie neutral, could be proven to affect one sex, the disadvantaged one, to a disproportionate extent and was not objectively justifiable (Sohrab, 1994a; Steiner, 1996). Defined thus, indirect discrimination did not necessarily involve intent. There is, therefore, an outcome orientation to it which renders structural causes, including family situation, for certain labour-market disadvantages relevant, albeit only to a degree (Scheiwe, 1994, p. 254). This, as well as the directives which preceded it on equal pay and equal treatment, were by any and all standards a landmark, however.

For a whole series of reasons – not least EU legal competence, political will and ambivalence in some quarters about whether and how to address the matter of women's disadvantage – the EU Directive adopted a very particular approach to equality in social security, ringfencing it and building into it a series of delimitations of application relating to the sphere of

---

[5]   This is true also of its sister Directives 86/378 (on equal treatment in occupational social security schemes) and 86/613 (on the application of the principle of equal treatment of men and women engaged in an activity, including agriculture, in a self-employed capacity and on the protection of self-employed women during pregnancy and motherhood). The discussion in this section will focus mostly upon Directive 79/7.

activity, the people covered and the risks and social security schemes covered. The image of a funnel comes to mind. The funnelling effect reduced its gender bite. Its list of exceptions was extensive (Burri and Prechal, 2013, p. 12). With regard to activity, for example, only employment was covered. Unpaid work, including care-related activities, was therefore placed outside the remit of the Directive. Confining it to employment in turn delimited the universe of people covered – those in the working population,[6] including retired people, invalided workers and those whose working life was interrupted by sickness, occupational accidents or involuntary unemployment. Excluded from the Directive, then, were people who were never employed, those who were never and are not currently seeking employment, and those whose occupation was not interrupted by one of the specified risk contingencies. Obviously, the bulk of those placed outside the personal scope of the Directive are women, especially lone mothers and other carers.[7] The third step in reining in the Directive was to limit coverage to specific risks, namely sickness, invalidity, old age, accidents at work, occupational diseases, and unemployment. It is instructive to think of what is not covered by limiting the provisions to these classic social security risks: family policies, caring-related cash transfers, survivor benefits, and the bulk of the minimum income schemes as well as publicly-provided social services are all provisions which are excluded from the Directives. Finally, particular conditions very pertinent to gender inequality (such as the pension age, the granting of benefits including pensions to those who have or are bringing up children, the granting of old age or invalidity entitlements based upon the derived entitlements of a wife, the granting of a benefit increase for a 'dependent' wife, among others) were specifically excluded. Such exclusions are contrary to the ethos of equality of treatment, and at the same time reveal the limits of this entire approach (specifically taking as the norm the typical male situation of employment over the life course and earned entitlement to benefits). In sum, the Directive overall operated with a much narrower notion than gender inequality – effectively sex inequality on the basis of a male norm.

In terms of impact, most analyses agree that the Directive furnished significant results. While some of the member states had already undertaken to address discrimination in their social security systems, the legally binding nature of this and other Directives forced change upon all and standardized approaches across the EU. The main type of reform called

---

[6] This, following the European Court of Justice (ECJ) judgment in *Johnson v Chief Adjudication Officer*, Case C-31/90 (1991), is defined also to include those seeking work.

[7] Although the ECJ judgment in the *Drake v Chief Adjudication Officer* case recognized caring for a person in receipt of invalidity benefits as coming within the scope of the Directive.

forth by the Directive involved the adoption of sex-neutral categories of entitlement or the transformation of existing categories of entitlement into sex-neutral ones. It is hard to believe that some of these conventions existed as recently as the 1980s and 1990s. Reformulations most often took the form of extending formal entitlement to the benefits concerned (sometimes to altered and even reduced benefits) (Sohrab, 1994b) to both sexes. As a strategy for change, it relied for the most part on equalizing access to benefits. But implementing the Directive also meant the abolition of some countries' automatic classification of married women as 'dependants' of their husbands, as well as getting rid of special conditions and lower rates of benefit that sometimes existed for female claimants as well as the limiting of benefit entitlement to the male breadwinner/head of household. Some analysts conclude that, together with the rulings of the European Court of Justice, a body of gender-related policies of substantial scope has been yielded by the Directives (Ostner and Lewis, 1995). It has also been said that a complex and broadly-defined principle of equality between women and men has been put in place as one strand in the law of the EU (Hoskyns, 1996, p. 197). Indeed, its sex equality policy has furnished the EU with one of the main strands of its social policy and lent it credibility as a social policy actor. Moreover, national laws and practice have been revised and modified and the EU's concern with sex discrimination became for at least two decades a necessary feature of the climate within which the dialogue between central EU and national policy making took place.

Overall, the advantages of this type of equality strategy are that it makes significant inroads into discrimination suffered by women and acts to counter stereotyping and labelling. But a key weakness is that formal equality measures may be surface in nature – a kind of 'add women and don't stir' prescription. As an overall judgement of Directive 79/7, I conclude that it provided for those women who are similarly situated to men to be treated equally with men in relation to the 'classic' social risks arising from employment. Significant as this might be, it is a form of equality in isolation. Being more or less limited to market-derived social security, it leaves untouched the whole other world of labour underpinning states, labour markets and societies with which feminist engagement has been so concerned.

6.2 GENDER MAINSTREAMING

The move to a different strategy partly followed from the recognition of the limits of an equal treatment approach but is also attributable to a new and vibrant concept appearing on the scene that seemed to offer better possibilities to bring about meaningful change, especially in the everyday world of policy making (Council of Europe, 1998). The EU's general turn in the 1990s to softer, more persuasive measures such as non-binding recommendations (as against legislation) also created a window of opportunity.[8] Gender mainstreaming was the new idea, and arguably remains the dominant EU approach (at least discursively). In an analysis of five areas of EU policy,[9] Pollack and Hafner-Burton (2000) argue that three factors can explain the turn to gender mainstreaming: political opportunities opened by EU institutions; networks of gender advocates; and strategic framing of gender mainstreaming by these and other actors to make it fit with the dominant frame.

It is important to say, however, that gender mainstreaming has not displaced the *de jure* approach to equal treatment – the two approaches exist side by side but from the 1990s on gender mainstreaming has had the greater energy and political commitment as compared with equal treatment through legally-binding measures (although some such activity has continued throughout the period).

As the term implies, gender mainstreaming focuses on gender rather than the specific needs of women or equal treatment between the sexes. The concept first appeared in international texts after the United Nations Third World Conference on Women in Nairobi, 1985, being grounded in discussions about the role of women in development (Council of Europe, 1998). In the EU context, it became official policy when it was made a central pivot in the European Commission's Fourth Medium-term Community Action Programme on Equal Opportunities for Women and Men (1996–2000) and the focus of a communication by the Commission in 1996 (Commission of the European Communities, 1996). Thus began gender mainstreaming's 'long march through the institutions',[10] in a context in which the Treaty of Amsterdam (1997) broke new ground in making equal opportunities between women and men – rather than the heretofore equal pay and equal treatment in the workforce – a central objective of the EU. But what exactly is gender mainstreaming and how was it developed in the European context?

In a context of lack of specificity and a clear definition of what constitutes gender mainstreaming, the Council of Europe (1998, p. 16) identified the following as common references in different originating conceptions

---

[8]   A significant factor in the latter turn was the increasing divergence of outlook and ideology among the member states which made agreement on laws more difficult to achieve.

[9]   Structural Funds, employment, development, competition, and science, research and development.

[10]   A term borrowed from Susan Watkins (2018, p. 14) who used it to describe the process whereby an anti-discrimination approach became hegemonic in American feminism.

and documents: setting gender equality as a goal; aiming for full participation of women in decision-making; developing and applying tools, such as the screening of policy proposals from a gender perspective; and effecting shifts in organizational cultures and ways of working and also in the actors involved, especially 'everyday' actors. It came up with the following definition: "gender mainstreaming is the (re)organisation, improvement, development and evaluation of policy processes, so that a gender equality perspective is incorporated in all policies at all levels and at all stages, by the actors normally involved in policy-making" (Council of Europe, 1998, p. 16). Of course, practice renders this something of a theoretical definition in that neither the process nor end goals necessarily follow this definition, or indeed use any clear definition at all. Nevertheless, it is important to bear in mind the point made by Pollack and Hafner-Burton (2000, p. 434) about how demanding gender mainstreaming is as a concept for it requires the adoption of a gender perspective by all the central actors in the policy process with the ultimate aim of transforming all the institutions.

Its distinctiveness is that it targets both values and institutional processes, aiming to embed gender-sensitive norms and practices in the structures, processes and operating environment of all public policy (Daly, 2005; Cavaghan, 2017). Rather than focusing on a centred or specialized policy field, gender mainstreaming aims for the horizontal integration of gender across policy domains – gender is relevant to all. In key respects, it seeks to supplant the heretofore special track of gender equality – or from another view 'isolated' nature of provisions – with integration and embeddedness across all spheres. With a strong focus on implementation and bringing about change in practice, it is especially developed as a set of policy-related tools, techniques and skills. Prominent in its toolkit are such methods as the production of gender-disaggregated statistics, gender impact assessment and gender budgeting – some pioneered by feminist engagement, these are all meant to lay bare the real picture. Gender mainstreaming is therefore more slanted towards policy analysis and delivery – a methodology oriented to the design and scrutiny of policy – rather than actually signifying a programme of action targeted at outcomes in which power processes are seen to be at play (Daly, 2005). The focus is shifted from political mobilization and a feminist agenda to gender expertise and administrative practice (de los Reyes, 2016, p. 31; Cavaghan, 2017).

Gender mainstreaming made quite a big impact at EU level, reaching widely into its policy on employment regulation especially. For example, in 1997 gender equality was mainstreamed into the European Employment Strategy (a system of EU governance based on coordination of national responses and strategies to a set of agreed objectives, especially for the creation of 'more and better jobs') (Villa, 2013). In line with the techno-rational nature of mainstreaming, a new 'field of knowledge' saw the setting of numerical targets for female labour market participation (as well as for male participation) and a detailed policy pathway identified, involving especially targets for childcare coverage, for both younger (under 3 years old, a target of 33 per cent) and older children (3 years of age and over, a target of 90 per cent) to be achieved by 2010. The numerical targets for participation in employment by sex were replaced later by a unisex target of a 75 per cent employment rate for those aged 20 to 64 years by 2020, in a move towards gender neutrality that has been seen as very significant. Impact and progress at member state level is uneven and patchy (Daly, 2005; Stratigaki, 2005; Villa, 2013). Overall, the high years of gender mainstreaming – for at least a decade from the mid-1990s – saw a transformation of the EU's approach from a narrow focus on equal opportunities in the workplace to a gradual acceptance of specific positive actions and an institutional commitment to mainstreaming gender across policies (Pollack and Hafner-Burton, 2000, p. 450).

However, the policy itself, as well as its achievements, are contested. Some disagreed on politico-philosophical grounds – seeing gender mainstreaming as a dilution of the underlying vision of gender equality – whilst others feared that the transversalizing approach would lead to the displacement if not demise of the structures and institutions that had been put in place around gender equality. The empirical research examining what has happened indicates that, rather than a single coherent approach to gender mainstreaming, there was a constellation of concepts and approaches (Daly, 2005; Verloo, 2005; Cavaghan, 2017).[11] One could argue that a lack of conceptual focus negatively affected progress in implementation. At root though, the failure to come up with a clear policy vision has been attributed to gender mainstreaming's lack of a theory of transformation beyond the policy process (Daly, 2005) – what else has to change apart from policy making for gender equality to be achieved? A further consequence was the risk of gender-related goals being subverted for other purposes. This, at root an instrumentalization, seems to have happened during the first decade of the 2000s, with employment participation increasingly promoted as an end in itself and gender equality 'co-opted' to serve economic goals (Stratigaki, 2004, 2005). For Jacquot (2015, p. 135), "there has been a shift from 'equality *within* the market' to 'equality *for* the market'".

There was another risk as well – depoliticization – given that gender mainstreaming accentuates the engagement of the policy-making actors

---

[11]   Jacquot (2015, pp. 86–8) identifies four major conceptions of gender mainstreaming: an extensive conception, a minimalist reductive one, a defensive one, and a conservative one.

(the technical) over that of the political actors (Lombardo and Meier, 2006; Verloo, 2006). Those who had placed gender mainstreaming on the EU agenda – the so-called 'velvet triangle' (Woodward 2004, cited in Jacquot, 2017, p. 34) of administrative, political, academic and activist agents – became distanced from it as it moved into the professional policy-making circles. The centre of expertise also became dispersed. There occurred what Jacquot (2015, p. 34) calls a 'professionalization' of gender equality policy, by which she means the marginalization of activist and feminist involvement.

Before we draw the curtain on an assessment of gender mainstreaming, there are two claims that can be made for it. One is that it has facilitated an advance in knowledge (for Watkins, 2018, p. 51, this is "the great gain"). The EU Gender Equality Index – which I have used in earlier chapters to assess progress – can be attributed to gender mainstreaming's focus on assessing and anticipating impact and progress and the need for data and evidence for that purpose.[12] As an index it is actually more broad-ranging and comparatively innovative as compared with other indices such as the Gender Inequality Index (GII) of the UNDP and the Gender Gap Index (GGI) of the World Economic Forum.[13] Its nearest competitor is the OECD Gender Index.[14] The latter includes 80 indicators of gender inequalities in the fields of education, employment, entrepreneurship, health and development, and governance. The data cover OECD member countries, as well as Brazil, China, India, Indonesia and South Africa. Notably, though, there is no set of indicators on financial well-being and inequality in that regard (other than on wage gaps). A second claim that can be made for gender mainstreaming – also along the lines of offering tools – is that it precipitated the use of gender budgeting and thereby spread the practice, knowledge and tools for analysing budgets and spending plans for their likely effect on gender equality (Quinn, 2016).[15] Of course I am not attributing the growing use of gender budgeting solely to the EU engagement with gender mainstreaming; rather there is

---

[12] See https://eige.europa.eu/gender-equality-index/about.
[13] Mention should also be made of The International Bank for Reconstruction/The World Bank Index of Women, Business and the Law at http://wbl.worldbank.org/. This follows a women sensitive employment life course model and uses eight sets of indicators of legal regulations/rights organized around the following: going places, starting a job, getting paid, getting married, having children, running a business, managing assets, getting a pension. See International Bank for Reconstruction/The World Bank (2019).
[14] See the data portal at http://www.oecd.org/gender/.
[15] See https://wbg.org.uk/resources/what-is-gender-budgeting/.

a wider move to popularize gender budgeting as a tool of policy analysis, promoted especially by women-oriented and feminist political agency.[16]

6.3   SUBSEQUENT DEVELOPMENTS

Charting developments in subsequent periods and especially through the 'Lisbon years' (2000–10), Jacquot (2015) sees gender equality as having become progressively marginalized or downsized in the EU's policy goals/priorities. She documents how it went from its headline status of one priority in four, to one in ten, and then to one in 24 (p. 119).[17] From the early to mid 2000s on, the push towards common action on all forms of discrimination intensified and with the advent of the first Barroso Commission and the departure of Commissioner Diamantopoulou in 2004 the internal Commission push for gender equality receded (Jacquot, 2015, p.123). The subsequent trajectory was to 'fold gender in' (in Jane Jenson's (2008) phrase) and to marry it with a broader anti-discrimination focus. The latter was especially consequential.

6.3.1   Multiple Grounds of Discrimination

While the topic of racism has been part of EU policy discourse for a while, in the mid-1990s the EU resorted to its classic approach to counter it: anti-discrimination, understood in a multi-dimensional or complex way. The Treaty of Amsterdam (1997) could be said to embody elements of an intersectional approach, as it recognized discrimination on six grounds – sex, racial or ethnic origin, religion or belief, disability, age and sexual orientation. The same six grounds of discrimination are addressed in the Lisbon Treaty (2007/C 364/01), which declares that the EU should aim to combat these forms of discrimination and may indeed take the appropriate action to do so. The Charter of Fundamental Rights of the European Union (2000/C 364/01) asserts adherence to non-discrimination on an even more expansive set of grounds, including sex, race, colour, ethnic or social origin, genetic features, language, religion or belief, opinions, membership of a national minority, property, birth, disability, age or sexual orientation.

In terms of policy, discrimination on the grounds of race and ethnicity (outside the labour market) was addressed by the Racial Equality Directive (2000/43/EC) while the Employment Equality Directive (2000/78/EC)

---

[16]   See https://wbg.org.uk/.
[17]   Villa (2013) charts a similar trajectory for gender in the European Employment Strategy.

focused on potential grounds of discrimination within the field of employment not covered by other directives (that is, religious belief, sexual orientation, disability and age) (Rolandsen Augustín, 2013, p. 51).[18] One can see from Table 6.1 that the Racial Equality Directive was the most extensive single directive which means that discrimination on racial grounds is banned across the six domains listed. Gender discrimination is the second most widespread form of anti-discrimination measure in the EU, but it is not present in healthcare or in education. The other grounds (of sexual orientation, religion or belief, dis/ability and age) are protected only in employment and vocational training and workers' and employers' organizations. There is another clue to the heart of the EU project in the table as well – the fact that employment is the area most protected by anti-discrimination legislation. We might note also that nationality as a ground is missing from the Racial Equality Directive, which means that discrimination on the ground of migrant background is also missing (Fredman, 2016). Absent also is socio-economic status as a justiceable inequality under EU legislation (Walby et al., 2012).

This 'integration' has had several consequences, especially as regards gender equality which we will recall has a much longer and more diverse history in the EU. First, integration has shifted the centre of gravity towards judicial machinery. This has also meant a move of gender equality bureaucracy from the Directorate General of Employment and Social Affairs to that of Justice and Consumers (Jacquot, 2015). Through this and other means, the role of social and employment policy in equality policy has been decentred. This, secondly, meant a change in approach. Not alone did gender become one of a number of grounds on which the battle for equality was to be fought but the problematization and 'solution' focused on individual rights and discrimination rather than social policy and social rights.

How does the EU's intersectionality approach work in practice? This has been the source of considerable criticism. For one, there are significant structural obstacles to intersectional claims at EU level. Among the difficulties identified by Fredman (2016) are: different grounds are lodged in different pieces of legislation (as Table 6.1 indicates); justification defences are framed differently for different grounds; and there is no scope for an expansion of the listed grounds without amending legislation. The view of Rolandsen Augustín (2013, p. 51) – shared by many others including

---

[18]   The Racial Equality Directive (2000/43/EC) prohibits discrimination on the ground of racial or ethnic origin in a broad range of fields, including employment, social protection and social advantages, education, and goods and services available to the public, including housing.

Table 6.1   Scope and legal basis of EU anti-discrimination directives

Ground	Employment and vocational training	Workers' and employers' organizations	Social protection including social security	Social protection including healthcare	Education	Public goods and services including housing
Racial or ethnic origin	Directive 2000/43	Directive 2000/43	Directive 2000/43	Directive 2000/43	Directive 2000/43	Directive 2000/43
Gender	Directive 2005/54 Directive 2010/41 (self-employment)	Directive 2006/54	Directive 79/7 (statutory social security only) Directive 2006/54 (occupational social security only)	N/A	N/A	Directive 2004/113
Sexual orientation	Directive 2000/78	Directive 2000/78	N/A	N/A	N/A	N/A
Religion or belief	Directive 2000/78	Directive 2000/78	N/A	N/A	N/A	N/A
Disability	Directive 2000/78	Directive 2000/78	N/A	N/A	N/A	N/A
Age	Directive 2000/78	Directive 2000/78	N/A	N/A	N/A	N/A

Source: Adapted from European Institute for Gender Equality (2019, Table 1, p. 9).

Jacquot (2015), Jenson (2015) and the European Commission (2015a) – is that the EU has slipped into a hierarchicalization of grounds in which race and ethnicity is the dominant of the grounds and gender – which had been dominant at the outset and of course was more institutionalized in the EU – has dropped in importance. A base problem here is that little thought or attention has been given to how the grounds interact and there is a reliance on relatively simplistic assumptions in this regard (Rolandsen Augustín, 2013; Fredman, 2016). Questions have also been raised about the meaning and depth of intersectionality in the EU context. Far from its roots as resistance to the mainstream, it has fed a 'diversity agenda', which works towards the goal of horizontal inclusion and is largely devoid of any understanding of inequalities of power. Diversity management tends to hide the impact of power relations and structural inequality – its tendency is to celebrate difference and play down racism. It also creates a 'paradigm of difference', normalizing the existence of different subject positions in terms of gender, ethnicity, age, and so forth (de los Reyes, 2016, p. 24). The treatment of the grounds in a rather silo manner also tends to construct them as characteristics of individuals or groups, thus breaching their non-reductive nature in the academic formulation, which views them more as multiple and interacting systems of inequality to be found at individual, meso and macro levels. There is also a question about implicit competition among the grounds (de los Reyes, 2016, p. 51).

6.3.2 Gender-specific Developments

Looking more broadly than at discrimination law, Jacquot (2015, 2017) depicts the developments during the most recent period as 'dismantling'. In her view, even though women and gender are mentioned, the recent programmes are not imbued with an awareness of gender inequality as a problem. Others name this 'degendering' (Rolandsen Augustín, 2013). On the basis of an analysis of the underpinning ideas, Jane Jenson (2015) develops a distinction between policy/discourse that is gender aware and that which sets out gender equality as an objective.[19] The former certainly references gender and speaks in gender-specific terms whereas the latter is oriented to problematizing gender inequality in regard to income, employment and care. This picks up on a point made in some of the literature reviewed in Chapter 2, whereby terms like 'familialization' and others can be gender neutral. As articulated by Mahon (2018b, p. 269), the gender aware policy inclines towards public support for childcare (possibly targeted at low-income families), maternity leave provisions and women's part-time work, whereas the gender equality oriented policy advocates for a universal approach for care-related services and measures to address the unequal division of domestic labour and redefine the working day for both women and men. Jenson's conclusion about the EU is that the discourse remains gender aware and may even have a strong vision of gender equality in mind but that the policy goals in regard to gender equality – such as sharing care – have been weakened along with the instruments. In her analysis, Jenson also discerns a disjunction between discourse and policy in the contemporary EU in that, while a structural approach to gender inequality is articulated discursively, the policies do not match such articulations.

This is something we encounter quite often in gender-related policy. We can appreciate it from a brief consideration of the current policy agenda in

---

[19] Note that Mahon (2018b) uses this perspective to interrogate the gender framings used by the OECD and Economic Commission for Latin America and the Caribbean.

the EU. Essentially the approach set out in the Roadmap for Equality for Women and Men 2006–10, adopted in March 2006, remains (more or less) the core set of gender-related policies in place. This 'stability' is notable in the EU context where policy is frequently reframed and reimagined. The Roadmap defined six priority areas for EU action on gender equality: economic independence for women and men, reconciliation of private and professional life, equal representation in decision-making, eradication of all forms of gender-based violence, elimination of gender stereotypes, and promotion of gender equality in external and development policies (i.e. beyond the frontiers of the EU) (European Commission, 2006). The Women's Charter (2010) basically prioritized more or less the same actions: equality in the labour market and equal independence for women and men; equal pay for equal work and work of equal value (in which the gender pay gap is targeted); equality in decision-making through EU incentive measures; dignity, integrity and an end to gender-based violence through a comprehensive policy framework; and the promotion of gender equality beyond the EU by pursuing the issue in external relations and with international organizations (European Commission, 2010b). The current European Pact for Gender Equality (2011–20), which followed the first five-year pact of 2006, calls on member states to close gender gaps in employment and social protection, promote work–life balance and combat violence against women. The Pact underscores the commitment to gender equality in the Treaty, acknowledges the gender-specific elements of the Europe 2020 Strategy and also mentions the need to reinforce governance through gender mainstreaming. The commitment to gender mainstreaming seems weaker in comparison with the first pact (Villa, 2013). In particular, in 2006, "measures to reinforce governance through gender mainstreaming and better monitoring" was one of the three stated headline areas of action, including the need to "ensure that gender equality effects are taken into account in impact assessments of new EU policies" (Council of the European Union, 2011). From 2011 this area for action was replaced by a strategy on combating violence against women, and the commitment to gender mainstreaming was moved to a final section on 'governance, implementation and monitoring'. The 2016–19 Commission Staff Working Document on Strategic Engagement for Gender Equality makes gender mainstreaming one of five areas for action but conceives of it primarily in terms of impact assessment, evaluation and regular monitoring (European Commission, 2015b).

Jenson (2015) identifies three reframings or shifts that have been key (associating them especially with social investment which will be discussed in Chapter 7): the move from promoting employment and women's participation to a more gender-neutral, adult worker model (which promotes part-time employment and supplements for low wages); the narrowing of women's identity for policy purposes to rights and responsibilities related to their maternal role; the folding of gender inequality into a wider range of intersectional and cultural inequalities and the associated turn to legal and judicial protection over positive action and policy intervention. Elomäki (2017) discerns the emergence of a new type of economic discourse – the economic case for gender equality – in the process (further) instrumentalizing gender equality for economic growth purposes. Emphasizing the macro-economic benefits, this brings together themes and arguments around women as a labour market reserve, women's unused human capital and women's employment, as a solution to the demographic challenge. What is new about this is not the market-oriented discourse which has long characterized EU engagement with gender equality but the promotion of gender equality for economic growth purposes. In the process gender equality – rather than an issue of justice and rights for women – is reduced to women's employment and the framing of this in terms of macro-economic benefit and specifically the GDP growth calculus.[20] Moves in this regard were evident from the early 1990s, intensifying over the Lisbon period (when gender equality was represented as serving social cohesion ends as well as economic growth) (see Lewis, 2006; Kantola, 2010) but the explicit development of the new economic case Elomäki dates from 2008, after which, she says, "the economic case became the backbone of gender equality policy documents of the EU institutions" (2017, p. 294). Hence long-term concerns that had some *sui generis* importance – such as the gender wage gaps – became matters of economic inefficiency, productivity and under-utilization of women's human capital.[21]

The European Institute for Gender Equality has been making a similar economic case, for example, by publishing a number of reports investigating this (e.g. European Institute for Gender Equality, 2017d). Closing the activity rate gap, they estimate, will provide an increase of between 3.5 million and 6 million jobs in 2050 as a result of additional women entering

---

[20] The OECD (2018) has also taken up this approach. Its *Is the Last Mile the Longest?* (produced in association with the Nordic Council of Ministers) makes the case for gender equality by attempting to calculate how past improvements in gender equality (specifically women's employment rate) in Denmark, Iceland, Norway and Sweden have led to GDP growth. Their estimates of the contribution are between 10 and 20 per cent. It is acknowledged that future growth in female employment rates will have a smaller yield. Given this, the suggestion is that the next stage should focus on closing gender gaps in hours worked.

[21] This trend is much wider than the EU. See the special section in the *Canadian Journal of Development Economics*, 38, 4, 2017 for an analysis and critique of economic efficiency as an argument for gender equality in a developmental context. See also Prügl (2017) for an analysis of how the World Bank is promoting gender equality for the purposes of economic growth, a change in policy from seeing gender equality as an outcome of growth to an enabler.

the labour force. GDP per capita is estimated to increase by 0.8–1.5 per cent in 2030 and by 3.2–5.5 per cent in 2050 (an increase in GDP of up to EUR280 billion by 2030 and up to EUR1.490 billion by 2050). Depending on a woman's educational level, the cost of exclusion from the labour market throughout the working life is estimated at between EUR1.2 million and EUR2 million (Eurofound, 2016). Chant and Sweetman (2012), looking more broadly to a world developmental context, term this approach 'smart economics'. One can see Elomäki's point here – women and gender equality become objects, their potential needing to be 'tapped' or exploited and the benefits of this sold to the policy community.

6.4   CONCLUSION

This chapter has shown that the EU trained the spotlight centrally on gender inequality for quite a long period and developed and applied different approaches to address it. Of these, legal regulation on equality in social security rights and employment conditions and a very different approach – gender mainstreaming – have been the most consequential. Gender's star has faded though in the last 15 years or so, especially if one drills down below the discourse into the measures that are promoted. The approach has changed to one of anti-discrimination on the one hand (with gender one of a number of other grounds) and a focus on promoting gender equality for its economic growth benefits on the other. While gender mainstreaming is still talked about and promoted, as Jane Jenson (2015) has said, the EU has some very strong diagnoses but rather weak policies. Gender equality has lost political momentum – there is a sense in which the challenge feels dated, the achievements are good enough to be getting on with and other considerations seem more urgent.

At root there is disappointment among feminist circles about the EU's commitment and approach to gender inequality. One criticism made in relation to gender mainstreaming is that it has been implemented in an integrationist rather than agenda-setting way (Pollack and Hafner-Burton, 2000, p. 452). The underlying set of insights here comes from Rees (1998) and Jahan (1995) to the effect that an integrationist approach does not challenge existing policy paradigms, whereas agenda setting involves a fundamental rethinking of the procedures but especially the ends and goals. Against this backdrop, some such as Kantola (2015) and Jacquot (2015) are calling for a regrounding of equality policy in economic policy rather than in anti-discrimination policy.

One could argue at length about the appropriate conceptualizations of equality – and the relative success of EU and other types of equality policy – but one of the most significant implications of treating equality as a multi-layered concept is that equality of access becomes an essential first step towards a higher-order equality. The EU recognized access problems in social benefits and took important steps in granting women equal access to social security benefits but it adopted a narrow, anti-discrimination approach and limited the remit to social security benefits. Such sex-neutral rules are important but they are not sufficient, mainly because they do not intervene enough to change the structures which perpetuate inequality and they may even reinforce the underlying sources of inequality.[22] We have seen in Chapter 4, for example, that greater numbers of women have access to the labour market but that sex segregation within and across jobs and occupations remains. There are at least two other types of response. One possible strategy is to change the conditions of accessing and receiving benefits, services and jobs that especially disadvantage women. This is in a sense a strategy to render the welfare and jobs systems more 'women friendly' and as a basis of reform it goes beyond the sex neutral or anti-discrimination strategy by involving the reformulation of the conditions of access and entitlement so as to make them more favourable than they were to women. There are major shortcomings of this approach to equality also, not least its grafting of reforms onto a system that remains fundamentally unchanged. A further strategy is more expansive in that it involves the recognition of (women's) unpaid caring work for benefit and public support purposes more broadly. Here the principle of care is incorporated into the social policy system so that undertaking this type of activity becomes a basis of entitlement. There has been movement towards this as we shall see in Chapter 7. While recognizing women's unpaid work for benefit support purposes may be underpinned by principles around female economic agency, they run the risk of further institutionalizing the sexual division of labour and of reinforcing caring as a female activity. A yet further strategy individualizes benefit entitlement and taxation provisions so that people secure entitlement independently of their family or household relations and status. Individualization of benefits represents a fundamental structural change in the benefit systems of the majority of member states. This is a good basis on which to start the explorations of the next chapter.

---

[22]   In addition as Sainsbury (1993, p. 16) points out, such reforms, in giving the impression that equality is being or has been taken care of, divert attention away from addressing the underlying factors creating female dependence and gender inequality.

7.   Gender and social policy more broadly

This chapter shifts the discussion, not just by moving from the EU level to that of the member states but also by considering gender and social policy in a more broad-ranging way. Chapter 6 indicated that women cannot expect equality policy from the EU. But this does not exhaust the policies (or politics) in play. This is not just because the national member states are more important and powerful actors in social policy than the EU but because 'equality policy' encompasses but a part of the relevant policy landscape. There are other visions and policy fields that directly or indirectly seek to influence women's and men's access to resources and the ways they organize their lives. Mindful of a point made earlier (in Chapter 2) about not being too policy-led (in the sense of directing attention to those areas of policy which are explicitly about gender), this chapter defines the relevant policy universe beyond whether gender equality is part of the nomenclature and target set of policy or not. I foreground the question of what kind of claims women and men can make on the state and on what basis. In the latter regard especially, the age-old question of the role and place of the family in policy endures.

We have seen from Chapter 6 (and also from Chapter 2) that reform towards gender equality in earlier decades functioned to rid the benefit system of sex discrimination (both direct and indirect). These reforms mainly concentrated on eliminating direct discrimination. But there were some relevant measures aimed at addressing indirect discrimination also. For example, women began to be treated as individuals in their own right rather than as 'dependants' of their husbands for some taxes and benefits (Land, 2011; Bennett and Daly, 2014). If not discrimination, then what is left? Feminist analysis suggests assumptions around and incentives/disincentives towards or away from certain kinds of activities in both 'public' and 'private' life, continuing a tradition in Europe of finding public solutions to issues in private life and utilizing the power of government to socialize some of the costs (Gornick and Meyers, 2003). This enjoins us to look at policy somewhat more obliquely, especially at policy's response to care giving and care receiving which, as we know from the preceding chapters, is one of the fields of most importance for gender relations and gender inequality. Outside the home as well as inside it – and across societies – women tend to be given and assume responsibility for care giving and family/work organization and they often carry this load without much recognition or support. We need to be conscious throughout, therefore, of the way gender assumptions and divisions around care are built into and underpin policy and provision and that these may come in diverse forms.

The chapter is organized as follows. The first part devotes attention to two important policy frames or rubrics: work–life balance and social investment. Subsequent sections of the chapter analyse the policy reforms that have sprung from these and other dominant considerations, examining in turn measures investing in parenting, in childcare and in care for older people. As with the other chapters, a short summary/overview draws the chapter to a close.

7.1 CONTEMPORARY POLICY FRAMES

One of the hallmarks of social policy in Europe today is the promotion of a more differentiated life course model as compared with the past. Social policy has always been focused on securing particular periods of the life course – in particular differentiating between being under and over working age and seeing the latter as a period necessitating income-smoothing measures especially (Falkingham and Hills, 1995). But nowadays, as well as the post-employment period, social policy is actively concerned with the earliest phase of life; the early education and care of very young children is of increasing interest along with the resourcing of the youngest phases of life more generally. There is both a more general focus on children's development and a greater differentiation of childhood into particular phases or stages (Daly, 2019). In addition, supporting the 'working periods of life' is foregrounded. Concerns about fertility play a role here. Two main discourses articulated by policy take these interests forward: work–life balance and social investment. Both have great significance for women and gender, although in my view neither is explicitly oriented to gender equality. Notably, these perspectives are multi-purpose and multi-functional. We will consider each briefly in turn before moving on to the policy constellation (of reforms) that is being spearheaded in their name and related considerations.

7.1.1 Work–life Balance

Work–life balance – a rather anodyne term which has become a wide-ranging policy rubric at EU level – was coined to represent the challenge for contemporary policy as one of managing the intersection between unpaid and paid work on the one hand and the accommodation of family life with labour market exigencies on the other (Lewis, 2009). A number of issues and concerns are bundled into this frame: demographic decline, the quality of family life, the role of both employment and family as contributing to social integration, and gender equality in an era when women's lives are becoming more like those of men. The term has a strong micro-level set of references. Individual women's (and increasingly men's) relative poverty of agency in regard to both employment and family is viewed as a problem – the rhetoric is of choice and positive choice around work and family life whereby both are rendered possible for women and to a lesser extent men. There are elements of what Rottenberg (2018, p. 171) calls 'the mobilization of affect', whereby a positive cognitive state, such as the pursuit of happiness, is to be aimed for and achieved by people changing their attitudes and behaviour so as to create a felicitous balance between public and private aspects of the self.[1] While she uses this term especially to illuminate the discourse of prominent elite women in the US, one can see the appeal to culture and emotional plane inhering also in some of the policy rhetoric around work–life balance in Europe. This leads work–life balance policies to seek to enable people to realize their plans to have children at the time of their choosing and to organize their lives in a manner that allows them to engage in both employment and family life (Adema, 2012, p. 489). Quality of life, and to some extent also quality of care, are inherent to it with the task for policy to 'soften' the intersections of public and family life. Calibrating policies from different spheres is called for. Underpinning the concept, in part anyway, is a desire to put back together a sense of collective life and especially prevent family life from becoming fragmented by the labour market and other demands. This discourse prioritizes families with children for intervention and support (rather than adults requiring care – although the EU is increasingly interested in the latter with the right to affordable long-term care services of good quality

---

[1] For Rottenberg this marks the beginnings of a reorientation of the liberal feminist discursive field away from notions of freedom, equal rights and social justice towards the importance of well-roundedness and well-being (2018, p. 28).

one of 20 principles enunciated in the European Pillar of Social Rights[2]). Power is not part of the balance emphasis.

As the use of the term 'reconciling' implies, reconciliation of work and family life is about more than the behaviour of individuals however. It is also directed at harmonization at a more macro level, of the institutions of market, family and state. Quite a sociological set of references underpins it. As it has been taken up by policy the problem has been interpreted in terms of poor synchronization between the main institutions patterning family and work life. The perceived solution, therefore, is to harmonize the rhythms and timings of family life with those of employment, and especially reduce the incompatibility between motherhood (and to a lesser extent fatherhood) and paid work, and rebalance the distribution of care activities within the family and between the family and other institutions (Lewis, 2009; Hobson, 2014). As a policy rubric, the work–life balance perspective has given the state licence to intervene in the rather fine details of family life, and in the process to shift the understanding of what is considered 'public' and 'private'. In particular, we see ongoing development and repurposing of maternity, paternity and parental leave provisions and general moves towards more flexible employment schedules as well as the provision of public services. There is a call for greater flexibility in the scheduling of paid work generally.

For feminists, equality in the distribution of paid and unpaid work is a bellwether of gender inequality; in the work–life balance frame equality per se is not necessarily the goal – as implied by the term 'balance' (one might even think that gender equality requires some imbalancing of the status quo). But there is a general recognition in it that a more equal balance of family-related responsibilities is necessary if women are to be able to be in the labour market in the numbers and to the degree desired. Hence, there are resonances in the work–life balance policy endeavour of a broader understanding of 'equality', or at least a sense that paid work intertwines with unpaid work and that egalitarianism in aspects of 'family life' is a legitimate policy focus. What is meant here particularly is the idea of (better) sharing between partners of the tasks associated with family life – especially those linked to child-rearing. The latter has been a high-level goal especially on the part of the EU which is a leader in the field of promoting a work–life balance frame for policy (Knijn and Smit, 2009). In such work–life balance policies, the primary 'good' for redistribution is time (with access to income as a more dormant consideration) with the more inchoate 'opportunities' signalling potential for a 'career employment'

---

[2] See https://ec.europa.eu/commission/priorities/deeper-and-fairer-economic-and-mon etary-union/european-pillar-social-rights/european-pillar-social-rights-20-principles_en.

trajectory as compared simply with employment. The frame also elevates services as a vital part of the supportive policy package. Feminist scholarship, of course, takes a much broader and deeper view, holding that we have to look at the lives of women and men in the round and that 'unpaid work' not only makes paid work possible but has a profound emotional and social register as well as an economic one (it is the latter that dominates the policy discussions). Such interdependence exists not just at the micro level but also at macro level (in terms of the distribution of responsibilities between and respective contributions of different institutional spheres).

7.1.2 Social Investment

As mentioned, European welfare states have long understood part of the task of social policy as being to manage the life course – they do this through defining and organizing support for particular events, phases, episodes and transitions (Leisering and Leibfried, 1999). The labour market has a key role here as well and in fact it is the interaction between the state and the labour market that is posited as so influential of outcomes in people's lives. The strategy plays out at a number of different levels. First, it helps to frame the very definition of stages of life (e.g. childhood, adulthood, old age); second, it influences the connections between these three standard phases of life and smooths the transition between phases; third, it affects people's life course by reinforcing particular normative models about appropriate behaviour and gainful activity at different periods of the life course. The social investment perspective – which is a dominant frame in the current rethinking and reanalysis of the welfare state in Europe – also prioritizes the distribution of resources across age groups. In representing the old welfare state frame as 'passive' and 'outmoded' in its preference for a male breadwinner model, this perspective seeks especially to reform the welfare state through better resourcing of the youngest age groups and a better balance between productive and unproductive (or so-called 'passive') redistribution (Jenson and Saint-Martin, 2006; Esping-Andersen, 2009; European Commission, 2010b). In its most expansive version in academic work, the philosophy underpinning social investment is said to focus on three main social policy functions: (i) the creation of capacities, which involves a shift in policy from an exclusive focus on present costs to a focus on current and future impacts; (ii) addressing social risks within life course dynamics, which involves a move from a clear-cut divide between those who pay and those who are recipients of welfare provision to a vision of contemporary social reality where individuals change status in different phases of their lives; and (iii) the reconciliation of work and family life (Hemerijck, 2017).

This perspective and view of social policy's functions has been subjected to critical scrutiny from a gender perspective, with questions raised especially about what the key goals of the policy are and whether gender inequality is centrally addressed (as against what might be called 'coincidental outcomes'). Chiara Saraceno (2015), amongst others, has pointed out that the perspective does not value women's participation in the labour market or gender equality in their own right (even if it has a view of these as outcomes). Rather, these are sought for their investment yield (similar to what we have seen regarding gender equality as a goal of policy in the EU in Chapter 6). Saraceno reserves particular criticism for the fact that the perspective fails to understand – and offer terms to deal with – the devaluing of care and other non-market-oriented activities.

We now look at the kinds of policies that have emerged from these and other rubrics, mindful that they set a general discursive context rather than being fully realized in contemporary European welfare states and that whatever changes are introduced they take place within national patterning, history and priorities.

7.2 EMERGING POLICY CONSTELLATIONS

As mentioned, both work–life balance and social investment turn the spotlight on parents and their chances and capacities for both child-rearing and employment. Leaves from employment are a primary policy mechanism for this purpose. A second emphasis is on the early welfare and development of young children – taken forward especially by changes in policy and provision on early childhood education and care (ECEC). This is located in a macro context of the information economy, future skill needs, and demographic changes (see Barcelona European Council, 2002; Mahon, 2010). Thirdly, there is the matter of care for older people, which is increasingly coming to be seen – especially within EU circles – as a matter of work–life balance.

7.2.1   Investment in Parents and Parenting

Of the different types of leave, maternity leave is the oldest in Europe and in fact in some countries was part of the foundational welfare state architecture. First introduced in the last decades of the nineteenth century, by the eve of the Second World War all developed countries, except for Canada and the US, had adopted some form of maternity leave (Gauthier, 1996, p. 50). In the following decades it developed apace but in the last 20–30 years (and longer in some countries) it has been accompanied by two other types of leave – parental leave and paternity leave. It is the latter two that have been the focus of policy reform and change over the last decades in Europe, with maternity leave more or less in a state of stasis. The thrust is to increase the length of both parental and paternity leave. Between 1980 and 2005 the average duration of paid parental leave increased from 18 to 53.6 weeks and the replacement rate went up considerably also – from 11.3 per cent to 30.9 per cent of the OECD's Average Production Worker's wage (Daly and Ferragina, 2018).[3] These are very strong movements, reflecting strong pressures. But there is considerable national and regional variation also. In regard to parental leave, for example, countries differ in whether they prioritized duration per se or financial compensation in the terms of the number of weeks of paid leave. Austria, Germany, Greece, Ireland, Italy, the Netherlands, Portugal, Spain and the UK tended to prioritize the unpaid route, whereas Finland, France, Luxembourg and Sweden significantly increased both over the last decades.

Paternity leave is another major development. However, in comparison to parental leave it is short. By 2015 the average duration of paid leave across 23 OECD countries studied by Daly and Ferragina was only 0.9 weeks. Looking at the patterns over time the forerunner countries in this regard in the EU are Belgium, Luxembourg, Spain and Sweden. A sizeable number of EU member states have no (paid or unpaid) paternity leave: Austria, Germany and Ireland. Overall though, the thrust of policy is to increase the duration of paternity leave, to make a part of it paid, and to introduce either bonuses or penalties to encourage fathers to take the leave (Moss, 2012; Keck and Saraceno, 2013). But paternity leave does not reflect fully social policy's reframing of the respective entitlements and roles of fatherhood and motherhood. One also has to consider the redistribution of leave between parents and in particular developments reserving a period of leave for the father within the overall leave period. This is a source of considerable policy innovation. In terms of the number of paid weeks for the father, for example, between 1990 and 2005 the average level went from 0.2 weeks to 4.9, and reached 9.4 weeks in 2015 (Daly and Ferragina, 2018).

The policy changes suggest, then, that the practice as well as the responsibilities of fathers is in the sights of policy. It is not uncommon any longer for fathers to be given entitlement to part of the period of maternity leave (e.g. Spain and the UK are just two countries where this

---

[3]   This is on the basis of an analysis of the following 23 countries: Australia, Austria, Belgium, Canada, Denmark, Finland, France, Germany, Greece, Iceland, Ireland, Italy, Japan, Luxembourg, the Netherlands, New Zealand, Norway, Portugal, Spain, Sweden, Switzerland, the UK and the US.

has happened). An even more suggestive example of a policy that seeks to activate and reconstruct the practice of fatherhood is the 'father's quota' introduced in Norway and Sweden during the 1990s. This measure sets aside a certain proportion of parental leave specifically for the father which, as a mandated period, is lost to the family if he does not take it. The significance of the change in the view of the father role should not be underestimated. Whereas fathers have always been expected to provide income for their families, fatherhood in some European countries today is also defined around providing care (or, rather, demonstrating a readiness to care). Moreover, it seems to be accepted that it is a legitimate role for public policy to encourage fathers to care. Hence, as law is becoming less regulatory (in its treatment of divorce for example – see Lewis, 2001), social policy appears to be increasingly regulatory. However, it is important not to get carried away by what is a minority practice.

Castro-García and Pazod-Moran (2016) closely examine the incentives and disincentives in the parenting-related leave schemes for engagement by mothers and fathers and suggest that their 21 (mainly EU) country cases can be divided into three groupings. The first consists of countries that promote co-responsibility between parents (all Nordic countries plus Portugal – non-transferability and high replacement levels are the critical policy dimension here); countries that consider men to be incidental collaborators in childcare (Belgium, Denmark, Finland, France, Germany, Slovenia and Spain), and countries that reinforce the gendered division of labour (Austria, Czech Republic, Greece, Hungary, Ireland, Italy, the Netherlands and the UK). Note that this relates to provisions in 2010 and so does not encapsulate changes since; some of these countries have introduced more generous leaves for fathers since. However, countries tend to have reformed by type (apart from Spain which has moved to equalize access to all leaves for mothers and fathers). Iceland is generally seen to be in the vanguard on equal parenting rights and incentives, with three months of leave each for the mother, the father and the couple.

Actually when one probes the conditions attaching to the leaves in more detail, it is clear that it is a 'light touch' fatherhood compared to a more profound mothering role that they encourage. Hence, one could liken paternity leave to a symbolic measure – a mildly positive, cultural suggestion. The reforms are not fundamental to the business of altering the genders in family relationships. Women's roles are as much the subject of reconstruction by social policy as are those of fathers. For if the policies incentivize fathers to take leave but there is no overall extension of the leave, then they are changing the incentives for mothers also. We can see this especially in the policies for women parenting alone. Whereas by the 1970s the family of a lone woman and her child(ren) appeared to have established a legitimate claim on public resources in many countries in the EU when her children were young, welfare states are now drawing back from this commitment, with employment activation seen as appropriate for mothers of young children (especially in Ireland, the Netherlands and the UK). As this process is played out in relation to lone-mother families, caring for children as a full-time component of motherhood is increasingly delegitimized.

One lesson that appears to have been learned is around the impact of the length of maternity leaves in that leaves of long duration act as a labour market disincentive for mothers. The bulk of the evidence suggests that a 'short parental leave' – between 20 and 30 weeks – seems to be associated with positive effects on mothers' employability and career chances, while long leaves appear to incentivize labour market withdrawal (Pettit and Hook, 2005; Del Boca et al., 2009; Akgunduz and Plantenga, 2013; Boeckmann et al., 2015).[4] The fact that policies are turning away from long leaves for mothers underlines the currency of the core principles of work–life balance.

There is no one interpretation of these and other developments, however. As Lang (2015) has pointed out, the parental leave reforms take forward and interconnect a complex configuration of concerns: a more equal division of parental leave, children's rights to care by both parents, women's labour market participation, and men's care-giving responsibilities. The tendency, therefore, is to construct gender equality as based on sameness, in terms of a type of dual earner/dual carer model. Lang also points out that the different policy solutions that exist in order to promote equality in parenthood problematize this either as an issue of structure, or as an issue of agency, which results in each of the solutions failing to problematize the other side of the structure/agency dichotomy (Lang, 2015).

7.2.2   Investment in Children

A primary focus of investment has been in ECEC. There is evidence of a strong international trend towards improving access for children to out-of-home education and care services. The fact that this orientation is being applied to young children (that is, those under 3 years of age) is another significant development.

There have been three main changes in childcare policy and provision. First, there has been a large growth in childcare provision. This is visible at EU level especially from the early 2000s, coinciding with the EU's setting

---

[4]   In the analyses by Budig et al. (2016), this is leave which is of over three years' duration.

the Barcelona Targets in childcare in 2002. These aimed for the following numerical targets of children in childcare to be achieved by 2010: at least 90 per cent of children between 3 years old and the mandatory school age and at least 33 per cent of children under 3 years of age (Barcelona European Council, 2002). In the inaugural document and discourse, these were framed as a good way to reduce barriers to maternal employment. The latest update on the targets takes a very different approach, emphasizing along with maternal employment developing the cognitive and social abilities of pre-school children and strengthening the social inclusion of children from disadvantaged backgrounds (European Commission, 2018). The evidence on policy roll-out in the member states shows that, while the target for the older age group is not problematic, progress on the target for the youngest children has been slow, although it has been reached for the EU as a whole on the latest evidence presented (for 2016) (European Commission, 2018). In terms of national and regional patterns, the Nordic countries were and continue to be forerunners, but not to an equal degree. With some 70 per cent of children under 3 in ECEC, Denmark is the frontrunner country, followed by the Netherlands, Sweden, Luxembourg, Portugal and France with around 50 per cent of the age cohort in ECEC. The low pole comprises some Central Eastern European countries (especially Slovakia, the Czech Republic and Poland) and Greece. There is considerable change over time. To pinpoint some developments at country level, Germany, Ireland, Italy, Luxembourg, Malta and Portugal are notable for the increase in the number of enrolments registered over the last five years. Greece and the UK have seen registration numbers go the other way, however.

The prioritization of children-oriented services is extremely interesting, in its own right and from a gender perspective. The discourse at EU level suggests that there is some ambivalence in whether ECEC is seen as a service for parents or children. Movement towards offering children personal guarantees is important to note as a child-focused measure – some seven EU member states now guarantee a legal right to ECEC for each child under 2 years old, often immediately after the end of parental childcare leave.[5] These are Denmark, Estonia, Finland, Germany, Latvia, Slovenia and Sweden. In most of these countries, the entitlement usually implies a full-time place. Other countries start the guarantee later. In Belgium, France, Hungary, Luxembourg, Malta, Spain and the UK, a place in publicly-subsidized ECEC is guaranteed from the age of 3 or a little earlier. So over half the EU member states grant children a right to ECEC. A somewhat different approach is to make attendance at ECEC

---

[5] See https://webgate.ec.europa.eu/fpfis/mwikis/eurydice/images/2/26/Early_Childhood_Education_and_Care_.pdf.

compulsory – for example, in Austria, Croatia, Cyprus, Greece, the Netherlands and Poland the last year of ECEC (pre-primary classes) is compulsory. These developments suggest some element of a children's rights approach. But there are limits to this. ECEC is not always a direct right to children – in some countries (e.g. Finland) it is a right given to parents and in others (Sweden) the right to full-time ECEC is conditional upon labour market engagement on the part of parents. This underlines the point that childcare-related guarantees (among other policy domains) also aim at managing both the distribution of employment among parents and maternal employment, in addition to aiding children's development.

Thinking intersectionally, one big tension is around whether there is a class gradient in the impact of ECEC-related policies from a gender perspective. There is, for example, an emerging line of analysis in the notion of a Matthew Effect which holds that the middle classes tend to be the main beneficiaries of social benefits and services (Cantillon, 2011, p. 446). When applied to childcare, such an effect would be indicated by socially-stratified participation in publicly-funded or provided childcare services in favour of higher-income groups. Although this line of research is still young, there is evidence to suggest that childcare in Europe is socially stratified and that such inequalities are hard to overcome. Van Lancker (2015), for example, examined childcare use for children aged 0–2 years by income quintile across EU countries and found that in none of the EU member states do lower-income families make greater use of childcare as compared with higher-income groups. The clear pattern is for significant gaps in favour of higher-income families and children. The UK is one of the European countries with very unevenly distributed ECEC usage by social class (along with Ireland, Luxembourg, the Netherlands and Spain). This has clear implications for gender inequality and no doubt helps to explain the differences in labour market participation by low-educated women in many countries. This is confirmed by research: one robust finding across countries is that childcare coverage and subsidies for children aged 3 years and younger seem especially vital for mothers with low education and income levels (Keck and Saraceno, 2013).

A pivotal question to pose is whether these and other developments indicate 'a new maternalism' in policy. Jenson (2015, p. 548) says that "Policy discourse that foregrounds children's needs and even rights defines women qua women primarily in terms of a maternal role." Jenson's analysis ranged wider than the EU, though, and was especially interested in the turn to conditional cash transfers in social policy more globally (Staab, 2010). In contrast to earlier forms of maternalism which made claims for women, modernized maternalism – according to Jenson – identifies motherhood and good mothering as cornerstones of economic development and societal well-being (2015, p. 548). Some components of this were examined in Chapter 6 in regard to the framing of gender equality as a potential tool of economic growth. One can certainly see some elements of this in the European policy landscape and it is in line with a social investment approach.

7.2.3 Policy on Older Care

Supporting care for older people is also part of the reform constellation but in comparison with childcare its reform tends to be more gradual and evolutionary and is rarely framed within a gender equality perspective.[6] A further comparison with childcare is also insightful: policy developments in regard to care for older people (or adults needing care more generally) are more reactive, in the sense of responding to growing and pressing need rather than driving forward particular agendas or strong visions. This might also be taken to indicate that care for children has received system recognition but care in the context of adulthood and old age has not.

What is the substance of provision today? Recent reviews (e.g. Courtin et al., 2014; Spasova et al., 2018) of these and other support policies to both carers and those needing long-term care underscore diversity and that recognition in the form of cash allowances to people providing care is not the norm. Only five of the 28 member states offer a financial payment directly to the carer: Croatia, Finland, Hungary, Ireland and the UK (Spasova et al., 2018). There does not appear to be any real move in this direction either, although more generally supportive services for carers – like respite care and information and training – are more widely available. It is far more common for EU member states to channel financial support to the person needing long-term care – this is the majority practice (although a few countries provide both types of support) and is tied to a growing trend towards personalization in the form of financial packages (Courtin et al., 2014). Four member states – Cyprus, Estonia, Latvia and Slovenia – do not provide any financial support. There is a 'choice' logic involved in the move towards personalization of benefits and the notion of care as a package (although payments for long-term care in Europe have roots in generally supporting care). This has also expedited a trend towards employing home-care help, the provider of which is quite often a migrant woman. Lutz (2008, p. 6) and others have underlined how families in Europe reconcile their work and private lives by 'outsourcing' parts of the care labour to migrant women.

---

[6] Although there is some movement on the part of the EU in this regard, especially in the context of the European Pillar of Social Rights – see Spasova et al. (2018).

Governments are subsidizing the provision of care by informal carers in other ways apart from cash payments. One policy direction is measures to encourage combining care and employment. These take various forms. They include, for example, pension credits for carers, which now exist in around half of EU member states (with no particular regional or regime patterning) and which grant credit of a period of time to the carer's working (and pension earning) record. Many of these are of long standing, with a history in offering some recognition and recompense to women (mainly) for time investment in family labour over the course of their lives. A more popular and contemporary way of linking employment with caring is through leaves from employment. We have considered these for parenthood above, but they exist also for caring for other age groups. In fact they are widespread. Only eight member states (almost all Central Eastern European or Baltic nations) have no leave in place. This type of leave is a world away from parent-related leave though in that it tends to be short term and mostly unpaid. It may also be different in another way as well, in that what it tries to do is normalize adult-related caring. The evidence confirms generally weak social rights attaching to care – these payments and entitlements are highly conditional and the official identification of informal carers and their needs is a weak point in most countries (Courtin et al., 2014, p. 88). A similar point has been made by Daly and Lewis (2000) and Knijn and Kremer (1997) who have underlined that care policy in general is characterized by a weak definition of rights as against a strong definition of responsibilities.

In a nutshell, countries are developing a mixed model approach and both out of home services and also cash for care programmes are being developed. Here too, like childcare, a balance is continually being sought between the volume of care provided privately (and especially in a familial context) and that provided by the state and the market.

What are the root tendencies? Surveying the scene in Asian and European long-term care policy, Kodate and Timonen (2017) see a (re)turn to family care and a stealthily growing role for family carers (interpreted to mean paid and unpaid carers). They identify three main channels or routes through which developments in formal home care bring about different modes of increasing, encouraging or necessitating family care across welfare states. The first is the integration of informal care into the broader care system in ways that sustain and enhance the supply of family care. A classic case here is the use of long-term care insurance – pioneered by Germany and available also in Austria, Japan and South Korea – which has not led to a decline in family care and in some countries is organized and reformed in such a way that it increases the family's involvement in care. The second way in which there is increased need for family care is somewhat more direct – the reduction or modification of formal services. Here they make reference to the rationing of formal care services, which is happening in most countries – even the Nordic ones – whereby care services are increasingly targeted at the most needy or most dependent. Thirdly, the moves to enable 'extremely flexible forms of care labour' are seen to require continued family involvement in care, in the role of care manager or purchaser, for example, or filling in for gaps. Here Kodate and Timonen make reference to the greater recourse to employed carers and even agencies which all need to be managed on the recipient side. They conclude that policies that are ostensibly about formal care often serve to enhance the centrality of family care by stealth (Kodate and Timonen, 2017, p. 8).

There is also, though, a decided movement towards the market and marketization (Simonazzi, 2009; Farris and Marchetti, 2017) in long-term care. The concept of 'marketization' is a widely used framework in this scholarship (Himmelweit, 2014). Some scholars have spoken of the 'corporatization of care' (e.g. Farris and Marchetti, 2017). However, one needs to be specific in the understanding of 'markets' and 'marketization'. There appear to be two trends involved. A first centres on increased provision of both home and institutional care by for-profit bodies, including the increasing use of paid carers by the public authorities. In both cases, the labour of migrants is often to the fore (sometimes as self-employed) (van Hooren, 2012; Williams, 2012b). A second related (but distinct) trend is a move away from institutional care as most countries are increasing the volume of home care. This is especially true of countries which have traditionally catered for elder care through a residential care model (the Scandinavian countries, the UK and France). Looked at in another light, this is a trend towards encouraging greater private provision in the form of an individual social care market (Meagher and Szebehely, 2013; León, 2014). This is linked to the first trend (in that family-based or other forms of home care are often organized through private provision) but it extends beyond it also to encourage especially greater involvement by for-profit and not-for-profit providers. The main driver here is cost but these moves can also be seen as associated with people's preferences to remain in their own homes for as long as possible. Countries are achieving this through various means – by providing more services and conventions to recognize and support carers for example (as in the UK) and through generic measures such as the adoption of new technology to prevent or delay institutionalization, and greater targeting of cash benefits or personal allowances. In England, the latter is part of a 'personalization' agenda whereby people have the option of taking charge of a sum of money and/or a set of services which can be oriented towards their own needs (Glendinning, 2008).

In an examination of patterns in 14 European countries,[7] Haberkern et al. (2015) underline the importance of institutional structures as well as cultural norms for continuing or changing gender inequality in regard to the provision of older age care. Gender inequalities in informal care provision are highest in countries with a high level of intergenerational care, high public spending on old age cash benefits, and a low provision of professional care services (inter alia). Da Roit et al. (2015) undertook an analysis to explain the gendered gap in informal caring, exploring the effect of four explanatory factors (care policies, problem pressure, labour market characteristics and gendered norms) in 13 European countries.[8] They found that women's labour market position and gendered care-related norms do not play a significant role in the production of a gender informal care gap in the countries analysed. What seems crucial is the relative presence or absence of public care services aimed at care-needing elderly. This factor – which was constructed by the researchers to encompass levels of expenditure on long-term care services as a proportion of GDP and the proportion of the population aged 65 and over using care services – was found to play a crucial role in all the paths to a gender gap in informal care, or its opposite. Hence, the authors conclude that both cash and care services are vitally important, although they sometimes work in opposite directions from a gender equality perspective. Furthermore, it is not just the presence of services but their volume and conditions of entitlement that make the most difference from a gender perspective.

This kind of development contributes significantly to the growth of a care market and to the private servicing of those needing care by employed care workers. There is a move to 'out-sourcing' or contracting-out of services formerly provided by the local authorities or municipalities (Estévez-Abe and Hobson, 2015; Morel, 2015). States support this often indirectly and in this regard migration policy and employment policy have been drawn to the fore of both policy making and policy analyses. One important factor conditioning what states do, for example, is the availability of and attitude towards (female) migrant labour. This is especially the 'solution' favoured in relation to the care of the elderly – it has become an alternative to institutional care in some countries (especially those in the Mediterranean region). So widespread is this in certain parts of Europe that the concept of the care mix might need to be extended to incorporate migrants as another 'partner'. Bettio et al. (2006) suggest that migrant

---

[7]   Austria, Belgium, Czech Republic, Denmark, France, Germany, Greece, Ireland, Italy, the Netherlands, Poland, Spain, Sweden, Switzerland.
[8]   Austria, Belgium, Czech Republic, Denmark, France, Germany, Greece, Ireland, Italy, Poland, Spain, Sweden, Switzerland.

workers help to ease reconciliation of work and family life as well as filling a widening gap, especially in regard to costs and public funding, between family care and professional care. They also, given generally low wages, strike a balance between the conflicting needs of publicly supporting care of the elderly and controlling public expenditure. One of the main messages of this work is a need to broaden the paradigm (see Razavi, 2011; Yeates, 2011). This would mean especially conceiving of care as part of not just a gender and care regime but also a migration regime and in turn recognizing that practices and conditions in parts of the world which appear remote from each other are actually very closely connected (Rodrigues et al., 2012).

The linking of care with the reproduction and circulation of the labour force in the global economy set in a broader context shows how the reorganization of gender is connected to the global strategy of capitalism (Verschuur, 2013, p. 146), not only in its neoliberal impulses but also its colonial constitution (de los Reyes, 2016, p. 40).

7.3   CONCLUSIONS

One of the messages from this chapter is that we have to look for new categories and policy developments but must always enquire or be open to the possibility that these are old categories recycled. Just as the scale, volume and contribution of care-giving are hidden, so too are many of the costs of inequalities in associated responsibilities. Pettit and Hook (2009, p. 170) concluded their cross-national study by saying that they struggled to identify even one country where women can have children without risking their economic fortunes. It is important to be explicit about these costs, both for individual women and men, and societies. In a more global context, Elson (2008, 2017) has suggested that policy in relation to care (and reproductive work more generally) should seek to recognize, reduce and redistribute care. Any progress in any of these regards in Europe is slow, especially in long-term care, although policy is targeting some redistribution of childcare from the family to extra-home care and one might say that there is increasing recognition of care, although not in a strong rights-based modality. That said, children's right to ECEC is an exceptional development to note. This is conceived as education more than care though – and indeed to generalize it states have had to reimagine childcare as education.

To sum up, there is a new familialism in place in Europe which is characterized by:

- A partial politicization of fatherhood for policy purposes, such that fatherhood is now a focus of political engagement. The 'problem' as policy sees it is to get men more involved and active in the rearing of their children and the main way of doing that is not through major redistributive or other structural/cultural change measures but a mild set of incentives oriented to cultural change.
- Women are being repositioned between family and work. The 'problem' here is constructed as one of getting women more active in paid work and somewhat less active in the rearing of their children. As Pfau-Effinger (2005, p. 325) has said, there has been a change in values such that a new type of home-caring mother is emerging. In place of the housewife model of the family, home care is now a transitional stage of women's life course, with new patterns of sequential or actual combinations of formal employment and informal care being promoted.
- A further repositioning is also taking place: as well as a rearrangement of family and work in the lives of individual women and men, family-related functions and agency are being refashioned vis-à-vis those of the state and market. Some individualization of benefits and services has taken place but there have been counter-tendencies in the direction of recognizing care provision in what seems to be a continuous round of reforms that lead states to put a brake on the extent to which care moves away from the family and individuals, women especially, move away from their care responsibilities.
- Policy concern with the family as an institution or structure remains, although the degree of support for a traditional family form is declining in most places (bar some of the Central Eastern European countries) and it is now the characteristics of the family as an economic unit and to some extent also a type of emotional investment (rather than a physical or organizational arrangement) that dominate. Hence, state policies continue to reproduce family responsibilities and labour, but they do so in somewhat different ways as compared with the past and arguably also more directly (in the sense, for example, of a greater degree of regulation of child-rearing and the employment-related behaviours of adult family members) (Papadopoulos and Roumpakis, 2019). The notion that family policy may now have a more instrumentalist, economic cast – as against resourcing the family as having moral authority (which was true especially in some of the Continental European countries in the past) – is also worth considering.

Saraceno (2015, p. 266) concludes: "Having family responsibilities continues to divide the opportunities of men and women even in the societies that are closest to the ideal model underpinning the social investment approach."

8. Scoping a future research agenda

This concluding chapter reflects upon and fleshes out a future research agenda. As interpreted here, such an agenda centres around identifying penetrating themes and questions meriting further reflection and study, rather than aiming for a definitive theoretical or empirical framework. The latter risks becoming too fixed, especially in a context of rapid – and sometimes unexpected – change. Hence, the aim is to provide reflection about and building blocks for a programme for future research, through identifying important concepts, lines of analysis and pertinent questions.

As I near the end of the book, it is helpful to recall the main questions posed: How do women's and men's situations compare and what role does social policy play in affecting these and shaping gender patterns? What are the different ways of addressing gender inequality in social policy and with what results? How is the intersection of gender with other inequalities managed, reproduced or changed by social policy? This chapter is divided into two main parts. The first recalls the main findings and highlights insights from the discussion and analysis in the preceding chapters, while the second part focuses attention on configuring a research agenda. An outline set of research questions brings the chapter to a close.

8.1 WHAT HAS BEEN HAPPENING IN PRACTICE?

In line with other work, the analysis undertaken underscores the uneven – asymmetrical even – nature of gender change (Pettit and Hook, 2009; England, 2010; Charles, 2011; Cooke, 2011). It is clear that women's lives have altered significantly, and those of men to a lesser degree. In particular, more women are in the labour market and a greater number have access to some income of their own. These kinds of changes are both reflected in and causal to an increase in dual earner households, which is now the dominant household arrangement among couples with children in the EU as a whole (again mainly because of changes made by women). But it is also obvious that speaking of women and men as global categories is inappropriate in light of the significant differences found between and within population sectors. In this regard, the role of family situation (allied with the varying effects of age or life course stage) together with the influence of socio-economic and ethnic group differences stand out. And, of course, national variations dissect the global picture also. I was unable to explore each of the variations – mainly due to data shortages but also because of the scale of the task – but the analyses undertaken leave no doubt about disparities in the experiences and opportunities available to different groups of women (and presumably men). It is important also to remind ourselves that, often when we speak about change and improvement, these tend to be read from the template of the lives of highly-educated, ethnic majority women (thereby also running the risk of over-estimating the degree of change).

Asymmetry also applies in another way. The degree or depth of change varies depending on which of the three spheres one has in focus. However, within this broader systemic asymmetry there is one symmetrical pattern: in the 'private sphere' of family life gender-segregated workloads and responsibilities are both widespread and resilient. A gendered division of family labour lives on despite increasing female employment and move-ments in class, racial and other lines of division (see also Cooke, 2011). There is a germinal insight about change here: that it is not taking the form of across-the-board degendering of social institutions but, rather, occurring through "processes of partial, domain-specific equalization" (Charles, 2011, p. 357). This is reflected in the outcome data reviewed, and specifically the equality scores (as measured by the Gender Equality Index). Of the three main dimensions considered – income, employment and time – any improvements in gender gaps have been driven by increases in women's employment participation and their level of financial resources. But these (rather global) indicators co-exist with little or no improvement over the last decade in gender gaps in overall economic situation, time expenditure (whether time on caring or social activities is the focus) or segregation in and quality of employment. As a result, the overall Gender Equality Index for the EU as a whole improved by just 4.2 percentage points in the ten years between 2005 and 2015, standing at 66.2 out of 100 in 2015 (European Institute for Gender Equality, 2017a).

Another asymmetric element relates to cross-national variation. The evidence confirms continued variation across countries. Again, to take the Gender Equality Index as a convenient summarizing measure, the overall gender gap in 2015 varied from a low of 50 in Greece to a high of 82.6 in Sweden. Relatively strong regional groupings prevail, especially at the extremes. The Nordic and Continental European countries together with Ireland and the UK tend to be at or above the EU average on the global equality indicator whereas the lowest equality scores are concentrated in the Baltic, Central Eastern European and Mediterranean nations. In the

Baltic and Central European countries especially, high levels of full-time, female and male employment co-exist with significant gender inequality in unpaid work. While the gaps have narrowed in some of the countries (especially Cyprus, Estonia, Italy and Slovenia) over the ten-year period covered by the Index, regional gaps and groupings generally persisted. The fact that the overall gap between the lowest and the highest countries was of a generally similar magnitude in 2015 as it was in 2005 (around 30 percentage points) suggests two things. The first is that countries vary in terms of the scale of gender inequality and that gaps are resilient (given that the ordering and relative placing of countries was generally similar in the two periods). Second, progress overall in reducing variation is rather minimal – a small number of countries made little or no progress over the ten-year period (European Institute for Gender Equality, 2017a, pp. 7–9). These include the Czech Republic, Slovakia and the UK as well as Finland, Hungary and Lithuania. Taken together, these results suggest that we may have to revise our understanding and expectation of change as gradual and progressive, and be open to the possibility of stalling and of structural limits to progress, in the sense of equality thrusts plateauing out.

The variation leads me to suggest that, taking account of the three types of resource considered here and the general policy approach, there are four main routes or patterns to gender equality in the EU at the present time. The first is 'equality mainly through the market' whereby women from all backgrounds have high labour market attachment and this is usually on a full-time basis. High public 'equality' coexists with high private inequality, however, for the division of labour in families is highly unequal with women carrying out most of the labour, as policy generally looks on but does not intervene. The Central Eastern European and Baltic countries, taken as a bloc (and of course there are exceptions), approximate this pattern as does Portugal. These countries are an interesting example of high female labour market participation without divided labour markets in terms of pay and segregation or female participation patterns riven by class (as Pettit and Hook, 2009, suggest is more generally the case). However, inequalities in unpaid work are strong and resilient, and poverty is more widespread than in the Nordic countries. The second route could be described as 'balanced equality in the public and private spheres' – employment patterns of mothers of young children are different to those of other women and men (lower rates, more part-time work) but the gender division of unpaid work is less than it is in the first route. This option is available to highly-educated women in most countries but it is really only in the Nordic countries (albeit with significant national differences) that it is widely available. These countries still provide the best-case scenario for dual income/dual caregiver outcomes (see also Morgan, 2009) and, speaking generally, they show the least inequality on the three dimensions considered. Public policies make a strong attempt at equalization across spheres. But it must be emphasized that this regional grouping breaks down once one starts to probe deeply, especially in regard to the relationships between mothers and the labour market. A third route is 'part-time equality' – whereby part-time work provides the pathway into employment for mothers. This is a pattern of limited equality across income, employment and time as a traditional division of labour in the home persists. It may not even be a half-way house towards equality. This pattern conjoins some of the Continental European countries (Austria and Germany, the Netherlands) with Ireland and the UK. Policy is not strongly committed to equality in the division of unpaid work. Fourthly, there is a pattern of 'selective but low-grade equality' for women – highly-educated women are in the labour market often on a full-time basis whereas women from other educational backgrounds tend to be home-based and large inequalities in unpaid work prevail across the board. Policy more or less fails to problematize gender inequality. Some national exemplars here include Cyprus, Italy and Malta.

This gives rise to two questions: Why has change been so uneven within and across countries? And why has it stalled in some?

My interest inheres in the role of social policy in relation to these and other questions. The legacy (both real life and academic) from the earlier periods highlighted that women have a relationship to and form of dependence upon the welfare state quite different to that of men, with the implications playing out in both micro everyday processes of life organization and more macro-level patterning and structuring. There is little to suggest that this gender-specific relationship pattern has changed significantly. If we think policy should have done better – and there is no reason to exonerate it of that responsibility – the review of policy undertaken showed three main policy-related factors that help explain the outcomes: policy has been selective in terms of which aspects of gender inequality have been targeted; the priority accorded to gender inequality has varied (especially at EU level which was the main locus considered for equality policy); and some of the prevailing social policy orientations and politics now sideline gender inequality as a problem or policy focus. And, in a fourth factor, policy equivocation reflects societal variations and ambivalence. For the European landscape is marked by continuing public support for maternal care of babies and young children in some quarters and systematic differences between the associated moral economy (the norms) and political economy (in terms of where the costs are borne) in others (Shalev, 2009).

In regard to the first, increases in women's involvement in the labour force and higher personal income for women (with the latter secondary to the former) have been prominent policy priorities, 'rounded out' by appeals to work–life balance. A rather innovative 'policy playbook' is adopted: paternity and maternity leave, parental leave, ECEC and better support for informal care of adults requiring care (through income and services). A result is a closer relationship now as compared with the past between employment/labour policies and social/family-related policy with the care-giving aspects of family relationships to the fore. 'Fathers' and 'parents' are more present as a focus of policy and more of young children's care is external to the family. However, the extent of the reforms and the gradual and piecemeal pace do not usurp women's role as mothers. The develop-ments have as yet failed to ignite substantial change in gendered patterns of parenting and there has been some correction in those countries (e.g. Sweden) which had moved strongly towards defamilialization.

Secondly, the EU, for long a leader in gender equality reform, does not treat it with the priority it once did, although rhetorically gender equal-ity is still prominent in EU discourse and gender equality programmes continue to exist. The single strongest thrust of the EU orientation over time has been its favouring of an anti-discrimination approach. This was consequential for gender between the 1970s and the 1990s especially, with a number of Directives addressing overt discrimination against women in social security systems and employment. It has also been deployed more recently to address discrimination on other grounds, especially race and disability. Gender mainstreaming – the competing social policy approach to gender inequality at EU level which targets change in the institutions and processes of policy making and seeks to generalize a concern with gender equality across the policy system – was actively pursued for a time from the 1990s but in the last ten years or so has been downgraded. It is important to note that gender mainstreaming yielded large advances in evidence and data, especially in regard to resources enabling cross-national comparisons, and in honing our understanding and assessment of 'progress'. Probably the EU's Gender Equality Index owes some of its origins to gender main-streaming, for example. Moreover, some of the ideas inherent in gender mainstreaming as an approach to policy have stuck – like a better sharing of domestic tasks and responsibilities and a 'work–life balance' – but, fatally in the views of some, they have been 'coopted' onto agendas centred upon economic and employment growth (Stratigaki, 2004, 2005). Overall, there is evidence of an economic growth rationale for equality acting to displace rationales deriving from equality, social justice and societal better-ment. Moreover, it is difficult to find leadership in gender equality policy also among the EU member states at the present time.

Third, the policy rubrics that hold court now – in particular work–life balance and social investment (both outlined in Chapter 7) – do not problematize gender equality as a policy priority (although they might view it as a beneficial effect especially if it results in higher female employment rates and – in some countries – higher fertility). These approaches tend to think in gender-neutral categories. The two-earner household is now seen to be the best chance for economic survival/prosperity. It has the twin advantage of effecting greater self-sufficiency on the part of individuals and households, and reducing public expenditure. The new model being promoted in Europe is not the full-time, dual earner arrangement but rather a combination model whereby women (and men to a lesser extent) are enabled to manage and combine care-related and employment activity. Here family considerations are central. On my reading Europe is not moving to a dual earner model in any unilinear way but it is shifting away from the expensive male breadwinner model that requires high subsidies from both the state and employers (in terms of the numbers of people that one wage has to support), regulation of the labour market and compromise if not sacrifice from many women.

That said, in many ways policy reflects public attitudes which still express significant affinity to traditional gender patterns, especially in a context of child-rearing and family life. This is the fourth causal factor. Maria Charles has pointed out that the most resilient gender inequalities are those that are not explicitly hierarchical and appear to reflect naturally distinct preferences of autonomous women and men (Charles, 2011, p. 367). Even when we take account of variation, it seems that Europe as a whole still favours a familialist response to gender equality challenges. This, among other things, complicates the politics involved (Morgan, 2009; Shalev, 2009).

In these times, it is striking how much pay and associated gender inequalities have come to be the dominant narrative in relation to financial inequality, reflecting on the one hand a general trend to downgrade the income support role of the welfare state in favour of the economy, and on the other a tendency to simplify and funnel complex issues into singular rubrics. Furthermore, there has been little movement to change the valuation of traditionally female activities and jobs, a change which feminist work has long identified as essential to gender equality. In the absence of such a shift, men have had little or no incentive to change and the incentive structures for women have pushed them in the direction of either gendered traditional or (for them) non-traditional activities and positions (England, 2010). The creeping thread of reform in social policy in Europe was to induct women into largely unchanged structures rather than a more integrated female and male perspective that would change those structures and/or provide a stronger basis for social justice and collective organizing. Put simply: it is difficult to see contemporary social policy developments coming out of a wish for a larger stake for women or even significant redistribution towards women. Note also that the mainstream in which the EU and member countries sought to integrate women has been itself increasingly reshaped by neoliberal policies (especially since the recession of 2008).

The next section of the chapter draws out a research agenda, thinking of this at both a conceptual and policy level. As the discussion proceeds, it will focus on a number of tensions central to the field.

8.2   A FUTURE RESEARCH AGENDA

Looking forward, a central plank of engagement has to be the underlying gender system and how it is maintained and changed. This may well mean circling around the same set of issues as in the past but we should not apologize for that. The gender system as conceived of here is constituted by the organizing principles and ideologies involved in the way the welfare state constructs relationships and resource differentials between women and men and governs the terms of family, kinship and reproductive/productive relations. Going forward, four main issues mark out key elements of researching the gender system: the meaning of gender equality and the role of social policy; the relationships and intersections among race, class, and gender (among other lines of differentiation) as axes of inequality; the significance of unpaid work and its relationship to paid work and gender equality; and the interconnections between local, national and global contexts. I will discuss each of these in turn, remaining mindful that they intersect and also involve core tensions that are beyond my capacity to resolve here.

8.2.1   Gender Equality and the Purpose of the Welfare State

A matter that needs continuing revisiting is how we should conceive of gender equality and what kind of vision of change is appropriate in a social policy and welfare state context. This, admittedly, is complex and difficult. Plantenga and Remery (2013, p. 36) point out that it is not obvious that women's position is strengthened or improved by virtue of being 'equal' to men in terms of hours of employment, for example. We might extend this point also to the Gender Equality Index and other similar indices that measure progress in terms of sameness and give the nod to equality by also including indicators of 'private life'.

There is no agreement in feminist or other circles regarding equality, although the unacceptability of inequality is widely shared. In both academic and policy work, a root question centres around sameness versus difference. For some, the ultimate goal is the elimination of the gender division of labour and of asymmetry between women and men such that both work for pay and participate in family-related care giving in equal measure (Gornick and Meyers, 2008, 2009). This kind of vision is inherent in the idea of the dual earner/dual carer household as an equality ideal which has been elaborated in the work of Nancy Fraser (1994), Diane Sainsbury (1999) and Janet Gornick and Marcia Meyers (2008), among others. An alternative vision – based on a philosophy that draws upon difference rather than sameness – focuses more on choice within a context of continuing gender differences. No particular overall household model is proposed here, not least because one of the theoretical foundations is of diversity in preferences. As articulated by Ann Orloff (2008, p. 4), this supports "political goals that would expand choice, or decisional autonomy, based in interdependence, and inclusive citizenship, emerging from a consideration of diversity in modern societies and from an understanding of gender as constitutive of subjects". There is a strong sense of open individual agency involved. Orloff is especially concerned that we take account of the persistence – and legitimacy – of continuing differences in gender-related attitudes and popular beliefs and people's deep investments in gender (the possibility that women and men do not want to be 'the same') and also the challenges to universalistic approaches and visions posed by difference and diversity, especially in a context of high immigration and population diversity. Another factor is the known significant variation in preferences along socio-economic, ethnic and other lines. Analysis indicates that a sameness understanding of equality tends to accord most with the orientations and lifestyles of highly-educated, ethnic majority women (Shalev, 2009).

These considerations should act as a caution in setting up normative models. And they, too, invite searching questions about the role of social policy. Thinking about choice and difference from a social policy perspective underlines the need for policy intervention and provision (rather than the more obvious obverse). Working in a more global context, Razavi and Staab (2018) remind us that for any policy reform to succeed a supportive infrastructure needs to be in place. Orloff (2008) in the quote above underlines this point with her reference to 'inclusive citizenship'. The idea of not constraining choice is in some ways also one of the key insights from the capabilities approach, although its focus is arguably on enabling choice with its emphasis on social policy's role in affecting means rather than determining ends (Sen, 1992, 1999; Nussbaum, 2000). As explained by Lewis and Giullari (2005, p. 88), the approach makes important distinctions between the resources available to a person (means), what she is and does (functionings), the personal, social and environmental factors that affect her ability to transform means into functionings (conversion factors) and the combination of 'beings' and 'doings' that she has the real freedom to achieve (her capability set). Agency is central but so too is the degree of value placed on different aspects of life (and their cognitive and cultural coding). This approach accords social policy quite an important place in either promoting or impeding people's ability to achieve capabilities (Hobson, 2014, p. 12). Kurowska (2018) points out that implicit in the approach is a role for policy in shaping the means available to people but at the same time allowing people to translate them into 'capabilities' and 'functionings'.

For this and other reasons, there are limits to a liberal interpretation of choice, especially if choice and freedom are read as calling for state disinvestment to allow for increasing incursion of the market. Then it means choice for some rather than all. The interpretation and realization of choice need to be carefully thought through, therefore. Indeed, as I said above, we may posit that a necessary condition of choice for all – especially those on low incomes or with fewer resources – is state provision. My sense is that we need to keep asking the question of what constitutes progress in gender equality and to view this exercise as involving problematizing the balance between choice and constraint and the policy packages associated with each for all categories of women and men. We must keep interrogating the mainstream neoliberal policy model (as an approach that targets women as economic actors only) while seeking alternatives to it. In this and other regards, I consider it important to keep the focus on resources and how policy affects resource holding/usage and associated inequalities. The vision that underpins this book – inequality as inhering in the gender division of resources of money, labour and time – seems like a serviceable framework going forward, although there are some blindsides regarding aspects of identity and immaterial welfare.

Thinking more broadly and in a manner inclusive of immaterial as well as material concerns, Sandra Fredman's (2016) conception of substantive equality is helpful to consider. Working in the context of the EU legal system, she develops her framework in the shadow of two challenges: to move from formal equality to substantive equality and to do so in a way that absorbs the challenges of an intersectional perspective. Rather than being based on sameness, it explicitly incorporates differences in power positioning and relationships. Thinking in terms of a legal framework and especially overcoming the limits of an anti-discrimination approach in EU law, she treats equality-oriented measures as having four complementary functions: redress disadvantage (the redistributive dimension); address stigma, prejudice, stereotyping and violence (the recognition dimension); facilitate participation and voice (the participative dimension); and accommodate difference through structural change (the transformative dimension). Power is central to her perspective in which intersecting relationships of power can be analysed according to the extent to which they (i) create socio-economic disadvantage; (ii) are stigmatic, prejudiced, stereotyping or violent; (iii) exclude or marginalize; and (iv) require conformity. This framework gives a sense of the breadth of the field. The different elements vary in the extent of their relevance for social policy – with the first three of most direct pertinence – but in key ways all are relevant and as an overall framework it shows promise in envisioning and interrogating what we might expect of law and policy.

8.2.2 Insights from Intersectionality

Intersectionality has to have a more central place in future studies of inequality. One can see why from some of the results of the analyses carried out in this book, albeit that it adopted what might be called a 'light-touch intersectional approach', systematically searching for differences in the situation of different groups of women – especially along family status, age and social class lines – and conceiving of people's lives, policies and associated inequalities as cutting across spheres and particular patterns of resource holding and usage. Proceeding in this way helped to reveal not just the inter-connections between different types of inequalities but gender as itself cut through by other axes of division. The results confirm some key lessons from existing work that should be taken seriously, especially the following points made by Choo and Ferree (2010) in their state-of-the-art review: the importance of recognizing that multiple stratification processes exist; that they are not independent of one another; and that it is vital not to leave uncritiqued the differences of the groups under study from an assumed norm.

That said, there are real challenges in employing an intersectionality approach. This is not just because of methodological or data issues but is also a function of conceptual challenges in holding questions of race, class, gender, sexuality, and other social categories and related processes in the frame at once (and doing so in a theoretically informed way). At the risk of being prosaic, intersectionality is a complex framework and way of thinking. There is also the fact that intersectionality has become rather elastic in its meaning and neoliberal in its application by policy (as we have seen in relation to the EU's engagement with the concept which frames it in a diversity management register). All of this raises questions about the approach's place in feminist studies and whether its origins in black feminism and Third World liberation movements are being erased and sanitized as it has moved to become a more mainstream approach

(Salem, 2018). I am convinced that we must continue to develop and integrate an intersectionality perspective in our work and that this must serve to focus on both marginalized groups and marginalizing processes. I am also convinced that gender can serve as one over-arching frame for it defines and organizes key commonalities that transcend particular lines of difference. So we can go in search of the underpinning gender system but treat it as a multi-dimensional entity (Htun and Weldon, 2018) and be open to the possibility that the underlying inequality or stratification is not solely gender-based.

The situation of men is especially pertinent in this context. Research in the social policy field has yet to incorporate a perspective on men as a heterogeneous social group in their own right and in relation to the lives of women (with some notable exceptions in the work of Hearn (2010), Hobson and Morgan (2002) and Dermott and Miller (2015)). In a lot of scholarship, men are either the residuals (but also the norm against which we (and society) construe and judge progress) or, in a more active vein, working and engaged fathers. Bringing men in is important in its own right, given the prevalence and consequences of hegemonic masculinity and the fact that gendered patterns of male behaviour are complicated by other social and cultural factors.

Some suggestions about how to take forward intersectional thinking in social policy studies can be gleaned from existing work. Ciccia and Sainsbury (2018) make the point that intersections have been most studied as outcomes (as here), whereas what is needed are "comparative approaches to disentangle the contextual and intersectional effects of inequalities in shaping the division of welfare" (p. 104). The underlying call here (on my reading) is to examine how intersections lead to and are based on diverse but connected marginalizations, understood in terms of access to power and grounded in material relations and resources, and how these play out in different settings within and across nations. Another line of thought comes from Siim and Borchorst (2017) who suggest that a vision of political intersectionality concerned with the interplay of 'redistribution policies' and 'recognition struggles' could be a useful strategy for revisioning gender and welfare regimes. Although I have not studied it specifically here, recognition merits a central place in gender and social policy studies. In regard to researching policy, Bacchi (2017) is in line with key elements of an intersectional perspective when she suggests moving away from categories or categorical distinctions in policy analysis altogether (because they hide the processes, practices and politics involved in the formation of these categories) and, rather, think in terms of processes generated by policy. This picks up on intersectionality's strong sense of needing to move beyond status markers. It means two things: that we can rely only to a limited extent on global, uni-dimensional gender indicators and that we need to try and divine the processes (the 'ing/ization') underlying them. This shifts the focus from how policies affect women and men to asking how they help constitute them. In this view, the questions we should pose to policy are 'complex how questions', such as: How is policy active or complicit in creating/perpetuating differences and inequalities between women and men in ways that are also racializing, and/or classing, and/or heteronorming, and so forth?

8.2.3 Familial Considerations, Care and Social Reproduction

The findings of this book underline the resource-related and other inequalities associated with care giving, for women especially. The direct costs involve the expenditure of time, energy and other material and immaterial resources in activities and commitments that have lesser public value in comparison to paid work. The indirect costs extend over the longer term and include such possible outcomes as insecurity in employment, career and income, reduced or no access to social protection benefits, delimited participation opportunities in education and training, all compounded in increased poverty risk, especially in old age.

As is clear from the foregoing – especially Chapter 2 – care has become a very important concept in the analysis of the material covered in this book. As an overarching concept it has developed to pick up on and organize some of the key lines of family-related policy development (and also health-related policy). While it does not encompass them and they pre-date care as a concept to some extent, the intelligence of the concept has allowed lines of analysis like maternalism or familialization/ defamilialization to flourish. Moreover, as a tool for policy analysis (and it is much more than that for some of its theorizations extend to existential philosophy and societal reorganization), care picks up on core aspects of the way that the welfare state is being reformed, keeping the spotlight on family considerations and their gendered framing (e.g. whether this is through increasing use of gender-neutral terminology like 'parent', 'carer' or something else).

As well as the above, there are a number of interesting and fruitful forms of enquiry in relation to care that are interesting to consider from a future-oriented view.

One prominent line of analysis is the care economy. This concept is being developed especially by feminist economists. Nancy Folbre is a leading scholar here (see Folbre, 2018) as is Sue Himmelweit (2014). In policy circles the Economic Commission for Latin America and the Caribbean is a noteworthy actor (ECLAC, 2004; Mahon, 2018b), shifting the focus from women's labour market participation to inequalities in the paid and unpaid division of labour and focusing on trends like the growth of paid domestic labour and of transnational care migration and 'care chains' which reach across the world. De Hanau et al. (2016)[1] conceptualize the care economy to include activities in education, care, health services and social care. Concerned especially about the concealed and under-resourced nature of much of care provision and increasing marketization, such theorizing seeks to make the hidden visible and to do so in a way that is sensitive to larger trends and global changes. Nancy Folbre (2009, p. 111 and *passim*) encourages us to think more broadly also; she emphasizes a framing of care that encompasses the organization and financial support for all care services (as against just child care). In underlining that "the social provision of a generous, equitable, sustainable, and efficient supply of care is a prerequisite of genuine gender equality" (p. 112), she makes three specific proposals for research and policy:

- Look beyond work–family policies such as paid parental leave and publicly provided child care to develop policies of economic support for all forms of family, friend, and neighbour care;
- Look beyond family care to the organization, cost and quality of paid care services;
- Develop better accounting systems for both economic growth and welfare state spending.

Folbre's call underlines the broad convening power of the concept of care. But – placed in a European context especially – it goes somewhat against the grain of recent scholarship in the field which has focused on the specificity of care (policies) for children as against those for long-term care for adults (e.g. Ranci and Pavolini, 2015; Dobrotić and Blum, 2019; Le Bihan et al., 2019). There is certainly a tension here, especially as both are becoming more diverse, and arguably more complex as policy fields (especially elderly care). The utility of a singular framing needs to be questioned by research going forward in my view. In the next section I will raise the question of the utility of care vis-à-vis social reproduction to pick up on the complex of factors driving gender inequality.

For now I wish to highlight that there are dangers in positioning care in economic and market terms. One risks, for example, thinking of care in terms of economic principles and economic rationalization. There are, then, reasons to keep a critical distance from conceptualizing care in

---

[1] Available at http://www.ituc-csi.org/IMG/pdf/care_economy_en.pdf.

economic terms. But whether that means that we should reject concepts like the care economy is open to question. It allows us to pose challenging questions like the degree to which the positioning of care in economic and market terms effects a commodification of care; the processes and consequences of promoting economic principles and economic rationalization in care as an activity that is fundamentally relationally based; and the contradictions of economization and marketization for those of us who hold that care workers/providers should not be treated as a source of cheap labour (Williams, 2018a, 2018b). And, of course, marketization is part of the political economy of care. We know something about the politics of ECEC through social investment-oriented analyses (e.g. Morgan, 2009) but long-term care as a social policy field is much less often seen through the lens of social investment and is also less analysed from a political economy perspective (in social policy anyway). In some respects, this is because it is only recently – with greater longevity and a less readily available supply of familial care – that it has become prominent and contested as a policy issue. While we do know something about the vested interests involved (corporations for example, or other providers – see Farris and Marchetti, 2017) and outsourcing (Estévez-Abe and Hobson, 2015; Morel, 2015), the alignment of the interests of commercial actors with those of other actors remains largely underexplored.

8.2.4 Crisis, Contemporary Global Capitalism and the State

Given the contemporary discourse about economic recovery, it may be tempting to consign the recession of 2008 to history. This would be ill-advised for its effects on our politics, economies, welfare states and philosophies around gender reach deeply and widely. The recession was generally taken as an opportunity in Europe – and on the part of the EU – to promote austerity as well as continuing to shift responsibilities and resources from the state to individuals, families, communities and markets. There is a risk also of seeing the recession and austerity as one-off events. I suggest that we should phrase our questions in the present and future tenses, mindful, of course, of the need for an account that is historically sensitive.

Making the link to prevailing economic models propels a question about which concepts and theories we should use to uncover and explain gender inequality. I want to frame this issue through a discussion of the strengths and merits of care as an analytical device as regards those of social reproduction. One can definitely claim for care a sensitivity to family and a capacity to encompass different modalities and dimensions of care (at different levels). However, Mignon Duffy's work (2005; see also Duffy and

Armenia, 2019) makes the case that much of the field remains dominated by studies of family care giving. This, it is claimed, has lent the scholarship a strong orientation towards care as nurturance (and hence, relationality and interdependence), thereby marginalizing another theoretical strand of (earlier) feminist work – domestic labour and social reproduction. The latter, while overlapping somewhat with the relationality field of work on care, is different in two key respects (Duffy, 2005). First, theoretically, the social reproduction perspective situates care-centred work in the economy and exigencies around the reproduction of the labour force. Secondly, expanding the field to include both nurturant and non-nurturant versions of care captures a much broader universe of workers (such as those involved in food preparation, house cleaning and laundry). Duffy's application of this categorization to employment data in the US Census of 2000 confirms this, as well as uncovering a racial divide whereby women of colour as compared with white women are over-represented among nurturant care occupations (although they remain over-represented compared to white women in non-nurturance jobs as well). This leads Duffy (2005, pp. 78–9) to conclude that a theoretical focus on care as nurturance appears to privilege the experiences of white women over the more varied experiences of women of colour and to exclude large numbers of very low-wage workers.[2]

Vershuur (2013) also picks up the criticism about care's focus on nurturing. Whilst recognizing the strengths and contribution of the scholarship on care, she is critical of it for focusing most attention on the nature of the labour involved as against the broader political economy and the articulation between the productive and reproductive spheres and how this changes over time (when care comes to be part of paid labour or a care economy, for example). While this may overstate care's focus on the relations and engagement involved and, indeed, underplay their significance, there is a serious point about the explanatory capacity and reach of both concepts. In earlier feminist work which used social reproduction as the leading framework of analysis, domestic labour was treated as embedded in a set of economic relations and linked to exploitation rather than devaluation. It could be argued to have stronger economic depth than care, being especially interested in the extent of the subsidy provided by social reproduction to public welfare and the economy in general (Kofman and Raghuram, 2018). In a prescient development of the concept, Rai et al. (2014) articulate the idea of 'depletion through social reproduction'

---

[2]   It is important to note that her definition of nurturant jobs includes such occupations as teachers, social workers, clergy, nursing, and a whole range of medical and dental practitioners.

to draw out the costs of non-recognition and lack of support for social reproduction. Depletion is for these authors a tipping point when resource outflows exceed resource inflows over a threshold of sustainability, making it harmful for those engaged in this work (whether individuals, households or communities). They identify three ways in which depletion can be reversed. The first is through mitigation (when individuals or other units might decide to pay for help, although they note that this can increase depletion further down the chain for those who cannot afford to pay). The second strategy is replenishment – whereby states or private bodies contribute to resource inflows (through services, financial help and so forth). Transformation is the third mode of reversal. Here they reference both a restructuring in the gender division of labour and recognizing and valuing social reproduction. There are clearly similarities with care here but work on it tends to go in a different direction.

I consider it important that we recognize the strengths and weaknesses of each concept and be conscious and judicious in our use of them. In the aim of adding context to the previous discussion, it is important to point out that studies using care have furnished a detailed and rich analysis of welfare and health policies. This, more a European than a US literature, has helped to open up and systematize the analysis of services to meet (care) needs. The service provision aspects of the welfare state have been especially elaborated (see e.g. Anttonen and Sipilä, 1996), providing an important corrective to the heavily transfer-related focus of welfare state studies. The concept of care has also, as I have said above, brought in familial considerations to a degree that work on social reproduction has not (yet).

Whichever concept we use it needs to be able to link developments across borders to bring in global capitalism and international development, especially in terms of the articulation between the national and global economies in relation to care-related labour and service organization. This will have to decentre the nation state as the unit of analysis to focus on global migrations and international patterns of resource flows, especially in a context of climate and other change. One of the foremost challenges is to identify and explain how and why the depletion of resources in the Global North is leading to depletion in the Global South and how social class, race and other axes of inequality are involved. Understanding the use of migrant (mainly female) workers to fill mounting gaps and deficits in care provision in the high-income countries as native-born women increasingly (re-)enter the workforce is an important link to powerful underlying processes (Budig and Misra, 2011; Hochschild, 2012). De los Reyes (2016, p. 39) sees some of the promise of an intersectional approach here: ". . . an intersectional perspective of the imbrications of class, race, sexuality and gender can be a point of departure for understanding the different ways that current capitalist accumulation models are recreating bio-political assumptions of the human through processes of commodification and the emergence of new modalities of governance".

We have already seen that scholarship is making such interconnections, broadening the scope of policy analysis courtesy of its interest in how policies on race, ethnicity and migration interact and are patterned in such a way as to render care giving (and often care receiving) a continued site and conduit of inequality within and across borders. Recognizing this starts to fill a gap in our understanding of how care is associated with complex inequality that both defines and transcends the national space. Williams (2018a, 2018b) has suggested a three-level framework: at a micro level the everyday experience of care and care work; at meso level the institutional infrastructure; and at macro level developments in global capitalism. Michel and Peng (2017) use what they call a multi-scalar approach (which also embraces micro, meso and macro interconnections) to examine three domains: care provisioning; the supply of and demand for care work; and the shaping and framing of care. In important respects, these scholars are merging insights from work on care and social reproduction.

One important way of ensuring that our perspectives are sufficiently sensitive to the exploitation caused by our lives in the global North is to enquire about the conditions under which they are sustainable and in particular whether they can be sustained only on the basis of an asymmetrical global economy (Hassim, 2009, p. 96). In other words, can the arrangements and privileges around care and welfare be universalized? Hassim sets out the conditions of global egalitarianism: we need to expand our model beyond the formal economy; be vigilant in regard to the socialization of care jobs; and acknowledge more overtly the global context of care and the need for global redistribution which guarantees access to the basic means of survival as well as the power to determine the content of international regulatory frameworks (2009, p. 105).[3] All of these questions become more urgent in a context of climate change.

8.3   KEY RESEARCH QUESTIONS

Overall, it is clear that examining the relationship between gender and social policy is not just a vibrant field of research but essential to understanding core aspects of contemporary lives. Regarding the relation-

---

[3]   See also Razavi and Staab (2018).

The gender system in social policy

- What gender-related assumptions and divisions does social policy take forward?
- What are the incentives/disincentives in policy from a gender perspective?
- Where is the relevant innovation (if any) in the social policy system, what are the origins and likely consequences?
- Are gender inequalities being reinscribed in new ways as policies develop and reform?
- Has equality plateaued out and are there structural limits to equality?
- How should we think of men and male interests and how do we find a way of deepening our conceptualization and critique of men's relationship to social policy (in a way that recognizes differences among men)?
- To what extent is the social policy system effecting gender inequality through other inequalities, and vice versa?
- What explains the different routes to gender equality found across countries and what are the divergences and convergences?

Political economy elements of social policy

- Who benefits from social policy provision?
- Who bears the costs of existing arrangements?
- Thinking in a more global context: where are the costs borne and what is the sub-national, national, regional and global patterning and relative privileging/disprivileging?
- Which are the actors involved in the reorganization of care and social reproduction, especially in its commodification and marketization? How is this connected to wider economic processes?
- What is the scale and nature of the role of the family (or relations of kinship) in resource exchange and support?
- What and where are the risks of care-related depletion?
- Which capabilities are essential for women and men and is choice only possible for well-off women and men?
- What are the racial interests and underpinnings in social policy and its reform?
- Has the approach that targets women only as economic actors been exhausted as a solution to gender inequality and what should replace it?
- How is the recession of 2008 and associated policy consensus transforming the welfare state and its place in economy and society?

Figure 8.1   Important questions for a future research agenda

ship between social policy and gender, the central concerns that have dominated scholarship – women's relationship to the welfare state project, the relationship between care, paid work, and welfare, the links between care, social reproduction and gender inequality – are as important as ever (Orloff, 2009). But they need to be considered and expanded through perspectives that take account of intersectional inequalities, a critical reconceptualization of unpaid work and care, and the interlinking of local, national, regional and global developments in a framework that problematizes resource flows and endangered sustainability. This book has attempted to illustrate, rather than exhaust, the possibilities. There are many ways in which the research reported here invites critical test and extension. I end with some potentially penetrating questions, loosely organized under two broad headings: the gender system and political economy (which of course are integrally related). These questions are envisaged to be applied at a range of levels.

References

Acker, J. (1992), 'From sex roles to gendered institutions', *Contemporary Sociology*, 21, 5: 565–9.

Ackerly, B. and True, J. (2013), 'Methods and methodologies', in Waylen, G., Celis, K., Kantola, J. and Weldon, L. (eds), *The Oxford Handbook of Gender and Politics*, Oxford: Oxford University Press, pp. 135–59.

Adema, W. (2012), 'Setting the scene: The mix of family policy objectives and packages across the OECD', *Children and Youth Services Review*, 34, 3: 487–98.

Akgunduz, Y. E. and Plantenga, J. (2013), 'Labour market effects of parental leave in Europe', *Cambridge Journal of Economics*, 37, 4: 845–62.

Altintas, E. and Sullivan, O. (2017), 'Trends in fathers' contribution to housework and childcare under different welfare policy regimes', *Social Politics*, 24, 1: 81–108.

Anderson, K. (2015), *Social Policy in the European Union*, London: Palgrave.

Anttonen, A. and Sipilä, J. (1996), 'European social care services: Is it possible to identify models?', *Journal of European Social Policy*, 6, 2: 87–100.

Anttonen, A. and Zechner, M. (2011), 'Theorising care and care work', in Pfau-Effinger, B. and Rostgaard, T. (eds), *Care between Work and Welfare in European Societies*, London: Routledge, pp. 15–34.

Arat-Koç, S. (2018), 'Migrant and domestic and care workers: Unfree labour, crises of social reproduction and the unsustainability of life under "vagabond capitalism"', in Elias, J. and Roberts, A. (eds), *Handbook of the International Political Economy of Gender*, Cheltenham, UK and Northampton, MA, USA: Edward Elgar Publishing, pp. 411–26.

Armstrong, K. A. (2011), 'The character of EU law and governance: From "Community method" to new modes of governance', *Current Legal Problems*, 64, 1: 179–214.

Atkinson, A. B., Casarico, A. and Voitchovsky, S. (2016), *Top Incomes and the Gender Divide*, Melbourne Institute Working Paper Series, Working Paper No. 27/16, Melbourne: University of Melbourne.

Aulenbacher, B., Lutz, H. and Riegraf, B. (2018), 'Introduction: Towards a global sociology of care and care work', *Current Sociology*, 66, 4: 495–502.

Avram, S., Popova, D. and Rastrigina, O. (2016), *Accounting for Gender Differences in the Distributional Effects of Tax and Benefit Policy Changes*, EUROMOD Working Paper No. EM7/16, Essex, UK: Institute for Social and Economic Research.

Bacchi, C. (1999), *Women, Policy and Politics: The Construction of Policy Problems*, London: Sage.

Bacchi, C. (2009), *Analysing Policy: What's the Problem Represented to Be?*, Malaysia: Pearson.

Bacchi, C. (2017), 'Policies as gendering practices: Re-viewing categorical distinctions', *Journal of Women, Politics, and Policy*, 38, 1: 20–41.

Baldassar, L. and Merla, L. (eds) (2013), *Transnational Families, Migration and the Circulation of Care: Understanding Mobility and Absence in Family Life*, London: Routledge.

Baldwin, P. (1990), *The Politics of Social Solidarity: Class Bases of the European Welfare States, 1875–1975*, Cambridge: Cambridge University Press.

Barcelona European Council (2002), *Presidency Conclusions Barcelona 15–16 March 2002*, Brussels: European Commission.

Barrett, M. (1980), *Women's Oppression Today: Problems in Marxist Feminist Analysis*, London: Verso.

Becker, G. S. (1981), *A Treatise on the Family*, Cambridge, MA: Harvard University Press.

Beechey, V. (1982), 'The sexual division of labour and the labour process: A critical assessment of Braverman', in Wood, S. (ed), *The Degradation of Work? Skill, Deskilling and the Labour Process*, London: Hutchinson, pp. 54–73.

Béland, D. (2005), 'Ideas and social policy: An institutionalist perspective', *Social Policy & Administration*, 39, 1: 1–18.

Béland, D. and Cox, R. H. (eds) (2011), *Ideas and Politics in Social Science Research*, Oxford: Oxford University Press.

Bennett, F. (1983), 'The state, welfare and women's dependence', in Segal, L. (ed.), *What Is to Be Done about the Family?* London: Penguin Books, pp. 190–214.

Bennett, F. (2013), 'Researching within-household distribution: Overview, developments, debates and methodological challenges', *Journal of Marriage and Family*, 75, 3: 582–97.

Bennett, F. and Daly, M. (2014), *Poverty Through a Gender Lens*, Oxford: Department of Social Policy and Intervention.

Berk, S. F. (1985), *The Gender Factory: The Apportionment of Work in American Households*, New York: Plenum Press.

Betti, G., Bettio, F., Geordiadis, T. and Tinios, P. (2015), *Unequal Ageing in Europe: Women's Independence and Pensions*, New York: Palgrave Macmillan.

Bettio, F. (2017), 'Can we call it a revolution? Women, the labour market, and European policy', in Auth, D., Hergenhan, J. and Holland-Cunz, B. (eds), *Gender and Family in European Economic Policy*, Cham, Switzerland: Palgrave Macmillan, pp. 15–39.

Bettio, F. and Plantenga, J. (2004), 'Comparing care regimes in Europe', *Feminist Economics*, 10, 1: 85–113.

Bettio, F. and Verashchagina, A. (2014), 'Women and men in the "great European recession"', in Karamessini, M. and Rubery, J. (eds), *Women and Austerity: The economic crisis and the future of gender equality*, London: Routledge, pp. 57–81.

Bettio, F., Simonazzi, A. and Villa, P. (2006), 'Change in care regimes and female migration: The "care drain" in the Mediterranean', *Journal of European Social Policy*, 16, 3: 271–85.

Bianchi, S. M. (2011), 'Family change and time allocation in American families', *Annals of the American Academy of Political and Social Science*, 638: 21–44.

Blackburn, S. (1995), 'How useful are feminist theories of the welfare state?', *Women's History Review*, 4, 3: 369–94.

Blyth, M. M. (1997), 'Any more bright ideas? The ideational turn of comparative political economy', *Comparative Politics*, 29, 2: 229–50.

Boeckmann, I., Misra, J. and Budig, M. (2015), 'Cultural and institutional factors shaping mothers' employment and working hours in postindustrial countries', *Social Forces*, 93: 1301–33.

Bonoli, G. (2005), 'The politics of the new social policies: Providing coverage against new social risks in mature welfare states', *Policy and Politics*, 33, 3: 431–49.

Bould, S., Crespi, I. and Schmaus, G. (2012), 'The cost of a child, mothers' employment behaviour and economic insecurity in Europe', *International Review of Sociology*, 22, 1: 5–23.

Bradley, H. (2013), *Gender*, 2nd edition, Cambridge: Polity Press.

Brady, D. and Kall, D. (2008), 'Nearly universal, but somewhat distinct: The feminization of poverty in affluent Western democracies, 1869–2000', *Social Science Research*, 37, 3: 976–1007.

Brady, D., Blome, A. and Kmec, J. A. (2018), 'Work–family reconciliation policies and women's and mothers' labor market outcomes in rich democracies', forthcoming in *Socio-Economic Review*, Open Science Framework, https://academic.oup.com/ser/advance-article-abstract/doi/10.1093/ser/mwy045/5288701?redirectedFrom=fulltext.

Brandth, B. and Kvande, E. (1998), 'Masculinity and childcare: The reconstruction of fathering', *Sociological Review*, 46, 2: 293–313.

Brocas, A.-M. (1988), 'Equal treatment of men and women in social security: An overview', *International Social Security Review*, 41, 3: 231–49.

Budig, M. J. and Misra, J. (2011), 'How care-work employment shapes earnings in cross-national perspective', *International Labour Review*, 149, 4: 441–60.

Budig, M. J., Misra, J. and Boeckmann, I. (2012), 'The motherhood penalty in cross-national perspective: The importance of work-family policies and cultural attitudes', *Social Politics*, 19, 2: 163–93.

Budig, M. J., Misra, J. and Boeckmann, I. (2016), 'Work-family policy trade-offs for mothers? Unpacking cross-national variation in motherhood earnings penalties', *Work and Occupations*, 43, 2: 119–77.

Budlender, D. (ed.) (2010), *Time Use Studies and Unpaid Care Work*, New York: Routledge.

Burri, S. and Prechal, S. (2013), *EU Gender Equality Law: Update 2013*, Brussels: European Commission.

Burström, B. (2015), 'Sweden – Recent changes in welfare state arrangements', *International Journal of Health Services*, 45, 1: 87–104.

Calnitsky, D. (2019), 'The high-hanging fruit of the gender revolution: A model of social reproduction and social change', *Sociological Theory*, 37, 1: 35–61.

Campbell, J. L. (2002), 'Ideas, politics and public policy', *Annual Review of Sociology*, 28: 21–38.

Cantillon, B. (2011), 'The paradox of the social investment state: Growth, employment and poverty in the Lisbon era', *Journal of European Social Policy*, 21, 5: 432–49.

Castellano, R. and Rocca, A. (2017), 'The dynamic of the gender gap in the European labour market in the years of economic crisis', *Quality and Quantity*, 51: 1337–57.

Castro-García, C. and Pazod-Moran, M. (2016), 'Parental leave policy and gender equality in Europe', *Feminist Economics*, 22, 3: 51–73.

Cavaghan, R. (2017), *Making Gender Equality Happen: Knowledge, Change and Resistance in EU Gender Mainstreaming*, London: Routledge.

Cavaghan, R. and Dwyer, M. (2018), 'European economic governance in 2017: A recovery for whom?', *Journal of Common Market Studies*, 56, S1: 96–108.

Chant, S. (ed.) (2010), *The International Handbook of Gender and Poverty: Concepts, Research, Policy*, Cheltenham, UK and Northampton, MA, USA: Edward Elgar Publishing.

Chant, S. and Sweetman, C. (2012), 'Fixing women or fixing the world?

"Smart economics", efficiency approaches, and gender equality in development', *Gender & Development*, 20, 3: 517–29.

Charles, M. (2011), 'A world of difference: International trends in women's economic status', *Annual Review of Sociology*, 37: 355–71.

Cho, S., Williams Crenshaw, K. and McCall, L. (2013), 'Toward a field of intersectionality studies: Theory, applications, and praxis', *Signs*, 28, 4: 785–810.

Choo, H. Y. and Ferree, M. M. (2010), 'Practising intersectionality in sociological research: A critical analysis of inclusions, interactions, and institutions in the study of inequalities', *Sociological Theory*, 28, 2: 129–49.

Ciccia, R. and Bleijenberg, I. (2014), 'After the male breadwinner model: Childcare services and the division of labour in European countries', *Social Politics*, 21, 1: 50–79.

Ciccia, R. and Sainsbury, D. (2018), 'Gendering welfare state analysis: Tensions between work and care', *European Journal of Politics and Gender*, 1, 1–2: 93–109.

Cipollone, A., Patacchini, E. and Vallanti, G. (2014), 'Female labour market participation in Europe: Novel evidence on trends and shaping factors', *IZA Journal of Economic Labour Studies*, 3, 18: 1–40.

Commission of the European Communities (1996), *Communication from the Commission: Incorporating Equal Opportunities for Women and Men into All Community Policies and Activities*, COM(96) 67 final of 21 February 1996.

Connell, R. W. (1987), *Gender and Power: Society, the Person and Sexual Politics*, Stanford, CA: Stanford University Press.

Connell, R. W. (2002), *Gender*, Cambridge: Polity Press.

Connell, R. and Pearse, R. (2015), *Gender: In World Perspective*, 3rd edition, Cambridge: Polity Press.

Connolly, S., Aldrich, M., O'Brien, M., Speight, S. and Poole, E. (2016), 'Britain's slow movement to a gender egalitarian equilibrium: Parents and employment in the UK 2001–13', *Work, Employment and Society*, 30, 5: 838–57.

Cooke, L. P. (2011), *Gender–Class Equality in Political Economies*, New York: Routledge.

Corsi, M., Botti, F. and D'Ippoliti, C. (2016), 'The gendered nature of poverty in the EU: Individualized versus collective poverty measures', *Feminist Economics*, 22, 4: 82–100.

Council of Europe (1998), *Gender Mainstreaming: Conceptual Framework, Methodology and Presentation of Good Practices: Final Report of Activities of the Group of Specialists on Mainstreaming*, Strasbourg: Council of Europe.

Council of the European Union (2011), *Council Conclusions of 7 March 2011 on European Pact for Gender Equality (2011–2020)*, Brussels.

Courtin, E., Jemiai, N. and Mossialos, E. (2014), 'Mapping support policies for informal carers across the European Union', *Health Policy*, 118, 1: 84–94.

Crenshaw, K. (1989), 'Demarginalizing the intersection of race and sex: A black feminist critique of antidiscrimination doctrine, feminist theory and antiracist politics', *University of Chicago Legal Forum*, 1989: 139–67.

Crompton, R. (1999), *Restructuring Gender Relations and Employment: The Decline of the Male Breadwinner*, Oxford: Oxford University Press.

Crompton, R. (2006), *Employment and the Family: The Reconfiguration of Work and Family Life in Contemporary Societies*, Cambridge: Cambridge University Press.

Da Roit, B., Hoogenboom, M. and Weicht, B. (2015), 'The gender informal care gap: A fuzzy-set analysis of cross-country variations', *European Societies*, 17, 2: 199–218.

Daly, M. (1996), *Social Security, Gender and Equality in the European Union*, Brussels: Commission of the European Communities.

Daly, M. (2000), *The Gender Division of Welfare*, Cambridge: Cambridge University Press.

Daly, M. (2002), 'Care as a good for public policy', *Journal of Social Policy*, 32, 2: 251–70.

Daly, M. (2005), 'Gender mainstreaming in theory and practice', *Social Politics*, 12, 3: 433–50.

Daly, M. (2011), 'What adult worker model? A critical look at recent social policy reform in Europe from a gender and family perspective', *Social Politics*, 18, 1: 1–23.

Daly, M. (2018), 'Towards a theorization of the relationship between poverty and family', *Social Policy & Administration*, 52, 3: 565–77.

Daly, M. (2019), 'Children and their rights and entitlements in European welfare states', *Journal of Social Policy*, first view, https://www.cambridge.org/core/journals/journal-of-social-policy/article/children-and-their-rights-and-entitlements-in-eu-welfare-states/D71FC89F64E54204 32486DD958361B32.

Daly, M. and Ferragina, E. (2018), 'Family policy in high-income countries: Five decades of development', *Journal of European Social Policy*, 28, 3: 255–70.

Daly, M. and Lewis, J. (2000), 'The concept of social care and the analysis of contemporary welfare states', *British Journal of Sociology*, 51, 2: 281–98.

Daly, M. and Scheiwe, K. (2010), 'Individualisation and personal obligations – social policy, family policy, and law reform in Germany and the UK', *International Journal of Law, Policy and the Family*, 24, 2: 177–97.

Davis, S. N. and Greenstein, T. N. (2013), 'Why study housework? Cleaning as a window into power in couples', *Journal of Family Theory & Review*, 5, 2: 63–71.

de los Reyes, P. (2016), 'When feminism became gender equality and anti-racism turned into diversity management', in Martinsson, L., Griffin, G. and Giritli Nygren, K. (eds), *Challenging the Myth of Gender Equality in Sweden*, Bristol, UK: Policy Press, pp. 23–47.

De Wachter, D., Neels, K., Wood, J. and Vergauwen, J. (2016), 'The educational gradient of maternal employment patterns in 11 European countries', in Mortelmans, D., Matthijs, K., Alofs, E. and Segaert, B. (eds), *Changing Family Dynamics and Demographic Evolution*, Cheltenham, UK and Northampton, MA, USA: Edward Elgar Publishing, pp. 140–78.

Del Boca, D., Pasqua, S. and Pronzato, C. (2009), 'Motherhood and market work decisions in institutional context: A European perspective', *Oxford Economic Papers*, 61 (Supplement 1), i147–i171.

Dermott, E. and Miller, T. (2015), 'More than the sum of its parts? Contemporary fatherhood, policy, practice and discourse', *Families, Relationships and Societies*, 4, 2: 183–95.

Dermott, E. and Pantazis, C. (2014), 'Gender and poverty in Britain: Changes and continuities between 1999 and 2012', *Journal of Poverty and Social Justice*, 22, 3: 253–69.

Dobrotić, I. and Blum, S. (2019), 'Inclusiveness of parental-leave benefits in twenty-one European countries: Measuring social and gender inequalities in leave eligibility', *Social Politics*, advance article, https://academic. oup.com/sp/advance-article-abstract/doi/10.1093/sp/jxz023/5523049.

Donnison, D. V. and Chapman, V. (1965), *Social Policy and Administration*, London: Allen and Unwin.

Dotti Sani, G. (2018), 'The economic crisis and changes in work-family arrangements in six European countries', *Journal of European Social Policy*, 28, 2: 177–92.

Dotti Sani, G. and Treas, J. (2016), 'Educational gradients in parents' child-care time across countries, 1965–2012', *Journal of Marriage and Family*, 78, 4: 1083–96.

Duffy, M. (2005), 'Reproducing labor inequalities: Challenges for feminists conceptualizing care at the intersections of gender, race, and class', *Gender & Society*, 19, 1: 666–82.

Duffy, M. and Armenia, A. (2019), *Paid Care Work around the Globe: A Comparative Analysis of 47 Countries Prepared for UN Women*, LIS

Working Paper Series No. 758, Luxembourg: Luxembourg Income Study.

Dwyer, R. (2013), 'The care economy? Gender, economic restructuring and job polarization in the US labor market', *American Sociological Review*, 78, 3: 390–416.

Economic Commission for Latin America and the Caribbean (2004), *Roads Towards Gender Equity in Latin America and the Caribbean*, prepared for the ninth regional conference of women in Latin America and the Caribbean, Mexico City, 10–12 June, Santiago, Chile: United Nations.

Elomäki, A. (2017), 'The economic case for gender equality in the European Union: Selling gender equality to decision-makers and neoliberalism to women's organisations', *European Journal of Women's Studies*, 22, 3: 288–301.

Elson, D. (2008), 'The Three R's of Unpaid Work: Recognition, Reduction and Redistribution', paper presented at the Expert Group Meeting on Unpaid Work, Economic Development and Human Well-Being, New York, 16–17 November, New York: UNDP.

Elson, D. (2017), 'Recognize, reduce, and redistribute unpaid care work: How to close the gender gap', *New Labour Forum*, 26, 2: 52–61.

England, P. (2010), 'The gender revolution uneven and stalled', *Gender & Society*, 24: 149–66.

Erel, U. (2018), 'Saving and reproducing the nation: Struggles around right-wing politics of social reproduction, gender and race in austerity Europe', *Women's Studies International Forum*, 68 (May–June 2018): 173–82.

Esping-Andersen, G. (1990), *The Three Worlds of Welfare Capitalism*, Cambridge: Polity Press.

Esping-Andersen, G. (2009), *The Incomplete Revolution: Adapting to Women's New Roles*, Cambridge: Polity Press.

Estévez-Abe, M. (2015), 'The outsourcing of house cleaning and low skill immigrant workers', *Social Politics*, 22, 2: 147–69.

Estévez-Abe, M. and Hobson, B. (2015), 'Outsourcing domestic (care) work: The politics, policies, and political economy', *Social Politics*, 22, 2: 133–46.

Eurofound (2015), *Families in the Economic Crisis: Changes in Policy Measures in the EU*, Dublin: Eurofound.

Eurofound (2016), *The Gender Employment Gap: Challenges and Solutions*, Luxembourg: Publications Office of the European Union.

Eurofound (2017a), *Work-life Balance and Flexible Working Arrangements in the European Union*, Luxembourg: Publications Office of the European Union.

Eurofound (2017b), *Sixth European Working Conditions Survey – Overview Report (2017 update)*, Luxembourg: Publications Office of the European Union.

Eurofound (2017c), *European Quality of Life Survey 2016: Quality of Life, Quality of Public Services, and Quality of Society*, Luxembourg: Publications Office of the European Union.

Eurofound (2018a), *Living and Working in Europe 2017*, Luxembourg: Publications Office of the European Union.

Eurofound (2018b), *In-Work Poverty in the EU*, Luxembourg: Publications Office of the European Union.

European Commission (2006), *Communication from the Commission to the Council, the European Parliament, the European Economic and Social Committee and the Committee of the Regions: 'A Roadmap for equality between women and men 2006–2010'*, COM(2006) 92 final, 1 March, Brussels, European Commission.

European Commission (2010a), *Europe 2020: A European Strategy for Smart, Sustainable and Inclusive Growth*, Communication from the Commission, COM(2010) 2020, Brussels, European Commission.

European Commission (2010b), *Communication from the Commission: A Strengthened Commitment to Equality between Women and Men A Women's Charter*, COM(2010) 78 final, 5 March, Brussels, European Commission.

European Commission (2015a), *Evaluation of the Strengths and Weaknesses of the Strategy for Equality between Women and Men 2010–2015*, Brussels: European Commission.

European Commission (2015b), *Commission Staff Working Document: Strategic Engagement for Gender Equality, 2016–2019*, SWD(2015) 278 final, Brussels: European Commission.

European Commission (2017a), *Reflection Paper on the Social Dimension of Europe*, COM(2017) 206, Brussels: European Commission.

European Commission (2017b), *2017 Report on Equality between Women and Men in the EU*, Brussels: European Commission.

European Commission (2017c), *Special Barometer 464 Gender Equality 2017: Gender Equality Stereotypes and Women in Politics*, Brussels: European Commission.

European Commission (2018), *2018 Report on Equality between Women and Men in the EU*, Brussels: European Commission.

European Commission (2019), *2019 Report on Equality between Women and Men in the EU*, Brussels: European Commission.

European Institute for Gender Equality (2016), *Poverty, Gender and Intersecting Inequalities in the EU: Review of the Implementation of*

Area A: Women and Poverty of the Beijing Platform for Action, Vilnius: European Institute for Gender Equality.

European Institute for Gender Equality (2017a), *Gender Equality Index 2017: Measuring Gender Equality in the European Union 2005–2012*, Vilnius: European Institute for Gender Equality.

European Institute for Gender Equality (2017b), *Poverty and Gender over the Life Cycle: Review of the Implementation of the Beijing Platform for Action*, Vilnius: European Institute for Gender Equality.

European Institute for Gender Equality (2017c), *Gender, Skills and Precarious Work in the EU: Research Note*, Vilnius: European Institute for Gender Equality.

European Institute for Gender Equality (2017d), *Economic Benefits of Gender Equality in the European Union: How Closing the Gender Gaps in Labour Market Activity and Pay Leads to Economic Growth*, Vilnius: European Institute for Gender Equality.

European Institute for Gender Equality (2019), *Intersecting Inequalities – Gender Equality Index*, Vilnius: European Institute for Gender Equality.

Fagan, C. and Norman, H. (2013), 'Men and gender equality: Tackling gender desegregation in family roles and in social care jobs', in Bettio, F., Plantenga, J. and Smith, M. (eds), *Gender and the European Labour Market*, London: Routledge, pp. 199–223.

Falkingham, J. and Hills, J. (1995), *The Dynamic of Welfare: The Welfare State and the Life Cycle*, London: Prentice Hall.

Falkner, G. (2013), 'The European Union's social dimension', in Cini, M. and Pérez-Solórzano Borragán, N. (eds), *European Union Politics*, 4th edition, Oxford: Oxford University Press, pp. 268–80.

Farris, S. R. and Marchetti, S. (2017), 'From the commodification to the corporatization of care: European perspectives and debates', *Social Politics*, 24, 2: 109–31.

Ferguson, M. L. (2017), 'Neoliberal feminism as political ideology: Revitalizing the study of feminist political ideologies', *Journal of Political Ideologies*, 22, 3: 221–35.

Fernandez-Macias, E., Hurley, J. and Storrie, D. (eds) (2012), *Transformation of the Employment Structure in the EU and USA 1995–2007*, London: Palgrave Macmillan.

Ferragina, E. (2019), 'Does family policy influence women's employment? Reviewing the evidence in the field', *Political Studies Review*, 17, 1: 65–80.

Ferree, M. M. (2009), 'An American roadmap? Framing feminist goals in a liberal landscape', in Gornick, J. C. and Meyers, M. K. (eds), *Gender Equality Transforming Family Divisions of Labour: The Real Utopias Project*, Volume VI, London: Verso, pp. 283–315.

Ferree, M. M. (2010), 'Filling the glass: Gender perspectives on families', *Journal of Marriage and Family*, 72, June: 420–39.

Ferree, M. M. (2015), '"Theories Don't Grow on Trees": Conceptualizing Gender Knowledge', http://www.ssc.wisc.edu/~mferree/wp/wp-content/uploads/2015/03/theories-dont-grow-on-trees.pdf.

Ferrera, M. (1996), 'The "Southern model" of welfare in social Europe', *Journal of European Social Policy*, 6, 1: 17–37.

Few-Demo, A. (2014), 'Intersectionality as the "new" critical approach in feminist family studies: Evolving racial/ethnic feminisms and critical race theories', *Journal of Family Theory and Review*, 6 (June): 169–83.

Finch, J. and Groves, D. (eds) (1983), *A Labour of Love: Women, Work and Caring*, London: Routledge.

Firestone, S. (1970), *The Dialectic of Sex: The Case for Feminist Revolution*, New York: Farrar, Straus and Giroux.

Fisher, B. and Tronto, J. (1990), 'Toward a feminist theory of caring', in Abel, E. K. and Nelson, M. K. (eds), *Circles of Care Work and Identity in Women's Lives*, Albany: State University of New York Press, pp. 36–54.

Folbre, N. (2009), 'Reforming care?', in Gornick, J. C. and Meyers, M. K. (eds), *Gender Equality Transforming Family Divisions of Labour: The Real Utopias Project*, Volume VI, London: Verso, pp. 111–28.

Folbre, N. (2018), *Developing Care: Recent Research on the Care Economy and Economic Development*, Ottawa: International Development Research Centre.

Francavilla, F., Giannelli, G. C., Mangiavacchi, L. and Piccoli, L. (2013), 'Unpaid family work in Europe: Gender and country differences', in Bettio, F., Plantenga, J. and Smith, M. (eds), *Gender and the European Labour Market*, London: Routledge, pp. 53–72.

Fraser, N. (1989), *Unruly Practices, Power, Discourse and Gender in Contemporary Social Theory*, Cambridge: Polity Press.

Fraser, N. (1994), 'After the family wage: Gender equity and the welfare state', *Political Theory*, 22, 4: 591–618.

Fraser, N. (2009), 'Feminism, capitalism and the cunning of history', *New Left Review*, 56: 97–117.

Fraser, N. (2013), *Fortunes of Feminism: From State-managed Capitalism to Neoliberal Crisis*, London: Verso.

Fraser, N. and Gordon, L. (1992), 'Contract versus charity: Why is there no social citizenship in the United States?', *Socialist Review*, 3: 45–67.

Fraser, N. and Gordon, L. (1994), 'A genealogy of dependency: Tracing a keyword in the U.S. welfare state', *Signs: Journal of Women in Culture and Society*, 19, 21: 309–34.

Fraser, N., Bhattacharya, Y. and Arruzza, C. (2018), 'Notes for a feminist manifesto', *New Left Review*, 114: 113–34.

Fredman, S. (2016), *Intersectional Discrimination in EU Gender Equality and Non-discrimination Law*, European Network of Legal Experts in Gender Equality and Non-discrimination, Brussels: European Commission.

Fuwa, M. (2004), 'Macro-level gender inequality and the division of household labor in 22 countries,' *American Sociological Review*, 69: 751–67.

García-Faroldi, L. (2018), 'Mothers' autonomy or social constraints? Coherence and inconsistency between attitudes and employment trajectories in different welfare regimes', *Social Politics*, early view, https://academic.oup.com/sp/advance-article-abstract/doi/10.1093/sp/jxy030/5184845?redirectedFrom=fulltext.

Gauthier, A. H. (1996), *The State and the Family: A Comparative Analysis of Family Policies in Industrialized Countries*, Oxford: Clarendon Press.

Gauthier, A. H., Smeeding, T. and Furstenberg, F. F. (2004), 'Are parents investing less time in children? Trends in selected industrialized countries', *Population and Development Review*, 30: 647–71.

Geist, V. and Ruppanner, L. (2018), 'Mission impossible? New housework theories for changing families', *Journal of Family Theory & Review*, 10, 1: 242–62.

Gershuny, J. and Kan, M. Y. (2012), 'Halfway to gender equality in paid and unpaid work? Evidence from the multinational time-use study', in Scott, J. Dex, S. and Plagnol, A. C. (eds), *Gendered Lives: Gender Inequalities in Production and Reproduction*, Cheltenham, UK and Northampton, MA, USA: Edward Elgar Publishing, pp. 74–94.

Giannelli, G. C., Mangiavacchi, L. and Piccoli, L. (2012), 'GDP and the value of family caretaking: How much does Europe care?', *Applied Economics*, 44, 6: 2111–31.

Glendinning, C. (2008), 'Increasing choice and control for older and disabled people: A critical review of new developments in England', *Social Policy & Administration*, 42, 5: 451–69.

Glendinning, C. and Millar, J. (eds) (1987), *Women and Poverty in Britain*, Brighton: Wheatsheaf.

Glenn, E. N. (2002), *Unequal Freedom: How Race and Gender Shaped American Citizenship and Labor*, Cambridge, MA: Harvard University Press.

Glenn, E. N. (2016), 'The social construction and institutionalization of gender and race', in Ferguson, S. J. (ed.), *Race, Gender, Sexuality, and Social Class: Dimensions of Inequality and Identity*, 2nd edition, Thousand Oaks, CA: Sage, pp. 108–19.

Glennerster, H., Hills, J., Piachaud, D. and Webb, J. (2004), *One Hundred Years of Poverty and Policy*, York: Joseph Rowntree Foundation.

Goldin, C. (2014), 'A grand gender convergence: Its last chapter,' *American Economic Review* 104, 4: 1091–119.

Gordon, L. (1990), 'The welfare state: Towards a socialist-feminist perspective', *Socialist Register*, 27: 171–200.

Gornick, J. (2004), 'Women's economic outcomes, gender inequality and public policy: Findings from the Luxembourg Income Study', *Socio-Economic Review* 2: 213–38.

Gornick, J. C. and Jantti, M. (2010), *Women, Poverty and Social Policy Regimes: A Cross-national Analysis*, LIS Working Paper 534, Luxembourg: Luxembourg Income Study.

Gornick, J. C. and Meyers, M. K. (2003), *Families that Work: Policies for Reconciling Parenthood and Employment*, New York: Russell Sage Foundation.

Gornick, J. C. and Meyers, M. K. (2008), *Institutions for Gender Egalitarianism: Creating the Conditions for Egalitarian Dual Earner/ Dual Caregiver Families*, New York and London: Verso.

Gornick, J. C. and Meyers, M. K. (eds) (2009), *Gender Equality Transforming Family Divisions of Labour: The Real Utopias Project*, Volume VI, London: Verso.

Gornick, J. C., Meyers, M. K. and Ross, K. E. (1997), 'Supporting the employment of mothers: Policy variation across fourteen welfare states', *Journal of European Social Policy*, 7, 1: 45–70.

Gottfried, H. (1996), 'Introduction: Engaging women's communities: Dilemmas and contradictions in feminist research', in Gottfried, H. (ed.), *Feminism and Social Change: Bridging Theory and Practice*, Urbana: University of Illinois Press, pp. 1–20.

Graham, H. (1983), 'Caring: A labour of love', in Finch, J. and Groves, D. (eds), *A Labour of Love: Women, Work and Caring*, London: Routledge & Kegan Paul, pp. 13–30.

Graham, H. (1991), 'The concept of caring in feminist research: The case of domestic service', *Sociology*, 25, 1: 61–78.

Graham, H. (1993), 'Social divisions in caring', *Women's Studies International Forum*, 16, 5: 461–70.

Grönlund, A., Halldén, K. and Magnusson, C. (2017), 'A Scandinavian success story? Women's labour market outcomes in Denmark, Finland, Norway and Sweden', *Acta Sociologica*, 60, 2: 97–119.

Guerrina, R. and Masselot, A. (2018), 'Walking into the footprint of EU Law: Unpacking the gendered consequences of Brexit', *Social Policy and Society*, 17, 2: 319–30.

Haberkern, K., Schmid, T. and Szydlik, M. (2015), 'Gender differences in intergenerational care in European welfare states', *Ageing and Society*, 25, 2: 298–320.

Hakim, C. (2000), *Work–Lifestyle Choices in the 21st Century: Preference Theory*, Oxford: Oxford University Press.

Halldén, K., Levanon, A. and Kricheli-Katz, T. (2016), 'Does the mother-hood wage penalty differ by individual skill and country family policy? A longitudinal study of ten European countries', *Social Politics*, 23, 3: 363–88.

Hancock, A.-M. (2007), 'When multiplication doesn't equal quick addition: Examining intersectionality as a research paradigm', *Perspectives on Politics*, 5, 1: 63–79.

Hankivsky, O. and Cormier, R. (2011), 'Intersectionality and public policy: Some lessons from existing models', *Political Research Quarterly*, 64, 1: 217–29.

Hankivsky, O. and Jordan-Zachery, J. S. (2019), *The Palgrave Handbook of Intersectionality in Public Policy*, Cham, Switzerland: Palgrave Macmillan; Springer Nature.

Harewood, A.-M. (2014), 'Exploring Gender Definition in Recent Sociological Scholarship', PhD thesis, Rutgers University, https://rucore. libraries.rutgers.edu/rutgers-lib/44113/.

Hassim, S. (2009), 'Whose utopia?', in Gornick, J. C. and Meyers, M. K. (eds), *Gender Equality Transforming Family Divisions of Labour: The Real Utopias Project*, Volume VI, London: Verso, pp. 93–109.

Hartmann, H. (1979), 'The unhappy marriage of Marxism and feminism: Towards a more progressive union', *Capital and Class*, Summer: 1–33.

Hays, S. (1996), *The Cultural Contradictions of Motherhood*, New Haven, CT: Yale University Press.

Hearn, J. (2010), 'Reflecting on men and social policy: Contemporary criti-cal debates and implications for social policy', *Critical Social Policy*, 30, 2: 165–88.

Hearn, J., Pringle, K. and Balkmar, D. (2018), 'Men, masculinities and social policy', in Shaver, S. (ed.), *Handbook on Gender and Social Policy*, Cheltenham, UK and Northampton, MA, USA: Edward Elgar Publishing, pp. 55–73.

Held, V. (2005), *The Ethics of Care: Personal, Political, and Global*, New York: Oxford University Press.

Hemerijck, A. (ed.) (2017), *The Uses of Social Investment*, Oxford: Oxford University Press.

Henwood, K. and Procter, J. (2003), 'The "good father": Reading men's accounts of paternal involvement during the transition to first-time fatherhood', *British Journal of Social Psychology*, 42: 337–55.

Hernes, H. (1987), *Welfare State and Women Power: Essays in State Feminism*, Oslo: Norwegian University Press.

Hill Collins, P. (1990), *Knowledge, Consciousness and the Politics of Empowerment*, New York: Routledge.

Himmelweit, S. (2014), 'The Marketisation of Care before and during Austerity', paper presented to IIPPE Annual Conference, Naples 16–18 September.

Hobson, B. (1990), 'No exit, no voice: Women's economic dependency and the welfare state', *Acta Sociologica*, 33, 3: 235–50.

Hobson, B. (ed.) (2002), *Making Men into Fathers: Men, Masculinities and the Social Politics of Fatherhood*, Cambridge: Cambridge University Press.

Hobson, B. (2014), 'Introduction: Capabilities and agency for worklife balance – a multidimensional framework', in Hobson, B. (ed.), *Worklife Balance: The Agency & Capabilities Gap*, Oxford: Oxford University Press, pp. 1–29.

Hobson, B. and Morgan, D. (2002), 'Introduction', in Hobson, B. (ed.), *Making Men into Fathers: Men, Masculinities and the Social Politics of Fatherhood*, Cambridge: Cambridge University Press, pp. 1–21.

Hochschild, A. R. (2000), 'Global care chains and emotional surplus value', in Hutton, W. and Giddens, A. (eds), *On the Edge: Living with Global Capitalism*, London: Vintage, pp. 130–46.

Hochschild, A. R. (2012), *The Managed Heart*, 3rd edition, Berkeley, CA: University of California Press.

Hook, J. (2010), 'Gender inequality in the welfare state: Sex segregation in housework 1965–2003', *American Journal of Sociology*, 115, 5: 1480–523.

Hook, J. (2015), 'Incorporating "class" into work-family arrangements: Insights from and for Three Worlds', *Journal of European Social Policy*, 25, 1: 14–31.

Hook, J. and Wolfe, C. (2012), 'New fathers? Residential fathers' time with children in four countries', *Journal of Family Issues*, 33: 415–50.

Hook, J. and Paek, E. (2018), *A Stalled Revolution for Whom? Change in Women's Labour Force Participation in 12 Countries, 1988–2015*. Mimeo, University of Southern California.

Hoskyns, C. (1996), *Integrating Gender: Women, Law and Politics in the European Union*, London: Verso.

Htun, M. and Weldon, L. (2018), *The Logics of Gender Justice: State Action on Women's Rights around the World*, Cambridge: Cambridge University Press.

Htun, M., Jensenius, F. R. and Nelson Nuñez, J. (2019), 'Gender discriminatory laws and women's economic agency', *Social Politics*, 26, 2: 199–223.

Ingold, J. and Hetherington, D. (2013), 'Work, welfare and gender inequalities: An analysis of activation strategies for partnered women in the UK, Australia and Denmark', *Work, Employment and Society* 27, 4: 621–38.

International Bank for Reconstruction/The World Bank (2019), *Women, Business and the Law 2019, A Decade of Reform*, Washington DC: International Bank for Reconstruction/The World Bank.

Jacquot, S. (2015), *Transformations in EU Gender Equality: From Emergence to Dismantling*, Basingstoke: Palgrave Macmillan.

Jacquot, S. (2017), 'A policy in crisis: The dismantling of the EU gender equality policy', in Kantola, J. and Lombardo, E. (eds), *Gender and the Economic Crisis in Europe: Politics, Institutions and Intersectionality*, Cham, Switzerland: Palgrave Macmillan; Springer Nature, pp. 27–48.

Jahan, R. (1995), *The Elusive Agenda: Mainstreaming Women in Development*, Atlantic Highlands, NJ: Zed Books.

Jaumotte, F. (2003), *Female Labour Force Participation: Past Trends and Main Determinants in OECD Countries*, Paris: OECD Economics Department Working Papers No. 376, OECD Publishing.

Javornik, J. (2014), 'Measuring state defamilialism: Contesting post-socialist exceptionalism', *Journal of European Social Policy*, 24, 3: 240–57.

Jenkins, S. (2008), *Marital Splits and Income Changes over the Longer Term*, ISER Working Paper 2008: 07, Colchester: Institute for Social and Economic Research, University of Essex.

Jenson, J. (2008), 'Writing women out, folding gender in: The European Union "modernises" social policy', *Social Politics*, 15, 2: 1–23.

Jenson, J. (2009), 'Lost in translation: The social investment perspective and gender equality', *Social Politics*, 16, 4: 446–83.

Jenson, J. (2015), 'The fading goals of gender equality: Three policy directions that underpin the resilience of gendered socio-economic inequalities,' *Social Politics*, 22, 4: 539–60.

Jenson, J. (2018), 'Social investment, poverty and lone parents', in Shaver, S. (ed.), *Handbook on Gender and Social Policy*, Cheltenham, UK and Northampton, MA, USA: Edward Elgar Publishing, pp. 197–214.

Jenson, J. and Nagels, N. (2018), 'Social policy instruments in motion: Conditional cash transfers from Mexico to Peru', *Social Policy & Administration*, 52, 1: 323–42.

Jenson, J. and Saint-Martin, D. (2006), 'Building blocks for a new social architecture: The LEGO paradigm of an active society', *Policy and Politics*, 34, 3: 429–51.

Kantola, J. (2010), *Gender and the European Union*, Basingstoke: Palgrave Macmillan.

Kantola, J. (2015), 'Gender equality governance and tools: The need for renewed focus and a clear vision', in Bettio, F. and Sansonetti, S. (eds), *Visions for Gender Equality*, Luxembourg: Publications Office of the European Union, pp. 72–4.

Kantola, J. and Lombardo, E. (2017a), *Gender and Political Analysis*, London: Palgrave.

Kantola, J. and Lombardo, E. (2017b), 'Gender and the politics of the economic crisis in Europe', in Kantola, J. and Lombardo, E. (eds), *Gender and the Economic Crisis in Europe: Politics, Institutions and Intersectionality*, Cham, Switzerland: Palgrave Macmillan; Springer Nature, pp. 1–26.

Karamessini, M. and Rubery, J. (2014), 'The challenge of austerity for equality: A consideration of eight European countries in the crisis', in Eydoux, A., Math, A. and Périvier, H. (eds), *European Labour Markets in Time of Crisis: A Gender Perspective*, Paris: Revue de l'OFCE, Debates and Policies, n 133, pp. 15–39.

Keck, W. and Saraceno, C. (2013), 'The impact of different social-policy frameworks on social inequalities among women in the European Union', *Social Politics*, 20: 297–328.

Klesment, M. and Van Bavel, J. (2017), 'The reversal of the gender gap in education, motherhood, and women as main earners in Europe', *European Sociological Review*, 33, 3: 465–81.

Knijn, T. and Kremer, M. (1997), 'Gender and the caring dimension of welfare states: Towards inclusive citizenship', *Social Politics*, 4, 3: 328–61.

Knijn, T. and Smit, A. (2009), 'Investing, facilitating, or individualizing the reconciliation of work and family life: Three paradigms and ambivalent politics', *Social Politics*, 16, 4: 484–518.

Knudsen, K. and Wærness, K. (2008), 'National context and spouses' housework in 34 countries', *European Sociological Review*, 24: 97–113.

Kodate, N. and Timonen, V. (2017), 'Bringing the family in through the back door: The stealthy expansion of family care in Asian and European long-term care policy', *Journal of Cross Cultural Gerontology*, 32, 3: 291–301.

Kofman, E. (2012), 'Rethinking care through social reproduction: Articulating circuits of migration', *Social Politics*, 19, 1: 142–62.

Kofman, E. and Raghuram, P. (2018), 'Gender, migration and social reproduction', in Elias, J. and Roberts, A. (eds), *Handbook of the International Political Economy of Gender*, Cheltenham, UK and Northampton, MA, USA: Edward Elgar Publishing, pp. 427–39.

Korpi, W., Ferrarini, T. and Englund, S. (2013), 'Women's opportunities under different family policy constellations: Gender, class, and inequality tradeoffs in western countries re-examined', *Social Politics,* 20: 1–40.

Kováts, E. (ed.) (2017), *The Future of the European Union: Feminist Perspectives from East-Central Europe*, Budapest: Friedrich-Ebert-Stiftung.

Koven, S. and Michel, S. (eds) (1993), *Mothers of a New World: Maternalist Politics and the Origins of Welfare States*, New York: Routledge.

Kremer, M. (2007), *How Welfare States Care: Culture, Gender and Parenting in Europe*, Amsterdam: University of Amsterdam Press.

Kurowska, A. (2018), '(De)familialization and (de)genderization – competing or complementary perspectives in comparative policy analysis', *Social Policy & Administration*, 52, 1: 29–49.

Land, H. (1978), 'Who cares for the family?', *Journal of Social Policy*, 7, 3: 257–81.

Land, H. (1980), 'The family wage', *Feminist Review*, 6: 55–77.

Land, H. (2011), 'Recognising care and sustaining carers: Challenges for economic and social policies in the twenty-first century', in Bertram, H. and Ehlert, N. (eds), *Families, Ties and Care: An International Perspective*, Leverkusen: Barbara Budrich Publishers.

Lang, L. (2015), 'Constructions of Gender Equality in Swedish Family Policy', Master's thesis, Lund University, Sweden.

Lareau, A. (2003), *Unequal Childhoods: Class, Race and Family Life*, Berkeley CA: University of California Press.

Le Bihan, B., Da Roit, B. and Sopadzhiyan, A. (2019), 'The turn to optional familialism through the market: Long-term care, cash for care, and care-giving policies in Europe', *Social Policy & Administration*, 53, 4: 579–95.

Lee, P. and Raban, C. (1988), *Welfare Theory and Social Policy: Reform or Revolution?* London: Sage.

Leibfried, S. (2015), 'Social policy: Left to judges and to the markets?', in Wallace, H., Pollack, M. A. and Young, A. R. (eds), *Policy-Making in the European Union*, 7th edition, Oxford: Oxford University Press, pp. 263–92.

Leira, A. (1992), *Models of Motherhood: Welfare State Policy and Scandinavian Experiences of Everyday Practices*, Cambridge: Cambridge University Press.

Leisering, L. and Leibfried, S. (1999), *Time and Poverty in Western Welfare States: United Germany in Perspective*. Cambridge: Cambridge University Press.

Leitner, S. (2003), 'Varieties of familialism: The caring function of the family in comparative perspective', *European Societies* 5, 4: 353–75.

Leitner, S., Ostner, I. and Schmitt, C. (2008), 'Family policies in Germany', in Ostner, I. and Schmitt, C. (eds), *Family Policies in the Context of Family Change*, Wiesbaden, Germany: Verlag für Sozialwissenschaften, pp. 175–202.

León, M. (ed.), (2014), *The Transformation of Care in European Societies*, Basingstoke: Palgrave Macmillan.

Lewis, G. (2000), *"Race," Gender, Social Welfare: Encounters in a Postcolonial Society*, New York: Wiley.

Lewis, G. (2013), 'Unsafe travel: Experiencing intersectionality and feminist displacements', *Signs: Journal of Women in Culture and Society*, 38, 4: 869–92.

Lewis, J. (1992), 'Gender and the development of welfare regimes', *Journal of European Social Policy*, 2, 3: 159–73.

Lewis, J. (2001), 'The decline of the male breadwinner model: Implications for work and care', *Social Politics*, 8, 2: 152–69.

Lewis, J. (2006), 'Work/family reconciliation, equal opportunities and social policies: The interpretation of policy trajectories at the EU level and the meaning of gender equality', *Journal of European Social Policy*, 13, 3: 420–37.

Lewis, J. (2009), *Work–family Balance, Gender and Policy*, Cheltenham, UK and Northampton, MA, USA: Edward Elgar Publishing.

Lewis, J. and Giullari, S. (2005), 'The adult worker model family, gender equality and care: The search for new policy principles and the possibilities and problems of a capabilities approach', *Economy and Society*, 34, 1: 76–104.

Lewis, J. and Meredith, B. (1988), *Daughters Who Care: Daughters Caring for Mothers at Home*, London: Routledge.

Lewis, J. and Ostner, I. (1991), 'Gender and the Evolution of European Social Policies', paper presented at workshop on 'Emergent Supranational Social Policy: The EC's Social Dimension in Comparative Perspective', 15–17 November, Center for European Studies, Harvard University.

Lewis, J. and Piachaud, D. (1992), 'Women and poverty in the twentieth century', in Glendinning, C. and Millar, J. (eds), *Women and Poverty in Britain: The 1990s*, Brighton, UK: Wheatsheaf, pp. 28–52.

Lister, R. (1990), 'Women, economic dependency and citizenship', *Journal of Social Policy* 19, 4: 445–67.

Lister, R. (1994), '"She has other duties": Women, citizenship and social security', in Baldwin, S. and Falkingham, J. (eds), *Social Security and Social Change: New Challenges to the Beveridge Model*, New York: Harvester Wheatsheaf, pp. 31–44.

Lister, R. (1997a), 'Dilemmas in engendering citizenship', in Hobson, B. and Berggren, A. M. (eds), *Crossing Borders: Gender and Citizenship in*

Transition, Stockholm: Swedish Council for Planning and Coordination of Research, pp. 57–114.

Lister, R. (1997b), *Citizenship: Feminist Perspectives*, Basingstoke: Palgrave Macmillan.

Lister, R. (2002), 'The dilemmas of pendulum politics: Balancing paid work, care and citizenship', *Economy and Society*, 31, 4: 520–32.

Lohmann, H. and Zagel, H. (2016), 'Family policy in comparative perspective: The concepts and measurement of familization and defamilization', *Journal of European Social Policy*, 26, 1: 48–65.

Lombardo, E. and Meier, P. (2006), 'Gender mainstreaming in the EU: Incorporating a feminist reading?', *European Journal of Women's Studies*, 13, 2: 151–66.

Lombardo, E., Meier, P. and Verloo, M. (eds) (2009), *The Discursive Politics of Gender Equality: Stretching, Bending and Policymaking*, New York: Routledge.

LSE Commission on Gender, Inequality and Power (2015), *Confronting Gender Inequality*, London: LSE.

Luckhaus, L. (1990), 'Changing rules, enduring structures', *The Modern Law Review*, 23, 5: 655–88.

Lutz, H. (2008), 'Introduction: Migrant domestic workers in Europe', in Lutz, H. (ed.), *Migration and Domestic Work: A European Perspective on a Global Theme*, Aldershot, UK: Ashgate, pp. 1–10.

Lutz, H. (2018), 'Care migration: The connectivity between care chains, care circulation and transnational social inequality,' *Current Sociology*, 66, 4: 577–89.

Lykke, N. (2011), 'Intersectional analysis: Black box or useful critical feminist thinking technology', in Lutz, H., Herrera Vivar, M. T. and Supik, L. (eds), *Framing Intersectionality: Debates on a Multi-faceted Concept in Gender Studies*, Farnham, UK: Ashgate, pp. 207–21.

Mahon, R. (2010), 'After neo-liberalism: The OECD, the World Bank and the child', *Global Social Policy*, 10, 2: 172–92.

Mahon, R. (2018a), 'Through a fractured gaze: The OECD, the World Bank and transnational care chains', *Current Sociology*, 4, 2: 562–76.

Mahon, R. (2018b), 'Shaping the way international organizations "see" gender equality: The OECD and ECLAC', in Shaver, S. (ed.), *Handbook on Gender and Social Policy*, Cheltenham, UK and Northampton, MA, USA: Edward Elgar Publishing, pp. 267–86.

Mandel, H. (2012), 'Winners and losers: The consequences of welfare state policies for gender wage inequality', *European Sociological Review*, 28: 241–62.

Mandel, H. and Semyonov, M. (2005), 'Family policies, wage structures and gender gaps: Sources of earnings' inequality in 20 countries', *American Sociological Review*, 70: 949–67.

Manoudi, A., Weber, T., Scott, D. and Hawley Woodall, J. (2018), *An Analysis of Personal and Household Services to Support Work Life Balance for Working Parents and Carers*, Synthesis Report ECE Thematic Review 2018, Brussels: European Commission.

Martinsson, L., Griffin, G. and Giritli Nygren, K. (eds) (2016), *Challenging the Myth of Gender Equality in Sweden*, Bristol, UK: Policy Press.

Mathieu, S. (2016), 'From the defamilialization to the "demotherization" of care work', *Social Politics*, 23, 4: 576–91.

McCall, L. (2005), 'The complexity of intersectionality', *Signs*, 30, 3: 1771–800.

McDowell, L. (2014), 'Gender, work, employment and society: Feminist reflections on continuity and change', *Work, Employment and Society*, 28, 5: 825–37.

McIntosh, M. (1978), 'The state and the oppression of women', in Kuhn, A. and Wolpe, R. M. (eds), *Feminism and Materialism*, London: Routledge & Kegan Paul, pp. 254–89.

McIntosh, M. (1981), 'Feminism and social policy', *Critical Social Policy*, 1, 1: 32–42.

McKinsey Global Institute (2015), *The Power of Parity: How Advancing Women's Equality Can Add $12 Trillion to Global Growth*, Brussels: McKinsey Global Institute.

McLaughlin, E. and Glendinning, C. (1994), 'Paying for care in Europe: Is there a feminist approach?', in Hantrais, L. and Mangan, S. (eds), *Family Policy and the Welfare of Women*, Loughborough: Cross-National Research Group, European Research Centre, Cross-National Research Papers, Third Series, pp. 52–69.

McRobbie, A. (2013), 'Feminism, the family and the new "mediated" maternalism', *New Formations*, 80–81: 119–37.

Meagher, G. and Szebehely, M. (eds) (2013), *Marketisation in Nordic Eldercare: A Research Report on Legislation, Oversight, Extent and Consequences*, Department of Social Work, Stockholm: University of Stockholm.

Meulders-Klein, M. T. and Eekelaar, J. (eds) (1988), *Family, State and Individual Economic Security*, vol. II, Brussels: E. Story-Scientia.

Michel, S. and Peng, I. (2012), 'All in the family? Migrants, nationhood, and care regimes in Asia and North America', *Journal of European Social Policy*, 22, 4: 406–18.

Michel, S. and Peng, I. (eds) (2017), *Gender, Migration, and the Work of Care: A Multi-scalar Approach to the Pacific Rim*, Cham, Switzerland: Palgrave Macmillan; Springer Nature.

Milkman, R. and Townsley, E. (1994), 'Gender and the economy', in Smelser, N. and Swedberg, R. (eds), *The Handbook of Economic Sociology*, Princeton, NJ: Princeton University Press and New York: Russell Sage Foundation, pp. 600–619.

Millar, J. and Bennett, F. (2017), 'Universal Credit: Assumptions, contradictions and virtual reality', *Social Policy and Society*, 16, 2: 169–82.

Millett, K. (1970), *Sexual Politics*, New York: Avon Books.

Mink, G. (1990), 'The lady and the tramp: gender, race and the origins of the American welfare state', in Gordon, L. (ed.), *Women, the State, and Welfare*, Madison: The University of Wisconsin Press, pp. 92–122.

MISSOC Secretariat (2012), *MISSOC Analysis 2012/2: Gender Differences in Social Protection*, Brussels: MISSOC Secretariat.

Montanari, I. (2000), 'From family wage to marriage subsidy and child benefits: Controversy and consensus in the development of family policy', *Journal of European Social Policy*, 10, 4: 307–33.

Morel, N. (2015), 'Servants for the knowledge-based economy? The political economy of domestic services in Europe', *Social Politics*, 22, 2: 170–92.

Morel, N., Palme, J. and Palier, B. (eds) (2012), *Towards a Social Investment Welfare State? Ideas, Policies and Challenges*, Bristol, UK: Policy Press.

Morgan, K. J. (2009), 'The political path to a dual-earner/dual-caregiver society: Pitfalls and possibilities', in Gornick, J. C. and Meyers, M. K. (eds), *Gender Equality Transforming Family Divisions of Labour: The Real Utopias Project*, Volume VI, London: Verso, pp. 317–37.

Moss, P. (2012), 'Parental leaves and early childhood education and care: From mapping the terrain to exploring the environment', *Children and Youth Services Review*, 34, 3: 523–31.

Mulinari, D. (2016), 'Gender equality under threat? Exploring the paradoxes of an ethno-nationalist party', in Martinsson, L., Griffin, G. and Giritli Nygren, K. (eds), *Challenging the Myth of Gender Equality in Sweden*, Bristol, UK: Policy Press, pp. 137–61.

Mun, E. and Jung, J. (2018), 'Policy generosity, employer heterogeneity, and women's employment opportunities: The welfare state paradox reexamined,' *American Sociological Review*, 83: 508–35.

Nelson, B. J. (1990), 'The origins of the two-channel welfare state: Workmen's compensation and mothers' aid', in Gordon, L. (ed.), *Women, the State and Welfare*, Madison: University of Wisconsin Press, pp. 123–51.

Nieuwenhuis, R., Need, A. and Van der Kolk, H. (2017), 'Is there such a thing as too long childcare leave?', *International Journal of Sociology and Social Policy*, 37, 1–2: 2–15.

Nieuwenhuis, R., Munzi, R., Neugschwender, J., Omar, H. and Palmisano,

F. (2018), *Gender Equality and Poverty Are Intrinsically Linked: A Contribution to the Continued Monitoring of Selected Sustainable Development Goals*, Discussion Paper No. 26, December, New York: UN Women.

Nussbaum, M. (2000), *Women and Human Development: The Capabilities Approach*, Cambridge: Cambridge University Press.

Oakley, A. (1974a), *Housewife*, Harmondsworth, UK: Allen Lane.

Oakley, A. (1974b), *The Sociology of Housework*, Oxford: Martin Robinson.

O'Connor, J. S. (1992), 'Citizenship, Class, Gender and the Labour Market: Issues of De-commodification and Personal Autonomy', paper presented to conference 'Comparative Studies of Welfare State Development: Quantitative and Qualitative Dimensions', University of Bremen, 3–6 September.

O'Connor, J. S. (1996), 'From women in the welfare state to gendering welfare state regimes', *Current Sociology*, 44, 2: 1–125.

OECD (2003; 2005; 2010; 2013), *Family Database*, http://www.oecd.org/els/family/database.htm.

OECD (2012), *Closing the Gender Gap: Act Now*, Paris: Organisation for Economic Co-operation and Development.

OECD (2017), *The Pursuit of Gender Equality: An Uphill Battle*, Paris: OECD.

OECD (2018), *Is the Last Mile the Longest? Economic Gains from Gender Equality in Nordic Countries*, Paris: OECD.

Ólafsson, S., Daly, M., Kangas, O. and Palme, J. (eds) (2019), *Welfare and the Great Recession: A Comparative Study*, Oxford: Oxford University Press.

Orloff, A. S. (1993), 'Gender and the social rights of citizenship: The comparative analysis of gender relations and welfare states', *American Sociological Review*, 58, 3: 303–28.

Orloff, A. S. (1996), 'Gender in the welfare state', *Annual Review of Sociology*, 22: 51–78.

Orloff, A. S. (2008), 'Should Feminists Aim for Gender Symmetry? Feminism and Gender Equality Projects for a Post-materialist Era', paper presented at the annual conference of the International Sociological Association Research Committee on Poverty, Social Welfare and Social Policy, RC 19, Stockholm, 4–6 September.

Orloff, A. S. (2009), 'Should feminists aim for gender symmetry? Why a dual earner/dual caregiver society is not every feminist's utopia', in Gornick, J. C. and Meyers, M. K. (eds), *Gender Equality Transforming Family Divisions of Labour: The Real Utopias Project*, Volume VI, London: Verso, pp. 129–57.

Ostner, I. and Lewis, J. (1995), 'Gender and the evolution of European social policies', in Leibfried, S. and Pierson, P. (eds), *European Social Policy: Between Fragmentation and Integration*, Washington, DC: Brookings, pp. 159–93.

Oxfam (2017), *Oxfam's Conceptual Framework on Women's Economic Empowerment*, Oxford: Oxfam.

Papadopoulos, T. and Roumpakis, A. (2019), 'Family as socio-economic actor in the political economy of welfare', in Heins, E., Rees, J. and Needham, C. (eds), *Social Policy Review 31: Analysis and Debate in Social Policy, 2019*, Bristol, UK: Policy Press, pp. 243–66.

Parreñas, R. (2001), *Servants of Globalization: Women, Migration and Domestic Work*, Stanford, CA: Stanford University Press.

Pascall, G. (1983), 'Women and social welfare', in Bean, P. and McPherson, S. (eds), *Approaches to Welfare*, London: Routledge & Kegan Paul, pp. 83–98.

Pascall, G. (1986), *Social Policy: A Feminist Critique*, London: Tavistock.

Pascall, G. and Lewis, J. (2004), 'Emerging gender regimes and policies for equality in Europe', *Journal of Social Policy*, 33, 3: 373–94.

Pateman, C. (1988), 'The patriarchal welfare state', in Gutman, A. (ed.), *Democracy and the Welfare State*, Princeton, NJ: Princeton University Press, pp. 231–60.

Paull, G. (2007), *Partnership Transitions and Mothers' Employment*, Department for Work and Pensions Research Report 452, Leeds: Corporate Document Services.

Paull, G. and Taylor, J. (2002), *Mothers' Employment and Childcare Use in Britain*, London: Institute for Fiscal Studies.

Peña-Casas, R., Ghailani, S., Spasova, S. and Vanhercke, B. (2019), *In-Work Poverty in Europe: A Study of National Policies*, Brussels: European Commission.

Peng, I. (2019), *The Care Economy: A New Research Framework*, Sciences Po LIEPP Working Paper No. 89, Paris: Sciences Po.

Périvier, H. (2014), 'Men and women during the economic crisis: Employment trends in eight European countries', in Eydoux, A., Math, A. and Périvier, H. (eds), *European Labour Markets in Time of Crisis: A Gender Perspective*, Paris: Revue de l'OFCE, Debates and Policies, n 133, pp. 41–84.

Perrons, D. (2015), 'The effects of the crisis on female poverty', in *Main Causes of Female Poverty, Compilation of In-depth Analyses*, Workshop 30 March, Brussels: European Parliament, pp. 39–67.

Pettit, B. and Hook, J. L. (2005), 'The structure of women's employment in comparative perspective', *Social Forces*, 84, 2: 779–801.

Pettit, B. and Hook, J. L. (2009), *Gendered Tradeoffs*, New York: Russell Sage Foundation.

Pfau-Effinger, B. (2004), *Development of Culture, Welfare States and Women's Employment in Europe*, Aldershot, UK: Ashgate.

Pfau-Effinger, B. (2005), 'Welfare state policies and the development of care arrangements', *European Societies*, 7, 2: 321–47.

Phoenix, A. and Pattynama, P. (2006), 'Intersectionality', *European Journal of Women's Studies*, 13, 3: 187–92.

Plantenga, J. and Remery, C. (2013), 'Measuring gender equality within the European Union', in Bettio, F., Plantenga, J. and Smith, M. (eds), *Gender and the European Labour Market*, London: Routledge, pp. 36–50.

Pollack, M. and Hafner-Burton, E. (2000), 'Mainstreaming gender in the European Union', *Journal of European Public Policy*, 7, 3: 432–56.

Ponthieux, S. (2013), 'Income pooling and equal sharing within the household: What can we learn from the 2010 EU-SILC Module?', *Eurostat Population and Social Conditions: Methodologies and Working Papers*, Luxembourg: European Commission.

Price, D. (2008), *Measuring the Poverty of Older People: A Critical Review*, Report of an ESRC Public Sector Placement Fellowship June 2007–January 2008, London: King's College London.

Price, D. (2009), 'Pension accumulation and gendered household structures: What are the implications of changes in family formation for future financial inequality?', in Miles, J. and Probert, R. (eds), *Sharing Lives, Dividing Assets: An Inter-disciplinary Study*, Oxford: Hart Publishing, pp. 257–82.

Prügl, E. (2017), 'Neoliberalism with a feminist face: Creating a new hegemony at the World Bank', *Feminist Economics*, 23, 1: 30–53.

Quadagno, J. S. (1994), *The Color of Welfare: How Racism Undermined the War on Poverty*, New York: Oxford University Press.

Quinn, S. (2016), *Europe: A Survey of Gender Budgeting Efforts*, IMF Working Paper No. 16/155, Washington, DC: IMF.

Rai, S., Hoskyns, C. and Thomas, D. (2014), 'Depletion', *International Feminist Journal of Politics*, 16, 1: 86–105.

Ramaekers, S. and Suissa, J. (2012), *The Claims of Parenting: Reasons, Responsibility and Society*, London: Springer.

Ranci, C. and Pavolini, E. (2015), 'Not all that glitters is gold: Long-term care reforms in the last two decades in Europe', *Journal of European Social Policy*, 25, 3: 270–85.

Rastrigina, O. and Verashchagina, A. (2015), *Secondary Earners and Fiscal Policies in Europe*, Brussels: European Commission.

Razavi, S. (2011), 'Rethinking care in a development context: An introduction', *Development and Change*, 42, 4: 873–903.

Razavi, S. and Staab, S. (2018), 'Rethinking social policy: A gender perspective from the developing world', in Shaver, S. (ed.), *Handbook on Gender and Social Policy*, Cheltenham, UK and Northampton, MA, USA: Edward Elgar Publishing, pp. 74–89.

Rees, T. (1998), *Mainstreaming Equality in the European Union: Education, Training and Labour Market Policies*. London: Routledge.

Risman, B. and Davis, G. (2013), 'From sex roles to gender culture', *Current Sociology*, 51, 5–6: 733–55.

Robeyns, I. (2003), 'Sen's capability approach and gender inequality: Selecting relevant capabilities', *Feminist Economics*, 9, 2–3: 61–92.

Rodrigues, R., Huber, M. and Lamura, G. (eds) (2012), *Facts and Figures on Healthy Ageing and Long-term Care*, Vienna: European Centre for Social Welfare Policy and Research.

Rolandsen Augustín, L. (2013), *Gender Equality, Intersectionality, and Diversity in Europe*, New York: Palgrave Macmillan.

Roll, J. (1991), *What Is a Family? Benefit Models and Social Realities*, London: Family Policy Studies Centre, Occasional Paper No 13.

Rose, H. (1981), 'Rereading Titmuss: The sexual division of welfare', *Journal of Social Policy*, 10, 4: 477–502.

Rose, H. (1986), 'Women and the restructuring of the welfare state', in Øyen, E. (ed.), *Comparing Welfare States and their Futures*, Aldershot, UK: Gower, pp. 80–95.

Rottenberg, C. (2014), 'The rise of neoliberal feminism', *Cultural Studies*, 28, 3: 418–37.

Rottenberg, C. (2018), *The Rise of Neoliberal Feminism*, Oxford: Oxford University Press.

Rubery, J. (2015), 'Regulating for gender equality: A policy framework to support the universal caregiver vision', *Social Politics*, 22, 4: 513–38.

Sainsbury, D. (1993), 'Dual welfare and sex segregation of access to social benefits: Income maintenance policies in the UK, the US, the Netherlands and Sweden', *Journal of Social Policy*, 22, 1: 69–98.

Sainsbury, D. (1994), 'Women's and men's social rights: Gendering dimensions of welfare states?', in Sainsbury, D. (ed.), *Gendering Welfare States*, London: Sage, pp. 150–69.

Sainsbury, D. (1996), *Gender, Equality and Welfare States*, Cambridge: Cambridge University Press.

Sainsbury, D. (ed.) (1999), *Gender and Welfare State Regimes*, Oxford: Oxford University Press.

Salem, S. (2018), 'Intersectionality and its discontents: Intersectionality as travelling theory', *European Journal of Women's Studies*, 25, 4: 403–18.

Sanchez-Mangas, R. and Sanchez-Marcos, V. (2008), 'Balancing family and work: The effect of cash benefits for working mothers', *Labor Economics*, 15, 6: 1127–42.

Sánchez-Mira, N. and O'Reilly, J. (2018), 'Household employment and the crisis in Europe', *Work, Employment and Society*, 33, 3: 422–43.

Sapiro, V. (1986), 'The gender basis of American social policy', *Political Science Quarterly*, 101, 2: 221–38.

Saraceno, C. (2011), *Family Policies, Concepts, Goals and Instruments*, Torino: Collegio Carlo Alberto, Carlo Alberto Notebooks, No 230.

Saraceno, C. (2015), 'A critical look at the social investment approach from a gender perspective', *Social Politics*, 22, 2: 257–69.

Saraceno, C. and Keck, W. (2010), 'Can we identify intergenerational policy regimes in Europe?', *European Societies*, 12, 5: 675–96.

Saxonberg, S. (2013), 'From defamilialization to degenderization: Toward a new welfare typology', *Social Policy & Administration*, 47, 1: 26–49.

Sayer, L., Gauthier, A. H. and Furstenberg, F. J. (2004), 'Educational differences in parents' time with children: Cross-national variations', *Journal of Marriage and Family*, 66: 1152–69.

Scheiwe, K. (1994), 'EC law's unequal treatment of the family: The case law of the European Court of Justice on rules prohibiting discrimination on grounds of sex and nationality', *Social and Legal Studies*, 3, 2: 243–65.

Schneebaum, A., Rehm, M., Mader, K., Klopf, P. and Hollan, K. (2014), *The Gender Wealth Gap in Europe*, Department of Economics Working Paper No. 186, Vienna: University of Economics and Business.

Scott, J. (1986), 'Gender: A useful category of historical analysis', *American Historical Review*, 91, 5: 1053–75.

Sen, A. (1985), 'Well-being, agency and freedom: the Dewey lectures 1984', *The Journal of Philosophy*, 82, 4: 169–224.

Sen, A. (1992), *Inequality Re-examined*, Oxford: Oxford University Press.

Sen, A. (1999), *Development as Freedom*, Oxford: Oxford University Press.

Shalev, M. (2009), 'Class divisions among women', in Gornick, J. C. and Meyers, M. K. (eds), *Gender Equality Transforming Family Divisions of Labour: The Real Utopias Project*, Volume VI, London: Verso, pp. 255–82.

Shaver, S. (1990), *Gender, Social Policy Regimes and the Welfare State*, Discussion Paper No. 26, Social Policy Research Centre, Sydney: University of New South Wales.

Shaver, S. (2018), 'Introduction to the *Handbook on Gender and Social Policy*', in Shaver, S. (ed.), *Handbook on Gender and Social Policy*, Cheltenham, UK and Northampton, MA, USA: Edward Elgar Publishing, pp. 1–18.

Shaver, S. and Bradshaw, J. (1993), *The Recognition of Wifely Labour by*

Welfare States, Discussion Paper No. 44, Social Policy Research Centre, Sydney: The University of New South Wales.

Showstack Sassoon, A. (ed.) (1987), *Women and the State: The Shifting Boundaries of Public and Private*, London: Hutchinson.

Sierminska, E. (in association with Girshina, A.) (2017), *Wealth and Gender in Europe*, Brussels: European Commission, Directorate General for Justice.

Siim, B. (1987), 'The Scandinavian welfare states – towards sexual equality or a new kind of male domination?', *Acta Sociologica*, 30, 3–4: 255–70.

Siim, B. and Borchorst, A. (2017), 'Gendering European welfare states and citizenship: Revisioning citizenship', in Kennett, P. and Lendvai-Bainton, N. (eds), *Handbook of European Social Policy*, Cheltenham, UK and Northampton, MA, USA: Edward Elgar Publishing, pp. 60–74.

Simonazzi, A. (2009), 'Care regimes and national employment models', *Cambridge Journal of Economics*, 33: 211–32.

Skocpol, T. (1995), *Protecting Soldiers and Mothers: The Political Origins of Social Policy in the US*, Cambridge, MA: The Belknap Press.

Sohrab, J. A. (1994a), 'Women and social security: The limits of EEC equality law', *Journal of Social Welfare and Family Law*, 16, 1: 5–17.

Sohrab, J. A. (1994b), 'An overview of the equality directive on social security and its implementation in four social security systems', *Journal of European Social Policy*, 4, 4: 263–76.

Sohrab, J. A. (1996), *Sexing the Benefit: Women, Social Security and Financial Independence in EC Equality Law*, Aldershot, UK: Dartmouth.

Spasova, S., Baeten, R., Costa, S., Ghailani, D., Peña-Casas, R. and Vanhercke, B. (2018), *Challenges of Long-term Care in Europe: A Study of National Policies 2018*, European Social Policy Network (ESPN), Brussels: European Commission.

Staab, S. (2010), 'Social investment policies in Chile and Latin America: Towards equal opportunities for women and children?', *Journal of Social Policy*, 39, 4: 607–26.

Stainback, K., Tomaskovic-Devey, D. and Skaggs, S. (2010), 'Organizational approaches to inequality: Inertia, relative power, and environments', *Annual Review of Sociology*, 36: 225–47.

Steiber, N. and Haas, B. (2012), 'Advances in explaining women's employment patterns', *Socio-Economic Review* 10, 2: 343–67.

Steiber, N., Berghammer, C. and Haas, B. (2016), 'Contextualizing the education effect on women's employment: A cross-national comparative analysis', *Journal of Marriage and Family*, 78, 1: 246–61.

Steiner, J. (1996), 'The principle of equal treatment for men and women in social security', in Hervey, T. K. and O'Keeffe, D. O. (eds), *Sex Equality Law in the European Union*, Chichester, UK: Wiley, pp. 111–36.

Stier, H., Lewin-Epstein, N. and Braun, M. (2018), 'Institutional change and women's work patterns along the family life course', *Research in Stratification and Mobility*, 57: 46–55.

Stratigaki, M. (2004), 'The co-optation of gender concepts in EU policies: The case of "reconciliation of work and family"', *Social Politics*, 11, 1: 30–56.

Stratigaki, M. (2005), 'Gender mainstreaming vs. positive action. An ongoing conflict in EU gender equality policy', *European Journal of Women's Studies*, 12, 2: 165–86.

Sullivan, O., Billari, F. and Altintas, E. (2014), 'Fathers' changing contributions to childcare and domestic work in very low fertility countries: The effect of education', *Journal of Family Issues*, 35, 8: 1048–65.

Sullivan, O., Gershuny, J. and Robinson, J. P. (2018), 'Stalled or uneven gender revolution? A long-term processual framework for understanding why change is slow', *Journal of Family Theory & Review*, 10, 1: 263–79.

Szelewa, D. (2019), 'Invention-institutionalization-implementation: The origins of childcare policies in Poland', *Social Politics*, 26, 1: 139–63.

Tambe, A. (2018), 'Reckoning with the silences of #MeToo', *Feminist Studies*, 44, 1: 197–202.

Taylor-Gooby, P. (2004), *New Risks, New Welfare*, Oxford: Oxford University Press.

Thévenon, O. (2016), 'Do "institutional complementarities" foster female labour force participation?', *Journal of Institutional Economics*, 12, 2: 471–97.

Thomas, C. (1993), 'Deconstructing concepts of care', *Sociology*, 27, 4: 649–69.

Treas, J. (2010), 'Why study housework?', in Treas, J. and Drobnič, S. (eds), *Dividing the Domestic Men, Women and Household Work in Cross-national Perspective*, Stanford, CA: Stanford University Press, pp. 3–18.

Treas, J. and Drobnič, S. (eds) (2010), *Dividing the Domestic: Men, Women and Household Work in Cross-national Perspective*, Stanford, CA: Stanford University Press.

Ungerson, C. (1995), 'Gender, cash and informal care: European perspectives and dilemmas', *Journal of Social Policy*, 24, 1: 31–52.

Ungerson, C. (1997), 'Social politics and the commodification of care', *Social Politics*, 4, 3: 362–81.

UNRISD (2016), *Policy Innovations for Transformative Change: Implementing the 2030 Agenda for Sustainable Development*, Geneva: Switzerland.

Uunk, W. (2015), 'Does the cultural context matter? The effect of a country's gender-role attitudes on female labour supply', *European Societies*, 17, 2: 176–98.

Van Hooren, F. J. (2012), 'Varieties of migrant care work: Comparing patterns of migrant labour in social care', *Journal of European Social Policy* 22: 133–47.

Van Kersbergen, K. and Vis, B. (2014), *Comparative Welfare State Politics: Developments, Opportunities, and Reform*, Cambridge: Cambridge University Press.

Van Lancker, W. (2015), 'Effects of poverty on the living and working conditions of women and their children', presented at Workshop on the Main Causes of Female Poverty, Workshop for the FEMM Committee, 30 March, European Parliament, Brussels.

Verloo, M. (2005), 'Reflections on the concept and practice of the Council of Europe approach to gender mainstreaming', *Social Politics*, 12, 3: 344–65.

Verloo, M. (2006), 'Multiple inequalities, intersectionality and the European Union', *European Journal of Women's Studies*, 13, 3: 211–28.

Verschuur, C. (2013), 'Theoretical debates on social reproduction and care: The articulation between the domestic and the global economy', in Oso, L. and Ribos-Mateos, N. (eds), *The International Handbook on Gender, Migration and Transnationalism*, Cheltenham, UK and Northampton, MA, USA: Edward Elgar Publishing, pp. 145–61.

Villa, P. (2013), 'The role of the EES in the promotion of gender equality in the labour market: A critical appraisal', in Bettio, F., Plantenga, J. and Smith, M. (eds), *Gender and the European Labour Market*, London: Routledge, pp. 135–67.

Vitali, A. and Arpino, B. (2016), 'Who brings home the bacon? The influence of context on partners' contributions to the household income', *Demographic Research*, 35, 41: 1213–44.

Wærness, K. (1978), 'The invisible welfare state: Women's work at home', *Acta Sociologica*, 21 (special issue): 193–207.

Walby, S. (1990), *Theorizing Patriarchy*, Oxford: Blackwell.

Walby, S., Armstrong, J. and Strid, S. (2012), 'Intersectionality: Multiple inequalities in social theory', *Sociology*, 46, 2: 224–40.

Waring, M. (1988), *If Women Counted: A New Feminist Economics*, London: Harper and Row.

Watkins, S. (2018), 'Which feminisms?', *New Left Review*, 109, Jan.–Feb.: 5–76.

West, C. and Zimmerman, D. H. (1987), 'Doing gender', *Gender & Society*, 1, 2: 125–51.

Williams, F. (1989), *Social Policy: A Critical Introduction*, Cambridge: Polity Press.

Williams, F. (1993), 'Gender, "race", and class in British welfare policy', in Cochrane, A. and Clarke, J. (eds), *Comparing Welfare States*, London: Sage, pp. 77–104.

Williams, F. (2012a), 'Care relations and public policy: Social justice claims and social investment frames', *Families, Relationships and Societies*, 1, 1: 103–19.

Williams, F. (2012b), 'Converging variations in migrant care work in Europe', *Journal of European Social Policy*, 22: 363–76.

Williams, F. (2018a), 'Care: Intersections of scales, inequalities and crises', *Current Sociology*, 66, 4: 547–61.

Williams, F. (2018b), 'Intersectionality, gender and social policy', in Shaver, S. (ed.), *Handbook on Gender and Social Policy*, Cheltenham, UK and Northampton, MA, USA: Edward Elgar Publishing, pp. 37–54.

Williams, J. C. (2010), *Reshaping the Work-Family Debate*, Cambridge, MA: Harvard University Press.

Wilson, E. (1977), *Women and the Welfare State*, London: Tavistock.

Women's Budget Group, Fawcett Society, #FaceHerFuture (2018), *Exploring the Economic Impact of Brexit on Women*, London.

Yeates, N. (2011), 'Going global: The transnationalization of care', *Development and Change*, 42, 4: 1109–30.

Yeatman, A. (2018), 'Gender, social policy and the idea of the welfare state', in Shaver, S. (ed.), *Handbook on Gender and Social Policy*, Cheltenham, UK and Northampton, MA, USA: Edward Elgar Publishing, pp. 21–36.

Index